LUCRETIU:
TRANSFOR1
GREEK WISDOM

This book is designed to appeal both to those interested in Roman poetry and to specialists in ancient philosophy. In it David Sedley explores Lucretius' complex relationship with Greek culture, in particular with Empedocles, whose poetry was the model for his own, with Epicurus, the source of his philosophical inspiration, and with the Greek language itself. He includes a detailed reconstruction of Epicurus' great treatise *On nature*, and seeks to show how Lucretius worked with this as his sole philosophical source, but gradually emancipated himself from its structure, transforming its raw contents into something radically new. By pursuing these themes, the book uncovers many unrecognised aspects of Lucretius' methods and achievements as a poetic craftsman.

David Sedley is Professor of Ancient Philosophy, University of Cambridge, and Fellow of Christ's College. He is the author, with A. A. Long, of *The Hellenistic Philosophers* (1987).

LUCRETIUS AND THE TRANSFORMATION OF GREEK WISDOM

DAVID SEDLEY

CAMBRIDGE
UNIVERSITY PRESS

PUBLISHED BY THE PRESS SYNDICATE OF THE UNIVERSITY OF CAMBRIDGE
The Pitt Building, Trumpington Street, Cambridge, United Kingdom

CAMBRIDGE UNIVERSITY PRESS
The Edinburgh Building, Cambridge CB2 2RU, UK
40 West 20th Street, New York NY 10011–4211, USA
477 Williamstown Road, Port Melbourne, VIC 3207, Australia
Ruiz de Alarcón 13, 28014 Madrid, Spain
Dock House, The Waterfront, Cape Town 8001, South Africa

http://www.cambridge.org

First published 1998
First paperback edition 2003

Typeset in Baskerville MT 11/12½ [SE]

A catalogue record for this book is available from the British Library

Library of Congress cataloguing in publication data

Sedley, D. N.
Lucretius and the transformation of Greek wisdom / David Sedley.
p. cm.
Includes bibliographical references and indexes.
ISBN 0 521 57032 8 hardback
1. Lucretius Carus, Titus. De rerum natura. 2. Didactic poetry,
Latin – History and criticism. 3. Lucretius Carus, Titus – Knowledge –
Greece. 4. Philosophy, Ancient, in literature. 5. Latin poetry –
Greek influences. 6. Theophrastus – Influence. 7. Empedocles –
Influence. 8. Epicurus – Influence. I. Title.
PA6484.S43 1998
187–dc21 97-35277 CIP

ISBN 0 521 57032 8 hardback
ISBN 0 521 54214 6 paperback

Transferred to digital printing 2003

For Tony Long

Contents

Preface

This book is the partial repayment of a debt. It was my desire to understand Lucretius better that led me into postgraduate research on Epicureanism. And, even more than the philosophy component of my Greats course at Oxford, it was that postgraduate research on Epicureanism that emboldened me to pursue the study of ancient philosophy as a career. It would therefore be only a small exaggeration to say that I learnt ancient philosophy in order to understand Lucretius. Until recently I have ventured little about Lucretius in print, but I have been thinking about him throughout my teaching career at Cambridge. This book is the outcome, and my way of thanking its eponymous hero.

My fascination with Lucretius was fuelled when as an Oxford undergraduate I had the good fortune, in 1966–7, to attend the wonderful lectures on Lucretius by the then Corpus Professor of Latin, Sir Roger Mynors. Mynors told us that he had himself in his early days been enthralled by Cyril Bailey's Lucretius lectures, none of whose brilliance, he remarked, showed through into Bailey's later monumental edition of the poet ('He had gone off the boil'). I like to think that some excitement from the real Bailey filtered through to me in those lectures.

Another debt is to David Furley, whose book *Two Studies in the Greek Atomists* I came across in Blackwell's while studying Aristotle for Greats. It was that book – which I bought for the then shocking sum of three pounds and nine shillings – that taught me not only how much interest Aristotle gained when he was read alongside other philosophers from a very different tradition, but also how much philosophical depth and subtlety there were to be found in Epicureanism, including that of Lucretius himself.

There are two other friends I should also like especially to thank. My copy of Martin Ferguson Smith's Loeb edition of Lucretius has finally fallen to bits during the writing of this book, a tribute to the fact that I rely on it at all times. His pioneering work on Diogenes of Oenoanda

xi

has also been a constant inspiration to me in my own studies of Epicureanism. And Diskin Clay, with his book *Lucretius and Epicurus*, has set a dauntingly high standard for anyone hoping to shed new light on Lucretius' poetry through the study of ancient philosophy. My book may be very different from his, but I have been constantly conscious of *Lucretius and Epicurus* as a model.

Many of my Cambridge colleagues, past and present – especially the ancient philosophers Myles Burnyeat, Geoffrey Lloyd, Malcolm Schofield, Nick Denyer, Robert Wardy, Mary Margaret McCabe and Dominic Scott, but also Ted Kenney and others – have engaged with me in debate about Lucretius at various times; and we have had three splendid Lucretius seminars. I have also learnt much from my students, especially from James Warren, with whom I have discussed Lucretian issues on many occasions.

Much of the background to this book lies in the Herculaneum papyri. In the nine months of 1971 I spent in Naples working on these uniquely difficult but rewarding texts, and during numerous return visits thereafter, I benefited from the help and hospitality of many, notably Marcello Gigante, Francesca Longo Auricchio, Albert Henrichs, Adele Tepedino Guerra, Giovanni Indelli, Gioia Rispoli, Salvatore Cerasuolo and Tiziano Dorandi. All of them, and others too numerous to mention, I thank warmly.

Those who have commented on earlier drafts of the material that found its way into this book include Jim Adams, Han Baltussen, Charles Brittain, Myles Burnyeat, Diskin Clay, Tiziano Dorandi, Don Fowler, Bill Furley, David Furley, Monica Gale, Philip Hardie, Ted Kenney, Mieke Koenen, Geoffrey Lloyd, Jaap Mansfeld, Roland Mayer, Catherine Osborne, Michael Reeve, David Runia, Samuel Scolnicov, Bob Sharples, Martin Smith, Voula Tsouna, Paul Vander Waerdt, Richard Wallace, Robert Wardy and David West. The penultimate draft of the entire book was read and commented on by Myles Burnyeat, Tony Long, Tom Rosenmeyer, Malcolm Schofield, Gisela Striker, Voula Tsouna and Robert Wardy. My warm thanks to all of these, and to many others who have contributed to discussion at various stages. Likewise to audiences who have responded to presentations of various parts of the book's thesis: at Berkeley, UCLA, Stanford University, Cornell University, the University of Wales, Duke University, the Bibliotheca Classica at St Petersburg, the Institute of Classical Studies in London, the Oxford Philological Society, the British Academy, the University of Leiden, the University of Durham, the Royal Netherlands Academy of

Arts and Sciences, and the University of Nottingham. Miriam Griffin was kind enough to lend me some valuable unpublished work of her own on Cicero's philosophical vocabulary. I have been most grateful for the advice of two anonymous referees for Cambridge University Press: even if, as I suspect, they have both been named at least once above, let me take the opportunity to thank them once again. Susan Moore's scrupulous copy-editing has saved me from numerous errors, unclarities and inconsistencies. Finally, warm thanks to Pauline Hire of the Cambridge University Press for all her advice and encouragement.

To the University of Cambridge and to Christ's College I am grateful for granting me sabbatical leave during Michaelmas Term 1996, when the bulk of the book was written.

Over the last twenty-seven years I have enjoyed innumerable conversations about Lucretius and Epicureanism with Tony Long – first my research supervisor, then my collaborator, and at all times a wonderful friend and supporter. It is to him that I have chosen to dedicate this book, with gratitude and affection.

David Sedley
Cambridge

Introduction

The old quarrel between poetry and philosophy may have simmered down, but in Lucretian studies the two do not always manage to be as willing allies as they ought to be. Lucretius used poetry to illuminate philosophy. My aim in this book is to use philosophy to illuminate poetry.

Lucretius' achievements as a poet to a large extent lie in his genius for transforming Epicurean philosophy to fit a language, a culture and a literary medium for which it was never intended. In order to understand how he has brought about this transformation, we need to know all we can about *what* he was transforming and how he set about his task.

In Chapter 1, 'The Empedoclean opening', I try to show how he defines the pedigree of his literary medium. It is the poetic genre of the hexameter poem on physics, pioneered by Empedocles. Lucretius' way of proclaiming this, I argue, is to write a proem which emphasises the nature and extent of his debt to Empedocles.

In Chapter 2, 'Two languages, two worlds', I turn to a neglected linguistic aspect of Lucretius' enterprise, his ambiguous relationship with the Greek language. The transition from Epicurus' technical Greek prose to Lucretius' largely untechnical Latin verse is not merely a formidable task of conversion, it is also an opportunity for Lucretius to map out an interrelation between two cultures. The result, I argue, is a powerful message, encoded in his linguistic imagery, about the true universality of Epicureanism, a universality demonstrated by its unique ability to transcend linguistic and cultural boundaries.

In Chapter 3, 'Lucretius the fundamentalist', I defend a quite traditional view, albeit one which is increasingly out of favour. It is that Lucretius had no significant contact with, or knowledge of, contemporary philosophy or science. I argue for a strong version of this claim: Lucretius was a true fundamentalist, nourished on the unmediated scriptures of his school's revered founder. To refute systematically every claim ever made about recent or contemporary influences on Lucretius would have resulted in a massive and tedious chapter. But equally, it is important not to content ourselves with impressionistic assertions or appeals to mere likelihood. I have therefore sought in this chapter to present a comprehensive argument for my case – at any rate, one fuller and more systematic than has previously been attempted so far as I am aware. The upshot is that Lucretius really does rely directly on Epicurus' own writings, just as he tells us he does in the proem to book III. His reverence for the master's scriptures is so all-consuming as to obviate any interest in later philosophical or scientific developments.

Chapters 4–5 form a single block. Between them they try to answer the questions (a) what was the hallowed Epicurean material which Lucretius was transforming, and (b) how did he proceed with the task of transforming it? This leads me into another rather traditional activity, one which many will think recent Lucretian scholarship to be well rid of. I mean the activity of *Quellenforschung*. But I hope what I have come up with will not seem like a return to the endless and inconclusive joustings of Lucretian scholarship in the first half of this century. The text which everyone agrees was in some sense Lucretius' ultimate source for physics, and which I among others believe to be his single direct source – I mean Epicurus' great treatise *On nature* – is one about which we possess a huge amount of information. Yet, extraordinarily, this information has never been assembled into a coherent overview, let alone adequately exploited by Lucretian scholars.

Therefore my Chapter 4, 'Epicurus, *On nature*', is devoted to a full-scale evaluation of this work. I try to show its probable structure, all the way down to the sequence of contents in individual books. I also offer a characterisation of its style, and try to explain why it held a unique place in the affections of Epicureans. Finally, I offer a partial chronology of its composition.

In Chapter 5, 'Lucretius' plan and its execution', I give reasons for regarding the first fifteen books of Epicurus' *On nature* as Lucretius' direct source on physics. This leads me on to what I consider the single most significant proposal in my book. I argue that we can discern in Lucretius' text his actual procedure when composing the poem. (Others have made the same claim, with very different results from mine, but they have never based it on an adequate look at *On nature*.) Initially he worked his way through *On nature* fairly systematically, following the order of topics which Epicurus himself had said was the correct one. He omitted a number of topics and individual arguments, but rarely deviated from Epicurus' sequence. However, as he wrote he began to see how the material should be eventually reordered, into something very much like the six-book structure in which we now know it. This crucially included the decision, taken quite early on, to reverse the material of books III and IV from Epicurus' order into that which we now find in the poem.

Much of the fine detail of this restructuring, however, was undertaken in a second phase, in which he only got half-way through reworking the poem. Books I–III are, to all intents and purposes, fully integrated into Lucretius' master plan. But books IV–VI as we have them are, I am convinced, not fully reworked. In Lucretius' proems, which represent the latest stages of his work, I claim to be able to detect what his further plans were for books IV and V – plans which remain unfulfilled in the text as it has come down to us. This in turn seems to me to offer strong support to those who have found themselves unable to believe that book VI, including its closing description of the Athenian plague, is in the final state that Lucretius envisaged for it. I thus end Chapter 5 with a proposal about how far he had got with his plans for the plague passage, based partly on what has proved to be his method of composition in the preceding books of the poem, and partly on a moral motif which I believe to play an important part in Lucretius' grand design.

I thus strongly resist the view, which is threatening to become an orthodoxy of Lucretian scholarship, that the *De rerum natura* is in fact finished. But although I am by implication endorsing the ancient tradition that Lucretius died before putting the final touches to the poem, I have nothing new to say about that tradition, including Jerome's story that Cicero was the posthumous editor. My sole contribution to Lucretian biography is to be found in Chapter 2: Lucretius had been to Greece.

One finding of Chapters 4–5 is that when the voice of Epicurus shows through in Lucretius' text, a primary source used by Epicurus sometimes shows through too. This is Theophrastus' great pioneering doxographical treatise, *Physical opinions*. In Chapter 6, 'The imprint of Theophrastus', I take the same theme forward, charting particular Lucretian passages where Theophrastus is being either borrowed from or implicitly criticised.

Chapter 7 rounds off the story by looking close-up at the structure and argument of a single book, the first. Doing so makes it possible to see in some detail how Lucretius' reworking of his Epicurean material has transformed Epicurus' primarily deductive chain of reasoning into a radically new style of discourse, governed even more by the requirements of rhetoric than by those of philosophical dialectic.

My single most earnest goal in writing this book is to be able to address readers who have themselves come to Lucretius through the study of Latin poetry. I hope to persuade some of them that there is much to learn about Lucretius, even as a poetic craftsman, by scrutinising the philosophical background to his poem in ways in which it is not usually scrutinised. I recognise that a certain proportion of the material in the later part of the book may be tough going for some readers. But I do very strongly urge even them at the very least to read the first two chapters, to skim the third and fourth, and to read the fifth and seventh. If they so prefer, they have my permission to ignore Chapter 6 altogether.

None of the chapters, with the exception of 3 and 6, assumes much prior philosophical knowledge on the part of the reader. All chapters involve some use of both Greek and Latin, but I have tried to translate all words and excerpts quoted in the main text.

Some of the material for this book can also be found in articles which I have already published or which are currently in press. They are the ones listed in the bibliography under my name for 1984 (Chapter 4), 1989a (Chapter 1), forthcoming (Chapter 7), 1997b (Chapter 5), 1998a (Chapter 6), and 1998b (Chapter 2). In all cases the material has been reworked and expanded for the book, and a good deal of it is entirely new.

CHAPTER I

The Empedoclean opening

1. CICERO'S LETTER

Lucreti poemata ut scribis ita sunt, multis luminibus ingeni, multae tamen artis. sed cum veneris, virum te putabo si Sallusti Empedoclea legeris, hominem non putabo.

Writing to his brother in 54 BC, Cicero supplies two unique testimonies (*Ad Q. fr.* II 9.4). In the first sentence he echoes Quintus' admiration for Lucretius' poem, thus providing the sole allusion to the *De rerum natura* likely to be more or less contemporary with its publication. In the second, he attests the publication of an *Empedoclea* by a certain Sallustius, presumably a Latin translation or imitation of Empedocles (compare Cicero's own near-contemporary use of the title *Aratea* for his translation of Aratus).

But even more striking than the two individual testimonies is their juxtaposition. Modern editors have taken to printing a full stop after *sed cum veneris*, understanding 'But when you come . . . (*sc.* we will discuss it).' This suppresses any overt link between the two literary judgements: the first breaks off abruptly with an aposiopesis, and the second, juxtaposed, is to all appearances a quite independent observation. On the equally natural and more fluent reading that can be obtained simply by reverting to the older punctuation,[1] as printed above, with a comma instead of the full stop, the letter is an explicit comparison between the *DRN* and the *Empedoclea*:

Lucretius' poetry shows, as you say in your letter, many flashes of genius, yet also much craftsmanship. On the other hand, when you come, I shall consider you a man if you have read Sallustius' *Empedoclea*, though I won't consider you human.

[1] This was the standard punctuation until the late nineteenth century. The repunctuation, with its aposiopesis *sed cum veneris* . . . (unique, but cf. partial parallels at *Ad Att.* XII 5a and XIV 20.3), appears to have been introduced by R. Y. Tyrrell in 1886, in his revised text of Cicero's Letters (Tyrrell (1885–1901)), but without offering any evidence or argument – since when it has been repeated, without comment, by all editors.

I

If this is right, the two works were being directly compared at the time of their publication, and Cicero, at least, judged the Lucretian poem vastly superior.

Why did this particular comparison suggest itself? It is well recognised that Empedocles is, along with Homer, Ennius, and others,[2] an important literary influence on Lucretius, and it has even been claimed that he was a philosophical influence.[3] But I do not believe that the depth and significance of the poem's Empedoclean character have yet been properly understood. If what I shall argue in this chapter is right, Cicero's comparison of the *DRN* with the *Empedoclea* will turn out to be an entirely natural one, which Lucretius would have welcomed and indeed invited. My case will be centred on the relation of Lucretius' proem to the proem of Empedocles' *On nature*.

2   EMPEDOCLES' TWO POEMS

There is plentiful evidence that it was principally if not exclusively in the hexameter poem usually known in antiquity as the *On nature* (Περὶ φύσεως) or the *Physics* (Τὰ φυσικά) — I shall discuss its actual title in §7 — that Empedocles expounded his world system. The central features of the cosmic cycle it described are well known: four enduring elements — earth, air (called 'aether'),[4] fire, and water — are periodically united into a homogeneous sphere by a constructive force called Love, then again separated out into the familiar stratified world by the polar force, Strife.[5] But there is a longstanding scholarly tradition, deriving primarily from Diels' editions published in 1901 and 1903, of attributing all the fragments concerning Empedocles' theories on the pollution and transmigration of the individual spirit, or 'daimon', to a second hexameter poem, the *Katharmoi*, or *Purifications*.

The original ground for this segregation was the belief that the physical doctrine of the cosmic cycle and the 'religious' doctrine of transmigration belonged to radically distinct and probably incompatible areas of Empedocles' thought. But Empedoclean studies have now reached a curious stage. On the one hand, the old dogma has been subjected to searching criticism, and is regarded by many as an anachron-

---

[2] The range of literary influences on Lucretius was considerably enlarged by the findings of Kenney (1970).   [3] Furley (1970), discussed below; also Bollack (1959).
[4] For 'aether', rather than 'air', as Empedocles' chosen designation of this element, see Kingsley (1995), ch. 2.
[5] The traditional belief that zoogony took place in both halves of this cycle, for which see especially O'Brien (1969), has been powerfully challenged by Bollack (1965–9), Hölscher (1965), Solmsen (1965), and Long (1974), and ably defended by Graham (1988).

istic imposition on fifth-century thought.[6] On the other hand, the conventional apportionment of fragments between the two poems, which was founded on that dogma, remains largely unchallenged, as if it had some independent authority. I believe that it has none.

One radical challenge to this picture, however, has been developed recently. Catherine Osborne[7] proposes that there were never two poems: rather, both titles name one and the same work. Although this proposal has found some favour,[8] and has certainly inspired some important reassessment of the doctrinal relation between the two sides of Empedocles' thought, I do not think that it can be right. Diogenes Laertius is unambiguously speaking of two separate poems when he tells us that '*On nature* and the *Katharmoi* (VIII 77, τὰ μὲν οὖν Περὶ φύσεως καὶ οἱ Καθαρμοί . . .) run to 5,000 lines.'[9] Moreover, a number of the surviving fragments of Empedocles are reported with explicit assignations to one or the other poem, yet not a single one with attributions to both the physical poem and the *Katharmoi*. Finally, as Jaap Mansfeld has brought to light, Giovanni Aurispa is known to have had a manuscript entitled (in Greek) 'Empedocles' *Katharmoi*' (now tragically lost) in his library at Venice in 1424.[10] Even if this evidence were thought insufficient, I hope that the matter will be put beyond doubt by my next section, where it will turn out that one major fragment cannot be placed in the *Katharmoi* without glaring inconsistency: Empedocles must have written at least two poems.

If we simply stick to the hard and the relatively hard evidence for what was in the *Katharmoi*, a different picture will emerge. We do at least have its opening lines.[11]

---

[6] E.g. Kahn (1960), Barnes (1979) II 93, Wright (1981), Osborne (1987), Inwood (1992), Kingsley (1995); reservations in Long (1966).   [7] Osborne (1987).

[8] Cf. its further development in Inwood (1992), pp. 8–19. The reply to Osborne and Inwood in O'Brien (1995) is unfortunately timed: it contains news of the recent papyrus find (see pp. 10 and 28 below), but not the specific information that this now virtually proves at least one 'Katharmic' fragment to belong to *On nature*.

[9] See Osborne (1987), pp. 28–9 on the unreliability of the figure 5,000. But as for the separation of the two titles, there is no compelling reason to doubt Diogenes' reliability, especially when no ancient source contradicts him on the point.

[10] Mansfeld (1994b), which should also be consulted for its further arguments for the existence of two separate poems. Of course his evidence is not strictly incompatible with the thesis that there was one poem, whose proponents may reply that this *was* that one poem. But it is uncomfortable for them, since it means that, if they are right, *Katharmoi* was the official title, contrary to the great bulk of the ancient citations.

[11] Empedocles B112. The square-bracketed words represent Greek words apparently corrupt or missing in the quotation as preserved. Here and elsewhere, I use the Diels/Kranz (1951–2) numbering of Empedocles' fragments, although a significantly better text is now available in the valuable edition of Wright (1981). Since the many available numerations are, as I shall argue, all equally misleading as regards the apportionment of fragments between the two poems, it is better for now simply to stick to the standard one.

Friends, who in the great town of the yellow Acragas dwell on the city's heights, caring about good deeds, I greet you. You see me going about as a divine god, no longer a mortal, honoured amongst all, it seems, and wreathed in ribbons and verdant garlands. [Whenever] I arrive in prosperous towns I am revered by men and women. They follow me in their thousands, asking me where lies their road to advantage, some requesting oracles, while others have asked to hear a healing utterance for ailments of all kinds, long pierced by troublesome [pains].

Thus Empedocles addresses the citizens of his native Acragas, telling how they revere him as a living god, 'no longer a mortal'. Men and women flock to follow him, pressing him with enquiries, requesting oracles and cures.

Why should we not suppose that the poem was nothing more nor less than a response to these requests, a set of purificatory oracles and 'healing utterances'?[12]

There is immediate support for this conjecture in the pseudo-Pythagorean *Carmen aureum*: 'But abstain from the foods that I spoke of in my *Katharmoi* and *Absolution of the soul.*'[13] This citation, or pseudo-citation, of the author's own *Katharmoi* invokes it for just the kind of self-purificatory advice that the title itself suggests. And that the allusion is inspired by Empedocles' work of the same name is confirmed just three lines later, where the poem closes with the words 'You will be an immortal, divine god, no longer a mortal' (ἔσσεαι ἀθάνατος θεὸς ἄμβροτος, οὐκέτι θνητός), pointedly recalling the famous opening of Empedocles' *Katharmoi*, 'You see me going about as a divine god, no longer a mortal' (B112.4–5, ἐγὼ δ᾽ ὑμῖν θεὸς ἄμβροτος, οὐκέτι θνητός, | πωλεῦμαι). Whatever the date of this forgery may be, its author clearly knows Empedocles' *Katharmoi*, and associates it with advice to abstain from certain kinds of food.

That a work with this title should be one dedicated to purificatory advice is unsurprising, since the very word *katharmoi* means ritual acts of purification. To adherents of the traditional interpretation, it is easy to assume that the poem was one about the wandering spirit's *processes* of purification, but I know no evidence that the word can mean that:[14] such processes would normally be called *katharseis*.

---

[12] For the scope and content of the relevant notions of pollution and purification, see Parker (1983). I have no particular suggestion to make about the function of the 'oracles'. The evidence of a purificatory role for oracles is meagre (Parker (1983), p. 86), and I would guess that it is Empedocles' assumed divinity that makes this an appropriate designation for his pronouncements.

[13] *Carmen aureum* 67–8, in Young (1971), 103–4: ἀλλ᾽ εἴργου βρωτῶν ὧν εἴπομεν ἔν τε Καθαρμοῖς | ἔν τε Λύσει ψυχῆς.

[14] The use of καθαρμοί is usefully surveyed by Guthrie (1969), pp. 244–5.

Better still, the hypothesis also fits the other two items of evidence known to me for *Katharmoi* as a literary genre. These two references also resemble the *Carmen aureum* in fathering the works in question on archaic figures of semi-legendary status. First, Epimenides the Cretan is said to have written *Katharmoi*, in verse and perhaps also prose,[15] and, although their content is not reported, it can hardly be a coincidence that Epimenides was celebrated above all for his ritual purifications, an expertise that led the Athenians to send for him to purify their city of plague.[16] Second, the remark at Aristophanes, *Frogs* 1033 that Musaeus taught 'healing and oracles' is glossed by a scholiast with the comment that Musaeus 'composed absolutions [?], initiations, and *katharmoi*'.[17] Healing and oracles are precisely the two services mentioned by Empedocles at the opening of his *Katharmoi*. Then why look further for the content of the poem?

Certainly no fragment explicitly attributed to the *Katharmoi* forces us to look further. Apart from the proem, there are just two such cases. One is B153a: according to Theon of Smyrna (104.1–3), Empedocles 'hints' (αἰνίττεται) in the *Katharmoi* that the foetus achieves full human form in seven times seven days. Aetius[18] confirms the report – though not the attribution to the *Katharmoi* – with the further information that the differentiation of limbs starts at thirty-six days. That Empedocles should only have 'hinted' this in the *Katharmoi* suggests that we are not dealing with an expository account of embryology. We learn from Censorinus[19] (third century AD) that in Greece the pregnant woman does not go out to a shrine before the fortieth day of her pregnancy. This is thought to be linked to the widespread belief that miscarriages are likeliest to occur in the first forty days.[20] There is a strong possibility that Empedocles' original remark occurred in the context of ritual advice to pregnant women, perhaps to avoid shrines for the first 'seven times seven' days. Here it is important to remember the opening of the *Katharmoi*, where it is made explicit that the demands for healing and oracles to which Empedocles is responding come from women as well as men.

The other explicit attribution to the *Katharmoi* – in fact to book II of the poem – occurs in a fragment first published in 1967, fr. 152 Wright:[21]

---

[15] 3A2 3 DK. [16] 3A1, 2, 4, 8 DK.
[17] 2A6 DK. There is a close parallel at Plato, *Rep.* II 364c–365a: Adimantus, as evidence of the belief that the gods can be bought off, cites the books of Musaeus and Orpheus, on the basis of which rituals are performed to bring about the λύσεις τε καὶ καθαρμοί of wrongs done by both the living and the dead. [18] Aetius V 21.1 = Empedocles A83.
[19] Censorinus, *De die natali* 11.7. [20] See Parker (1983), p. 48.
[21] Wright (1981), pp. 151 and 298; not, of course, to be found in Diels/Kranz (1951–2).

'For those of them which grow with their roots denser below but their branches more thinly spread . . .' Trees, or more generally plants, of this kind were singled out for a reason which cannot now be recovered.[22] The context may well have been one concerning the avoidance of certain leaves. According to Plutarch, in a probable but unprovable citation of the *Katharmoi*, Empedocles urged that all trees should be 'spared', but especially the laurel:[23] 'Keep completely away from the laurel's leaves' (B140). This has every chance of tying in with Empedocles' views on transmigration – he holds, for example, that the laurel is the best tree to transmigrate into (B127)! But it is significant that here once again, if the link with the injunction about laurel leaves is accepted, the actual fragment may well contain moral or purificatory advice rather than the doctrinal exposition characteristic of the physical poem. To repeat, ritual advice is just what we should expect in a work entitled *Katharmoi*.

The expectation finds further strong support in the story surrounding fragment B111. We learn that the biographer Satyrus quoted this fragment as confirming the suspicion that Empedocles dabbled in magic.[24] Since, according to Apuleius,[25] it was Empedocles' *Katharmoi* that brought upon him just such a suspicion, there is a strong likelihood that B111 is from this poem.[26] Significantly, the fragment is once again not a doctrinal exposition but ritual advice: how to influence the weather and to summon up the dead.

B111 uses the second person singular: 'You [singular] will learn . . .' Because the *On nature* was addressed to an individual, Pausanias, whereas the opening lines of the *Katharmoi* address the citizens of Acragas in the plural, it has often been thought that any fragments containing the second person singular must be assigned to the former poem. This is a very dubious criterion, since changes of address within a single didactic poem are quite normal. Hesiod's *Works and days* switches in its first three hundred lines between addresses to the Muses, to Perses, and to the 'bribe-swallowing princes'.[27] That the *Katharmoi* should, after its opening, move into the second person singular may merely reflect the fact that Empedocles is by now answering the individual requests from his audience of which the proem spoke.

---

[22] According to Theophrastus, *HP* 1 6.4, all plants have their roots more densely packed than their parts above ground, but some, e.g. the olive tree, have a particularly dense mass of slender roots.

[23] Plut. *Quaest. conv.* 646b, see preamble to B140 DK.   [24] DL viii 59.   [25] Apuleius, *Apol.* 27.

[26] This attribution is supported, as Inwood (1992), p. 16 has shown, by the fact that Clement (*Strom.* vi 30.1–3) directly associates B111 with the opening lines of the *Katharmoi*.

[27] See further, Osborne (1987), pp. 31–2, who appositely compares Lucretius' own switches of address.

There are no further unambiguously attested fragments of the *Katharmoi*. But we may, with caution,[28] consider as potential fragments of it any citations of Empedocles whose sources explicitly call them *katharmoi*. The clearest case of this is in Hippolytus,[29] who describes prohibitions on marriage and on certain foods as tantamount to teaching the *katharmoi* of Empedocles. Given this remark, along with the association of the *Katharmoi* with food prohibitions in the *Carmen aureum*, it seems safe to assume that the poem carried Empedocles' advice to abstain from slaughter, meat-eating, and perhaps even beans.[30] And it seems that abstention from marriage was a further injunction to be found in the same work.[31]

Another plausible such candidate is a fragment preserved by Theon of Smyrna.[32] Comparing philosophy as a whole to a religious ritual, Theon calls Plato's five propaedeutic mathematical studies in *Republic* VII a *katharmos*, which he immediately proceeds to link with Empedocles' injunction to cleanse oneself by 'cutting from five springs (in a bowl of) indestructible bronze' (B143).[33] We are here firmly in the territory of ritual self-purification. Theophrastus' godfearing character, for example, refuses to set out on his daily rounds until he has washed his hands at three springs.[34]

Deciding just which other verbatim fragments should be assigned to the *Katharmoi* is a problem to pursue on another occasion. The argument to which I shall now turn relies on a primarily negative conclusion: there

---

[28] B139, which in Sedley (1989a) I incautiously left in the *Katharmoi*, can now be shown to belong to the physical poem: see p. 30 below.

[29] Hippolytus, *Ref.* VII 30.3–4; see preamble to B110 in Diels/Kranz.

[30] Empedocles B141, carrying the Pythagorean advice to abstain from beans, is condemned as inauthentic by Wright (1981), p. 289, perhaps rightly.

[31] Hippolytus *loc. cit.* presents the advice not to marry as itself Empedoclean: 'You are dissolving marriages made by God, following the doctrines of Empedocles, in order to preserve the work of Love as one and undivided. For according to Empedocles, marriage divides the one and makes many.' This is a curious view to take of marriage, although it could well apply to the *family*.

[32] Theon of Smyrna 14–15.

[33] I here translate the Diels/Kranz text, based on Theon, κρηνάων ἄπο πέντε ταμόντ' <ἐν> ἀτειρέι χαλκῷ. Aristotle, *Poet.*1457b13 quotes (without attribution) the words τεμὼν ἀτειρέι (Λ, τανακέι Β) χαλκῷ, explaining that 'cutting' here is used to mean 'drawing'. This leads van der Ben (1975), 203–8, and Wright (1981), 289–90, to follow the lead of Maas and conflate the two quotations in the form κρηνάων ἄπο πέντε τεμὼν (or ταμὼν) <u>τανατήκεϊ</u> χαλκῷ, with the further inevitable conclusion that the reference is to drawing blood with a knife – which of course Empedocles would be condemning. This seems to me too high a price to pay, since it totally contradicts Theon's report that Empedocles with these words is advising us to cleanse ourselves.

[34] Theophrastus, *Char.* 16.2. See Parker (1983), pp. 226–7. Cf. Apollonius Rhodius III 860, where Medea, before preparing an ointment which confers invulnerability, bathes herself in seven streams.

is no reason to attribute to this poem any fragments of Empedocles beyond those offering ritual advice.[35]

3. THE PROVENANCE OF EMPEDOCLES B115

There is a decree of necessity, an ancient resolution of the gods, sworn by broad oaths, that when one of the daimons which have a share of long life defiles . . . its own limbs, or does wrong and swears a false oath, for thirty thousand years it must wander, away from the blessed ones, being born during that time as every form of mortal creature, exchanging for each other the arduous paths of life. The might of the aether drives it to the sea, the sea spits it out onto the threshold of land, the earth sends it into the rays of the gleaming sun, and the sun hurls it into the whirling aether. One receives it from another, and all hate it. I too am now one of these, a fugitive from the gods and a wanderer, who trust in raving Strife.

These lines (B115),[36] which are crucial for explaining the daimon's migrations, have been assigned to the *Katharmoi* by every editor of Empedocles since Diels.[37] The attribution has been questioned by N. van der Ben, and subsequently defended by D. O'Brien.[38] But this renewed debate has so far focused excessively on the contexts in which the lines are quoted by our sources, as if one could settle the question of their provenance by counting the allusions in those contexts to *katharsis* and cognate terms and likewise those to the cosmic cycle. Given the improbability that any ancient reader of Empedocles might have expected the physical poem and the *Katharmoi* to conflict doctrinally, the provenance of the lines will have mattered less to those who cited them than their value as evidence for Empedocles' views on the *katharsis* of the soul – a topic on which Platonism had conferred an absolutely pivotal importance.

Plutarch reports that Empedocles used these lines 'as a preface at the beginning of his philosophy'.[39] Is this too vague to be helpful? 'Philosophy' certainly might describe the content of the physical poem.[40] It might also be appropriate to the *Katharmoi*, on the tradi-

---

[35] I agree with Kingsley (1996), p. 109 that the *Katharmoi* must have contained some indication of how it is the facts of transmigration that make meat-eating a sin. But Empedocles' declared celebrity at the time of writing this poem hardly suggests that he would need to do very much explaining of his doctrine. I certainly see no necessity on this ground to attribute any specific known fragment (e.g. B137, as Kingsley suggests) to it, beyond those I have listed.

[36] I have avoided engaging with the textual difficulties of this passage, which are well discussed by Wright (1981). They do not affect any of the issues I am addressing here.

[37] This of course applies to Inwood (1992) only in so far as he identifies the *Katharmoi* with the whole of Empedocles' poetic *œuvre*.   [38] Van der Ben (1975), pp. 16ff.; O'Brien (1981).

[39] Plut., *De exilio* 607c: ἐν ἀρχῇ τῆς φιλοσοφίας προαποφωνήσας.

[40] Kingsley (1996) argues, in reply to Sedley (1989a), that 'philosophy' to Plutarch would normally

tional view of that poem's content as expository and doctrinal. But it is very much less appropriate if, as I have argued, the *Katharmoi* was not a doctrinal work but a set of purificatory pronouncements. Indeed, if that suggestion is correct, Plutarch's expression 'at the beginning of his philosophy' would immediately gain a much clearer sense. If Empedocles wrote two doctrinal poems, the words 'his philosophy' are a desperately vague way of referring to either one of them. But if he wrote just one, they become an entirely natural way of referring to that one.[41]

Plutarch's description in no way indicates that these were the very opening lines of the poem to which they belonged, just that they preceded the philosophy proper. Hence there is little value in the argument[42] that since we have the opening of the *Katharmoi* and it differs from these lines, they must have opened the physical poem instead. Much more mileage can be got out of the content of the disputed lines. First, it is hardly insignificant that they name five of the six cosmic entities on which Empedocles' physical system is based: the daimon's wanderings are graphically described in terms of its being tossed into and out of each of the four elements in turn; and Strife is named as the cause of its downfall. This at least supports the *coherence* of the passage with the physical poem.

But far more important, and strangely absent from the debate about its provenance, is the following consideration. In these disputed lines, Empedocles is himself a fallen daimon: 'I too am now one of these, a fugitive from the gods and a wanderer, who trust in raving Strife.' Is it credible that these words came in the introductory passage of a poem in whose opening lines Empedocles had moments earlier described himself

mean the kind of moral precepts, tinged with myth and religion, that are associated with the *Katharmoi.* This may not seem much of a challenge to my position, since I argue that there was a good deal of this kind of material in *On nature.* But Kingsley's claim is that 'philosophy' is precisely the word Plutarch would use to distinguish the 'philosophical' *Katharmoi* from the other, merely 'physical' poem. However, his evidence crumbles on examination. At *De gen. Socr.* 580c Plutarch's speaker Galaxidorus does (on a plausible restoration of the text) say that Pythagoras' philosophy, already full of 'visions and myths and religious dread', became positively 'Bacchic' in the hands of Empedocles. But in no way does this, as Kingsley seems to think, delimit what Plutarch would mean by the expression 'Empedocles' philosophy', and thus exclude physics from it. Plutarch's other speakers often make it abundantly clear that, like anybody else, they regard 'philosophy' as including physics (*De def. or.* 420B, *De facie* 942B) and logic (*De Is. et Os.* 387A), as well as contemplation of first principles (*ib.* 382D E). And although, as Kingsley notes, at *De poet. aud.* 14F and 15F, Plutarch recommends the couching of philosophy in versified myth as a didactic device, that tells us nothing about what he means by the *word* 'philosophy', especially when at least one of his speakers, Theon (*De Pyth. or.* 406E), takes an almost diametrically opposed view of philosophy. [11] Cf. Osborne (1987), pp. 29ff.
[12] Van der Ben (1975), p. 16.

as 'a divine god, no longer a mortal'?[43] Without the straitjacket of the
old prejudice that science and religion do not mix, it is hard to believe
that anyone would ever have thought of assigning the former text to the
Katharmoi. The most natural interpretation is that B115 comes from a
poem in which Empedocles classed himself as a fallen daimon still
working through its long cycle of transmigrations, whereas in the
Katharmoi, opening as it does with his confident self-proclamation as a
god, 'no longer a mortal', he presented himself as having now completed
the cycle and recovered his divinity. I therefore feel a reasonable degree
of confidence in placing Empedocles' major fragment on the wanderings of the daimon somewhere in the proem to the *On Nature*.

Since I first developed this argument several years ago,[44] it has
received welcome confirmation in the discovery of papyrus fragments
from book 1 of Empedocles' *On nature*.[45] They include lines denouncing
animal slaughter[46] – lines which editors have always hitherto assigned to
the *Katharmoi*. The taboo on slaughter is, famously, one which
Empedocles based on his doctrine of transmigration. Hence the transfer of these lines to the opening book of the *On nature* should do much to
obviate any remaining resistance to the conclusion that B115, on the
migrations of the daimon, belongs to the proem of that same book.

This conclusion will prove important at a later stage in my argument.
Earmarking it for future use, we can now at last turn to Lucretius.

4. LUCRETIUS AND EMPEDOCLES

Numerous echoes of Empedoclean passages have been recognised in
Lucretius' poem, with varying degrees of certainty.[47] It is no part of my
purpose to catalogue these. But two observations seem in order. First, the
500 or so extant lines of Empedocles[48] represent around one-tenth of his

---

[13] B112.4, reinforced by B113.2 ('if I am superior to frequently-perishing mortal human beings'), if,
as Sextus' juxtaposition of B113 with B112 suggests, it is also from the *Katharmoi*. In Empedocles'
world, even the generated gods perish eventually, i.e. at the end of each cosmic cycle: hence they
are not immortal but 'long-lived' (B21.12, B23.8; cf. B115.5 on the daimons). By contrast, mortals
are 'frequently-perishing', πολυφθερέων, see Wright (1981), p. 269.   [14] In Sedley (1989a).

[45] The exciting new Strasbourg papyrus of Empedocles has its *editio princeps* in Martin/Primavesi
(1998). Although, at the time of completing the present book, I had not seen this edition, Oliver
Primavesi was kind enough to send me a copy of his *habilitationsschrift* (the basis of Primavesi
(forthcoming)), and both he and Alain Martin have been extremely generous in keeping me
informed about their work.   [46] B139, see n. 107 below.

[47] Esp. Furley (1970); also Kranz (1944), Castner (1987), Gale (1994a), pp. 59–75. I have not seen
Jobst (1907), but I understand from Don Fowler that he anticipated Kranz's most important findings. For other studies, see Tatum (1984), p. 178 n. 5.

[48] This figure tries to take some account of the new papyrus find. I understand from the editors,

poetic output, if we are to trust Diogenes Laertius' figure of 5,000 lines in total,[49] and even on the most conservative estimates of Empedocles' total output,[50] not more than one-fifth. Or supposing (as I am inclined to suppose) that Lucretius' interest was exclusively in the *On nature*, what is extant of that is still likely to be less than a quarter – roughly 450 lines out of 2,000.[51] This raises the probability that if we had Empedocles' poems intact a great deal more Empedoclean influence would come to light, and our understanding of the *DRN* be immensely enriched.

Second, I would suggest that Lucretius is likely to owe rather more to Empedocles in terms of poetic technique than is generally recognised. For example, at 1 271–97 Lucretius argues for the corporeality of air by means of an intricate analogy between the destructive power of wind and that of water. David West has observed that the number of distinct points of correspondence between the description of the wind and the description of the water greatly exceeds that normally found in the similes of Homer and Apollonius.[52] Lucretius is thus, in West's terminology, a practitioner of the 'multiple-correspondence simile', a legacy that he was to pass on to Virgil. What I would myself add is that, although Homer and Apollonius may offer no adequate model for the technique, Empedocles does. In his description of the eye's structure and function as analogous to those of a lantern,[53] Empedocles reinforces the idea with a set of carefully engineered correspondences between the two halves of the simile.[54] As in Lucretius, so already in Empedocles, the multiplicity of correspondences has an argumentative motive, and not merely a descriptive one: the more correspondences there are, the more persuasive the analogy becomes. Here then is a technique, singularly at home in philosophical poetry, which has almost certainly passed from Empedocles, through Lucretius, into the Latin poetic tradition.

Lucretius' reverence for Empedocles is evident in the paean of praise with which he prefaces his criticism of Empedocles' four-element theory at 1 716–41:

Alain Martin and Oliver Primavesi, that they have detected in them some new examples of locutions imitated by Lucretius.   [49] DL VIII 77; for discussion see Osborne (1987), pp. 28–9.
[50] Wright (1981), p. 21.
[51] 2,000 lines seems to be the figure for the length of the physical poem given by the *Suda*, *s.v.* 'Empedocles' (= Empedocles A2 DK), despite the slightly odd grammar.
[52] West (1970).
[53] Empedocles B84. For discussion see Wright (1981), pp. 240–3, Sedley (1992b).
[54] These are contained principally in the close linguistic parallelism of lines 4–5 with the final two lines. For comparable prose uses of complex analogy in Hippocratic authors, cf. Lloyd (1966), pp. 345–8.

quorum Acragantinus cum primis Empedocles est
insula quem triquetris terrarum gessit in oris,
quam fluitans circum magnis anfractibus aequor
Ionium glaucis aspargit virus ab undis,
angustoque fretu rapidum mare dividit undis   720
Aeoliae terrarum oras a finibus eius.
hic est vasta Charybdis et hic Aetnaea minantur
murmura flammarum rursum se colligere iras,
faucibus eruptos iterum vis ut vomat ignis
ad caelumque ferat flammai fulgura rursum.   725
quae cum magna modis multis miranda videtur
gentibus humanis regio visendaque fertur,
rebus opima bonis, multa munita virum vi,
nil tamen hoc habuisse viro praeclarius in se
nec sanctum magis et mirum carumque videtur.   730
carmina quin etiam divini pectoris eius
vociferantur et exponunt praeclara reperta,
ut vix humana videatur stirpe creatus.
hic tamen et supra quos diximus inferiores
partibus egregie multis multoque minores,   735
quamquam multa bene ac divinitus invenientes
ex adyto tamquam cordis responsa dedere
sanctius et multo certa ratione magis quam
Pythia quae tripodi a Phoebi lauroque profatur,
principiis tamen in rerum fecere ruinas   740
et graviter magni magno cecidere ibi casu.

Of these [*sc.* the four-element theorists] the foremost is
Empedocles of Acragas, born within the three-cornered terrestrial coasts of the island [Sicily] around which the Ionian Sea,
flowing with its great windings, sprays the brine from its green
waves, and from whose boundaries the rushing sea with its
narrow strait divides the coasts of the Aeolian land with its
waves. Here is destructive Charybdis, and here the rumblings of
Etna give warning that they are once more gathering the wrath
of their flames so that her violence may again spew out the fire
flung from her jaws and hurl once more to the sky the lightning
flashes of flame. Although this great region seems in many ways
worthy of admiration by the human races, and is said to deserve
visiting for its wealth of good things and the great stock of men
that fortify it, yet it appears to have had in it nothing more
illustrious than this man, nor more holy, admirable, and precious. What is more, the poems sprung from his godlike mind
call out and expound his illustrious discoveries, so that he
scarcely seems to be born of mortal stock.
    But this man and the greatly inferior and far lesser ones whom

I mentioned above, although in making their many excellent
and godlike discoveries they gave responses, as from the shrine
of the mind, in a holier and much more certain way than the
Pythia who makes her pronouncements from Apollo's tripod
and laurel, nevertheless came crashing down when they dealt
with the elementary principles of things. Great as they were,
their fall here was a great and heavy one.

This is remarkable praise[55] to lavish on a philosopher who did, after all,
radically misconceive the underlying nature of the world. Where does
the emphasis lie? Lucretius speaks highly both of Empedocles' 'illustrious discoveries' (*praeclara reperta*, 732), and of his poetry, which is so
sublime as almost to prove his divinity – an honour that in the end
Lucretius will reserve for Epicurus alone.[56] With regard to Empedocles'
'discoveries', I am inclined to agree with those who hold that Lucretius
is implicitly commending, among other things, the clarity of their
exposition, especially by contrast with the obscurities of Heraclitus
denounced in the preceding passage.[57] This, I would further suggest, is
supported by the closing remarks in the passage quoted above, where
Lucretius expresses his approval both of Empedocles and of his 'lesser'
colleagues in the pluralist tradition[58] for revealing their findings 'in a
holier and much more certain way than the Pythia who makes her pronouncements from Apollo's tripod and laurel' (738–9). This has standardly been understood as crediting those philosophers with an
authority comparable to that of an oracle. It would be safer, however, to
say that it relies on a contrast – between religious oracles, which
Lucretius like any good Epicurean deplores, and the philosopher's rational alternative, delivered 'as from the shrine of the mind' (737).[59] That

---

[55] Contrast Edwards (1989), who takes this passage and others in Lucretius as treating Empedocles
with a certain disdain.

[56] First at III 15. It is unwise to be too confident that Lucretius is alluding to Empedocles' own pro-
fession of divinity at the beginning of the *Katharmoi*, if, as I would maintain, his interest is otherwise focused entirely on Empedocles' *On nature*. But the legend of Empedocles' plunge into Etna
in a bid to establish his own divinity was probably well enough known by this date to give the
remark extra point (cf. Wright (1981), pp. 15–16 and Hor. *Ars poet.* 463–6).

[57] I 635–44, cf. Kollmann (1971), and especially Tatum (1984).

[58] The reference is vague, but perhaps picks up the proponents of two elements in I 712–13 as well
as the four-element theorists of 714–15. On the Epicurean background to their belittling description, see pp. 142–3 below.

[59] On this reading, Lucretius' words distance him from approval of (literal) oracles as effectively as
the way in which, for example, those who praise the 'university of life' distance themselves from
approval of (literal) universities. Thus Lucretius' application of oracular language to his own
pronouncements, here and at V 111–12 (*fundere fata*), is ironic: cf. Obbink (1996), pp. 568–9, commenting on the irony in Philodemus, *Piet.* 2044–5 (ἐχρησμῳ[ι]δήσαμεν) and in Epicurus *SV* 29,
with a comprehensive set of Epicurean parallel uses of oracular language. The evidence listed

would amount to a contrast between, on the one hand, the clear, rational and unambiguous assertions of the pluralists, and, on the other, the Delphic ambiguities so characteristic of Heraclitus.[60] If so, we must be wary of exaggerating the extent to which this eulogy of Empedocles expresses special admiration for his teaching as such. It is largely as an eloquent and straight-talking expositor of his teaching that he is canonised. Empedocles' language may be densely metaphorical (as is Lucretius' own), but at least, as Lucretius sees it, it lacks the multi-layered evasiveness and trickery of Heraclitean prose. About Lucretius' very reserved evaluation of Empedocles' actual teachings I shall say more below.

What purpose is served in this passage by the fulsome praise of Sicily? One object, no doubt, is to compare Empedocles favourably with that other wonder of Sicily, Etna.[61] But it also has the job of illustrating why Sicily was the birthplace of the four-element theory.[62] The four elements are intricately worked into the travelogue. Empedocles was born within Sicily's 'terrestrial coasts' (*terrarum . . . in oris*, 717: literally 'coasts of lands') – and here *terrarum* is no 'otiose addition' (Bailey), but Lucretius' way of identifying the land of Sicily with the element earth. The elements water and fire are abundantly in evidence in the descriptions of the surrounding sea, of the whirlpool Charybdis, and of the flames of Etna (718–25). Finally (725), those flames are borne 'to the sky' (*caelum*). Now the sky, as the abode both of air and of the heavenly bodies, might in principle symbolise either of the elements air and fire. What surely clinches its identification with air, and thus completes the catalogue of four ele-

---

by Smith (1975), pp. 60–1, note b, does not militate against this picture: in Epicurus SF 29, χρησμῳδεῖν is associated with unintelligibility; Cic. *Fin.* II 20, 102 and *ND* I 66 do use *oracula* of philosophical pronouncements (some of them Epicurean), but only in the mouths of Epicurus' critics; the epigram of Athenaeus (ap. DL x 12) speaks of Epicurus not as himself oracular but as *inspired* either by the Muses or by the Delphic oracle. Cf. Smith (1996), p. 130 n. 75 for further comment.

[60] For *certus* = 'unambiguous' see *OLD s.v.*, 9. The same sense fits perfectly into v 111–12, where these lines recur: Lucretius is saying that his quasi-oracular prediction that the world will one day perish (see Chapter 6) is a firm and unambiguous one, unlike those associated with the Delphic oracle. For Heraclitus' 'Delphic' ambiguity, cf. his B93 DK. As for *sanctius*, in a comparison with an oracle this must primarily imply 'holier', but the basic meaning of *sanctus* (from *sancire*) is 'ratified' or 'confirmed', and it also has connotations of 'above board' or 'honourable' (*OLD s.v.*, 4).

[61] If the thesis developed below about Lucretius' literary debt to Empedocles is right, it may not be too fanciful to see in the imminent new eruption of Etna (722ff.) a hint at the scheduled rebirth of Empedoclean poetry. And is it really just a coincidence that at 730 Lucretius praises Empedocles as 'carus', his own cognomen (for the point, see Fowler (1996), p. 888)? The adjective is not part of his regular vocabulary, this being one of only two occurrences in his poem.

[62] This was well spotted by MacKay (1955) and Snyder (1972).

ments, is the fact that Empedocles himself uses 'sky' (οὐρανός) as a name for his element air (B22.2).[63]

And the Empedoclean influence goes deeper still. The very idea of using individual phenomena like sea, rain, wind and sun to symbolise the four elemental stuffs is thoroughly Empedoclean. So too is the poetic device of interweaving the four elements into the language of a descriptive passage: we have already seen Empedocles do the same at B115, when he described the tossing of the fallen daimon from aether (= air) to sea, to land, to the sun's rays, and then back once more into the eddies of the aether.

At the very least, then, Lucretius' description of Sicily reveals his intimate knowledge and exploitation of Empedoclean poetry. And it would be unwise to rule out a further possibility: that it is itself a direct imitation of a lost passage of Empedocles.

5. THE ENIGMA OF LUCRETIUS' PROEM

We are now ready to turn to the most hotly and inconclusively debated passage in Lucretius, the proem to book 1.[64] It is structured as follows:

1–20:	praise of Venus as *Aeneadum genetrix* and the life force of all nature;
21–8:	prayer to Venus to inspire Lucretius' poem, because she alone is responsible for making things pleasing, and because Memmius has always been her favourite;
29–43:	prayer to Venus to intercede with her lover Mars and bring peace to the Roman republic;
44–9:	it is not in the divine nature to concern itself with our affairs;
50–61:	programmatic address to Memmius about the content of the poem;
62–79:	praise of Epicurus' intellectual achievement;
80–101:	attack on the evils of religion, as illustrated by the sacrifice of Iphigeneia;
102–35:	warning to Memmius not to be enticed by false religious tales about the survival and transmigration of the soul;
136–45:	the difficulty of Lucretius' poetic task.

---

[63] As Kingsley (1995), ch. 2, shows, Empedocles' own designation of air is 'aether', and aether in early Greek epic is intimately associated with οὐρανός.

[64] The huge bibliography on this passage prominently includes Giancotti (1959), Kleve (1966), Kenney (1977), pp. 13–17, Clay (1983), pp. 82–110, Gale (1994a) ch. 6, and all the major commentaries.

The most enigmatic feature of the proem lies in the first three sub-divisions, 1–43. How can Lucretius, as an Epicurean, praise Venus as a controlling force in nature, and even beg her to intervene in human affairs? In Epicureanism, the gods emphatically do not intervene in any way in human affairs – as Lucretius himself paradoxically goes on immediately to point out (44–9 = ii 646–51).

To respond that the proem's treatment of Venus is allegorical is not in itself a solution to the puzzle. As Lucretius himself warns at ii 655–60, allegorical use of divinities' names, e.g. 'Neptune' for the sea and 'Ceres' for corn, is permissible only if one avoids any false religious implications. Although Venus might, on this principle, get away with symbolising nature, or even perhaps Epicurean pleasure,[65] the opening address to her as ancestress of the Romans can hardly be judged equally innocent, nor can the prayers to her to intervene in Roman affairs and to inspire Lucretius' poetry.

It is not that these allegorical explanations do not carry any weight at all. I think there is much truth in them. But the most they can do, for readers who have read on and been surprised to learn that this is an Epicurean poem, is mitigate their bafflement. The question remains, what can have impelled Lucretius to start out so misleadingly, under-mining exactly that attitude to the gods that the rest of the poem will so energetically promote? It would scarcely be an exaggeration to say that he spends the remainder of the poem undoing the damage done by the first forty-three lines.

6. FURLEY'S THESIS

In short, the opening of the proem simply is not like Lucretius. But it is very like Empedocles. In his outstandingly important study of the proem, David Furley has observed the high level of Empedoclean content to be found in it.[66] My object here will be to augment his observations with further evidence of Empedoclean echoes, but then, in the remainder of the chapter, to propose a very different explanation from his for their presence here.

[65] The suggestion of Bignone (1945), pp. 437–44, but one which faces the difficulty that Lucretius' Venus controls all natural coming-to-be (esp. 21ff.), not just animal reproduction. Asmis (1982) proposes that Venus is here an Epicurean deity invented to take over the role assigned to Zeus by the Stoics; but against the supposition that Lucretius is concerned to resist the Stoics, see Ch. 3 below.

[66] Furley (1970). The range and depth of Empedoclean nuances in the proem are further enriched by Clay (1983), pp. 22–3, 49ff., 82–110, 253–7.

First, notice the by now familiar technique of working the four elements into a descriptive passage. The poem begins as follows (1–5):

> Aeneadum genetrix, hominum divomque voluptas,
> alma Venus, caeli subter labentia signa
> quae mare navigerum, quae terras frugiferentis
> concelebras, per te quoniam genus omne animantum
> concipitur visitque exortum lumina solis.   5

> Ancestress of the race of Aeneas, delight of humans and gods,
> nurturing Venus, who beneath the gliding beacons of the sky
> pervade the ship-bearing sea and the crop-carrying lands,
> because it is due to you that every race of living beings is con-
> ceived, and born to look upon the sunlight.

Planted in the text already are references to the sky (which we have seen to represent the element air in Empedoclean imagery),[67] to the heavenly bodies and the sunlight (i.e. fire), to the sea, and to the land. We then launch into a second catalogue of the same four (6–9):

> te dea, te fugiunt venti, te nubila caeli
> adventumque tuum, tibi suavis daedala tellus
> summittit flores, tibi rident aequora ponti
> placatumque nitet diffuso lumine caelum.

> From you, goddess, and your approach the winds and the clouds
> of the sky flee away. For you the creative earth pushes up sweet
> flowers. For you the sea's surface laughs, and the sky, made calm,
> shines with diffused light.

Again, the four elements feature: the winds and clouds of the sky, the earth, the sea, the sunlight. And if all this is still not enough, we need only move on to 29–43, Lucretius' prayer to Venus to intercede with her lover Mars. It has long been recognised that here we have a striking allusion to the joint-protagonists of Empedocles' physical poem, Love and Strife – whom Empedocles himself sometimes calls Aphrodite and Ares.

Furley has noted two other Empedoclean echoes in the proem, to which we will come shortly. But first the question must be asked: why should an Epicurean poem start with an Empedoclean prologue?

It is here that I part company with Furley. He argues that Lucretius' act of piety to Empedocles is the acknowledgement of a philosophical debt. Although Lucretius was himself a committed follower of Epicurus, Furley suggests, he recognised Empedocles as the inaugurator or champion of two traditions to which, as an Epicurean, he too adhered. The

---

[67] I offer this as a ground for going beyond Furley and detecting all four elements even in lines 1–5.

first of these is the insistence on absolutely unchanging physical elements. The second is the rejection of a teleological world-view, with all its implications of divine intervention.

But this could hardly explain Lucretius' decision to open with a tribute to Empedocles. No reader of the proems to books III, V, and VI can doubt that Lucretius' other philosophical debts pale into insignificance when compared with his acknowledged dependence upon Epicurus. Why then would he give his putative philosophical obligation to Empedocles the undeserved and thoroughly misleading prominence that it gains from a position at the poem's opening?

Moreover, the unwritten rules of philosophical allegiance in the ancient world do not normally permit the imputation of authority to anyone other than the founder of your own school, or, at most, to his own acknowledged forerunners.[68] The Epicurean school was second to none in observing this principle. It seems certain that Empedocles was not regarded by Epicurus or his successors as any sort of philosophical forerunner; and even an acknowledged forerunner like Democritus was treated with limited respect in the school.[69] Now Lucretius is admittedly in certain ways a non-standard Epicurean, and I shall be arguing in Chapter 3 that he was not a participating member of any Epicurean group. Even so, his declarations of absolute loyalty to Epicurus as the very first philosopher to liberate the human race from fear of the divine[70] hardly suggest that he was an exception to this usual style of school loyalty. In any case, he certainly knew his Epicurean source texts well enough to be aware of Epicurus' own reserve with regard to his forerunners.

Even on the two philosophical issues picked out by Furley, element theory and anti-teleology, it is doubtful whether Lucretius or any other Epicurean would have been as generous in acknowledging Empedocles' contribution as Furley proposes. Indeed, so far as concerns element theory, Lucretius is emphatic at I 734–41 (translated above pp. 12–13) that this is not a topic on which Empedocles acquitted himself with distinction.

---

[68] As argued in Sedley (1989b).

[69] For Democritus as an acknowledged precursor of Epicurus, see Plut. *Col.* 1108E–F; for Epicurus' reserved praise of him in *On nature*, see pp. 142–3 below. Epicurean attacks on Empedocles include those of Hermarchus (see Longo Auricchio (1988), pp. 66–73, 92–9, 125–50, and Vander Waerdt (1988), pp. 89–90, n. 13) and Colotes (Plut. *Col.* 1111F ff.); see also Cic. *ND* I 29, Diogenes of Oenoanda 6 II–III Smith (1992), with the further passages assembled by Vander Waerdt. In my view (Sedley (1976a)) Epicurus' attitude to his predecessors was more respectful and lenient than that adopted by his followers, but it undoubtedly showed enough coolness to authorise and encourage their attacks.   [70] I 62–79, III 1–22, V 9–13.

That there is something, singular or plural, that somehow persists through all cosmogonical and other changes is common ground for all physical philosophers from Anaximander on. No doubt Empedocles' elements were more emphatically unchanging than those of his predecessors. At least, he says that as the elements intermingle they both become different things at different times and remain always alike (B17.34–5). He probably means that they form different compound substances but nevertheless retain their own distinctive properties in the mixture. But other interpretations were possible – for example, that in mixtures the elements do retain their original properties, but that these remain dormant until the compounds separate out again. And, at any rate, I see little sign that Lucretius was prepared to give him the benefit of the doubt on this point. In criticising the four-element theory, he makes no gesture of respect even for the well-advertised indestructibility of Empedocles' elements (B8, B9, B12): on the contrary, his principal ground for rejecting the theory is that stuffs like earth, air, fire, and water are inevitably perishable (I 753–62). As for their unchangeability, he mentions this as no more than a possible interpretation of the theory, and one that would rob it of what little explanatory power it has (I 770–81).

Does Empedocles fare any better in Lucretius' eyes as a champion of anti-teleology? It cannot be denied that Aristotle casts him in that role: in defending the teleological structure of organisms, Aristotle contrasts his view with the zoogonical thesis of Empedocles that originally a set of randomly composed monsters sprang up – graphically described by Empedocles as 'ox-children man-faced'[71] – of which only the fittest survived. This anticipation of one of the principles of Darwinism has earned Empedocles widespread respect, including, it is sometimes suggested, the respect of the Epicureans. For Lucretius testifies (v 837–77) that they adopted a similar-sounding theory of the survival of the fittest as their basis for the origin of species.

I would not want to deny the probability of a historical link between the Empedoclean and Epicurean theories. But it is a large leap from that to the supposition that the Epicureans acknowledged a debt to Empedocles. Indeed, it can be precisely in those cases where a school is drawing on the ideas of another that it is most at pains to minimise the resemblance and to stress its own originality. This appears to have been the Epicurean attitude to the Empedoclean theory of evolution. Plutarch[72] tells us explicitly that the Epicureans derided Empedocles'

---

[71] Empedocles B61.2. Cf. Aristotle, *Phys.* 198b32, 199b10–12, *PA* 640a19ff.   [72] Plut. *Col.* 1123B.

'ox-children man-faced'. And well they might, for Empedocles' monsters were themselves the bizarre product of random combinations of
limbs and organs that in an even earlier stage had sprung up and wan-
dered about on their own![73] There is nothing like this in the Epicurean
theory, as we hear about it from Lucretius; and I can see no attempt in
Lucretius book v to restore to Empedocles the credit which the
Epicurean school traditionally denied him.[74]

Indeed, since Lucretius certainly knew Empedocles' physical poem at
first hand and did not have to rely exclusively on Aristotelian-influenced
doxography,[75] it certainly should not be assumed that he read Empedocles
as a pioneering opponent of teleology. If Aristotle chooses Empedocles
rather than the far more suitable Democritus for that role, it is surely
because Empedocles, perhaps alone among the Presocratics, has actually
supplied him with an illustration of what a non-teleological explanation
of an organism would look like. It does not follow that Empedocles' own
intention, taken in context, came over as anti-teleological.[76] As is well
known, he is supposed to have postulated four stages of animal evolution,
of which the compounding of the ox-children man-faced was only the
second. Either in the first stage, that of solitary animal parts, or perhaps
in the third stage, that of the so-called 'whole-natured forms', he
described the creation of individual animal parts in terms that could
hardly have won him the friendship of an anti-teleologist like Lucretius.
In B84, already mentioned above, Empedocles describes how Aphrodite[77]
cunningly created the eye, just like someone fitting together a lantern for
the preconceived purpose of lighting their way at night. Even if one strips
from this the figurative personification of Love as a divine artisan, one is
left with the impression of an intelligent and purposive creative force. The
architectonic role of Love in Empedocles' cosmic cycle makes it a very
hard task indeed to portray him as a pure mechanist.

---

[73] Empedocles A72, B57.

[74] Furley (1970), p. 61 with n. 15, supports his thesis with the claim that Lucretius v 837–41 is a translation of Empedocles B57. Although it may pointedly recall the Empedoclean lines, it is hardly
a translation. Where Empedocles describes isolated limbs, Lucretius describes whole organisms
with congenital defects — and that represents a crucial difference between the two zoogonical
theories.

[75] Cf. Clay (1983), pp. 22–3, 289–90 nn. 43–4. Rösler (1973) correctly stresses Lucretius' use of doxography in his critique of Empedocles at 1 714–829; but this is, I believe, a special case, in so far
as the passage is almost certainly based on Epicurus' own criticism of earlier physical theories in
On nature xiv and xv, which in turn will have relied heavily on Theophrastus' *Physical opinions* (see
Ch. 4, §10; Ch. 5, §4; Ch. 6, §7).

[76] Teleology was not in Empedocles' day an issue on which sides had to be taken. In what follows,
I am describing the impression he was likely to make on later readers attuned to such a debate.

[77] B86 confirms that Aphrodite was the artisan in question; see Sedley (1992b).

Why, then, does Lucretius nevertheless speak approvingly of Empedocles' 'discoveries' (1 732–3)? To see this in perspective, it is important to note that only four lines later he speaks with equal approval of the 'discoveries' of other, unnamed natural philosophers whom he brackets with Empedocles. Lucretius is not, in effect, singling out Empedocles as a uniquely important authority but is expressing an Epicurean's qualified respect for the work of the Presocratic natural philosophers in general. Following Epicurus, he applauds the Presocratic tendency to seek physical, as opposed to theological, explanations for such cosmic phenomena as celestial motions, eclipses, and earthquakes. The Epicurean school's method of handling these phenomena was to catalogue with approval all the available physical explanations of each, adding that any or all might be correct, so that to choose between them would be arbitrary and unscientific. Both Epicurus, in his *Letter to Pythocles*, and Lucretius, in books v (509–770) and vi, thus come to list as possibilities a range of explanatory theses deriving in large measure from the Presocratic philosophers, including Empedocles. For example, both Epicurus (*Letter to Pythocles* 101) and Lucretius (vi 204–12) accept as one of the possible explanations of lightning the thesis of Empedocles (A63) that it is fire from the sun trapped in the clouds. It is, I am convinced, only at this level of detail that the Epicureans, Lucretius included, are prepared to applaud the 'discoveries' of Empedocles.

7. EMPEDOCLES AS LITERARY FOREBEAR

If, then, Lucretius is not thanking Empedocles for the content of the *DRN*, perhaps he is thanking him for its form. There are, after all, well-recognised formal correspondences between the two hexameter poems.

Take first their titles. *De rerum natura* is usually thought to translate Περὶ φύσεως, a title conventionally assigned to many Greek cosmological texts, including Empedocles' physical poem, as well of course as being the title of Epicurus' great prose treatise on which, I shall argue in Chapters 4–5, Lucretius was relying. As a matter of fact, though, one late source[78] reports Empedocles' title as *On the nature of the things there are* (Περὶ φύσεως τῶν ὄντων), which would be closer still to *De rerum natura*. There is no independent evidence to confirm this title, but it seems highly plausible. The simple 'On nature' is so widespread that it has been suspected of being, at least for fifth-century BC authors, no more than a standard

---

[78] *Suda, s.v.* 'Empedocles' = 31A2 DK.

title assigned to their works by later scholars.[79] But someone like Empedocles who wrote at least two poems, not to mention prose works, is less likely to have left them untitled, and we have seen no reason not to accept the title *Katharmoi* as entirely authentic. As for *On the nature of the things there are*, his near-contemporary Melissus published a work entitled *On nature, or on what there is* (Περὶ φύσεως ἢ περὶ τοῦ ὄντος), the singular 'what there is' proclaiming his Eleatic monism. That Melissus' reported title is authentic is confirmed by the parody published by Empedocles' follower Gorgias, *On what there is not, or on nature* (Περὶ τοῦ μὴ ὄντος ἢ περὶ φύσεως). Against this background, Empedocles' choice of *On the nature of the things there are*, with its plural form τῶν ὄντων, as a title for what was above all else a pluralist manifesto, makes ready sense.

Apart from the titles, there are other striking formal resemblances. In particular, Lucretius' poem is addressed to a friend, Memmius, as Empedocles' physical poem is to his friend Pausanias. And both at certain points turn to address an invocation to the muse Calliope.[80]

I am now ready to unveil my own hypothesis: *the proem of the DRN is, and is meant to be recognised as, an imitation of the proem to Empedocles' physical poem.*

The letter of Cicero with which I opened the present chapter constitutes strong evidence that contemporary readers could be expected to recognise this imitation, if such it was. For it attests a literary climate in which Empedocles was on the list of acknowledged Greek authors,[81] familiar to the well-educated either through direct acquaintance or through Latin translations and imitations. (Even if other Roman literati shared Cicero's inability to struggle through to the end of Sallustius' *Empedoclea*, many could be assumed, like him, at least to have read the opening.) Above all, it shows us Lucretius being thought about by his contemporaries in an Empedoclean context.

On my hypothesis, Lucretius' purpose is to establish from the outset the precise Greek literary mantle he is assuming (rather as Virgil's *Aeneid* announces with the opening words *arma virumque cano* that it will be a combined *Iliad–Odyssey*). Lucretius, in his poetic manifesto at 1 921–50 and his appreciation of Ennius' pedigree at 1 117–26 (see pp. 31–2 below), shows himself to be no less concerned with literary pedigree than other Roman poets of his era.

---

[79] Schmalzriedt (1970).   [80] Empedocles B3, B131; Lucretius vi 92–5. See Clay (1983), pp. 253–7.
[81] For a judicious discussion of Ennius' possible use of Empedocles, see Skutsch (1985), pp. 160, 164 n. 18, 260, 394ff., 758. Ovid's extensive use of Empedocles in the speech of Pythagoras in *Met.* xv is impressively discussed in Hardie (1995).

To amplify the hypothesis: Lucretius is imitating Empedocles' proem, but adapting it, as he goes along, (a) to a Roman patriotic theme, and (b) to Epicurean philosophy, at the same time steering us gently away from Empedocles' actual doctrines. His object? To announce himself as *the Roman Empedocles* – the great Roman poet of nature. In short, he is laying claim to a literary, not a philosophical, heritage. For there can be little doubt that it was to Empedocles, rather than to the only other available candidate, Parmenides, that Lucretius looked as his great Greek forebear in the tradition of cosmological poetry. This was certainly the comparison that regularly occurred to Roman readers,[82] and rightly so. (I shall be exploring Empedoclean features of Lucretius' writing not only in the present chapter but also in Chapter 2, §5, and in Chapter 7, §6.)

A glaring weakness of this hypothesis will already be obvious. We do not have the proem to Empedocles' *On nature*.[83] How then can we say anything at all about its resemblance or otherwise to Lucretius' proem?

My answer is twofold. First, we are not altogether without evidence about its content, as I hope to show. Indeed, there is little doubt that some of our familiar fragments of Empedocles are in fact from it. Moreover, thanks to the exciting papyrus find that has been made since I first formulated the argument of this chapter,[84] we now have considerably more of Empedocles' proem than was available even a few years ago. The new fragments are believed all to come from a single scroll, which contained book 1 of Empedocles' physical poem.[85]

Second, if the proposed hypothesis proves capable of explaining features of Lucretius' proem that otherwise remain inexplicable, that in itself would provide some degree of confirmation.

1 1–49. I shall begin my defence of the hypothesis with a re-examination of the opening lines (translated above p. 17):

> Aeneadum genetrix, hominum divomque voluptas,
> alma Venus, caeli subter labentia signa
> quae mare navigerum, quae terras frugiferentis
> concelebras . . .

The linguistic case for a direct Empedoclean model seems to me a rather strong one. The first two words are, of course, a distinctively Roman

---

[82] E.g. Quintilian *Inst.* 1 4.4; Lactantius, *Div. inst.* II 12 14.
[83] Van der Ben (1975) offers his own wholesale reconstruction of Empedocles' proem. Most of it rests on guesswork. My grounds for rejecting it will simply be the arguments I offer below for accepting a different reconstruction, based largely on Lucretius. [84] In Sedley (1989a)
[85] See above p. 10.

invocation. But *hominum divomque voluptas* already bears an Empedoclean fingerprint. The identical phrase recurs, with a small change of syntax, at VI 92–5, in an address to Calliope that has long been recognised as an Empedoclean touch on Lucretius' part.[86] *Hominum divomque* could translate some variant on the regular hexameter ending ἀνδρῶν τε θεῶν τε, used in Homer's formulaic designation of Zeus as 'father of men and gods'. Such reworkings of Homeric locutions are an integral feature of Empedocles' poetry.[87] And *voluptas* picks up Γηθοσύνη, 'Delight', used by Empedocles, like 'Aphrodite', as a title for his goddess Love (B17.24). Next, *alma*, 'nurturing', might represent ζείδωρος, 'life-giving', an attested Empedoclean epithet for Aphrodite (B151); but as a matter of fact there is a much better candidate among the new fragments of Empedocles. These include (in a fragmentary context) the adjective φυτάλμιος, 'nurturing', commonly used in Greek poetry as a stock epithet for divinities.[88] In addition to being virtually synonymous with the Latin *almus*, it also shares its leading syllable. It would be easy to imagine 'Κύπρι φυτάλμιε . . .' as an Empedoclean line-beginning, matching Lucretius' *alma Venus . . .*

We then proceed, in 2–9 (quoted p. 17 above), to the elaborate double interweaving of the four elements into the hymn. For Lucretius to expect any reader to identify these as the Empedoclean four in the very opening lines of the poem, without any prior clue, would be wildly optimistic. It is far more credible that he found them already present in his Empedoclean original. We have already noted that interweaving the four elements into a descriptive passage is an authentic Empedoclean device.

Line 3 is remarkable for its pair of compound adjectives: *quae mare navigerum, quae terras frugiferentis . . .* Lucretius has a well-known penchant for these quasi-Greek formations,[89] and we will see in the next chapter how they sometimes combine with Greek loan words to build up an evocative context that transports his reader to the Greek world. But there are two unusual features of this particular pair. First, both accurately translate actual Greek compound adjectives – respectively, *navigerum* = ναυσίπορον and *frugiferentis* = καρποφόρους (or a participial equivalent from καρποφορεῖν).[90] Second, although the bold deployment of compound

---

[86] VI 94, *Calliope, requies hominum divomque voluptas.*

[87] See the seminal study by Bollack (1965–9), I 277ff. Aristotle, in his lost *On poets*, called Empedocles Ὁμηρικός (DL VIII 57).

[88] There seems little possibility that in the actual fragment the adjective is serving this role.

[89] See Bailey (1947), I 132ff. for a convenient catalogue of Lucretius' compound adjectives.

[90] This is not unique in Lucretius – for instance *florifer* (III 11) corresponds to ἀνθοφόρος and *ignifer* (V 459 etc.) to πυρφόρος – but I have spotted very few such cases.

adjectives in pairs, or even in trios, is among the most prominent features of Empedocles' verse,[91] it is one Empedoclean practice which elsewhere Lucretius studiously avoids. In his whole poem, in fact, such a grouping occurs uniquely here.[92] The double idiosyncrasy suggests that in line 3 some exceptional motivation is at work. The supposition that Lucretius was consciously seeking to capture and reproduce in Latin an actual Empedoclean line would provide such a motivation. In fact, his line practically tumbles unaided into a characteristically Empedoclean Greek hexameter: πόντον ναυσίπορον καὶ γαίας καρποφορούσας.[93]

Lines 10–20 present Lucretius' entrancing portrait of the reproductive frenzy which Venus inspires throughout the animal kingdom in spring. Then in line 21 Venus emerges as the controller of all *natura*, in the passage (21–8) which also, in line 25, effectively delivers to us the title of the poem:

> quae quoniam rerum naturam sola gubernas
> nec sine te quicquam dias in luminis oras
> exoritur neque fit laetum neque amabile quicquam,
> te sociam studeo scribendis versibus esse
> quos ego de rerum natura pangere conor   25
> Memmiadae nostro, quem tu, dea, tempore in omni
> omnibus ornatum voluisti excellere rebus.
> quo magis aeternum da dictis, diva, leporem.

> Since you alone control the *natura* of things, and without you nothing springs forth into the realm of light or becomes joyful and delectable, I am eager for you to be my partner in writing the verses which I am trying to set out about the nature of things (*de rerum natura*) for our friend Memmius, whom you, goddess, have wanted to be at all times outstanding in all things. All the more then, goddess, bestow on my words an everlasting charm.

As Diskin Clay has pointed out, in this context *natura* (21) tends towards the sense 'birth' (through its association with *nasci*, 'be born') rather than

---

[91] Empedocles B20.6 7, B21.11 12, B40, B60 1, B76.1–2, etc. The forms ἐμπεδόφυλλα and ἐμπεδόκαρπα (B77.1) are unique to Empedocles, and suggest a heightened consciousness of the etymology of his own name as a further compound adjective, 'eternally renowned'.

[92] The closest groupings of compound adjectives, outside 1 3, are at II 1081–3 and V 864–6. In both cases they occur two lines apart, qualifying items which are respectively first and third in a list.

[93] In Sedley (1989a) I placed the first two words in the reverse order (perhaps metrically preferable but cf. e.g. Empedocles B84.6) ναυσίπορον πόντον καὶ γαίας καρποφορούσας. Gisela Striker has persuaded me to avoid the jingle which this creates in the second to third foot. Her own suggestion is to retain my original order but change the cases throughout to genitives. This could well be preferable. I retain the accusative merely in order to maximise the isomorphism with the Lucretian line.

simply 'nature', thus echoing Empedocles' characteristic use of φύσις with precisely the same shift from the more familiar 'nature' to 'birth'.[94]

Leaving aside these linguistic and conceptual echoes, it is in any case eminently plausible that Empedocles' poem should have opened with a hymn to Aphrodite. Hesiod's *Works and days*, with its opening hymn to Zeus, would constitute ample precedent within the tradition of didactic poetry; and it goes without saying that Aphrodite would be Empedocles' preferred divinity. In B128 he makes it a mark of the Golden Age, in which among other things there was no animal slaughter, that Aphrodite was the only divinity worshipped:

Nor did they have Ares or Strife as a god, nor was Zeus or Cronos or Poseidon their king, but Cypris was queen . . . Her they propitiated with pious images . . .

I am not suggesting that this fragment itself comes from Empedocles' proem. But it does reveal a feature of his religious thought that Lucretius could himself use to advantage — namely the idea that the identity of a person's divinities is a function of that person's own moral state.[95] If you are a peaceful person, Ares is not your god, but Aphrodite is. Lucretius, as an Epicurean, must hold the somewhat similar view that the gods' true nature is peaceful, and that people's tendency to endow them with angry and warlike temperaments is a projection of their own moral maladjustment.[96] The essence of god is blessed detachment; anger, jealousy and the like are accretions misleadingly superimposed by us on that essence.

This may offer us a lead on the much debated lines 44–9, in which Lucretius presents the correct Epicurean view of the gods as tranquil and detached:

> omnis enim per se divom natura necessest
> immortali aevo summa cum pace fruatur   45
> semota ab nostris rebus seiunctaque longe;
> nam privata dolore omni, privata periclis,
> ipsa suis pollens opibus, nil indiga nostri,
> nec bene promeritis capitur neque tangitur ira.

> For the entire nature of the gods, in its essence, must of necessity enjoy everlasting life along with perfect peace, removed and far separated from our affairs. Without any pain, without

[94] Empedocles B8. See Clay (1983), pp. 83–95, with the parallels he cites at p. 308 n. 29.
[95] Cf. B17.23, where Love is 'she by whom mortals think friendly thoughts and perform peaceful deeds'.
[96] See Long/Sedley (1987), 1 139–49. The point stands whether or not, as argued there, Lucretius was wrong to understand Epicurus' gods as objectively real life-forms.

dangers, strong through its own resources, with no need of us, it
is neither won over by favours nor touched by anger.

These lines occur also at II 646–51, where they are superficially much
more at home, and many editors believe that they are an intrusive gloss
in the proem:[97] it seems anomalous for Lucretius to stress the total
detachment of the gods from human affairs directly after his prayer to
Venus to intervene and save the Roman republic from war. And yet the
sudden reversal is too characteristic of Lucretius to be lightly dismissed.
Even when these same lines recur in book II, they are used similarly to
reverse the religious implications of what precedes, this time a seductive
allegorical reading of the worship of Cybele as symbolising (at least in
its last lines) her direct interest in human affairs.

Imagine now in addition an original Empedoclean proem in which
Aphrodite, as Love, is asked to propitiate Ares, as Strife. What
Empedocles would have intended by this is not so much an attempt to
interfere with the inevitable progression of the cosmic cycle, as a plea
to human beings to let their peaceful tendencies calm and suppress the
bloodthirsty side of their nature.[98] If so, Lucretius would welcome this
essentially moral use of myth and prayer, and could readily apply it to
the current war-torn state of his own country. But since Empedocles
regards Ares/Strife as a real, if less palatable, god, Lucretius might very
naturally want to add an Epicurean corrective: that Venus' hoped-for
propitiation of Mars represents no more than people's return to the one
true conception of the divine nature as tranquil and detached, instead
of angry and warlike. Hence the connexion of thought found in the
text: Venus, make Mars peaceful, because that alone is the *essential*
nature of divinity (*omnis enim per se divom natura . . .*). Or, translated into
Epicurean moral terms: Romans, let your belief in a peaceful god overcome your belief in a warlike god, because peacefulness is the true
essence of godlike happiness. The connexion of thought could no
doubt have been made clearer; but I would be reluctant to rob
Lucretius of this important Epicurean modification to Empedoclean
theology.

---

[97] See the arguments marshalled by Courtney (1987), pp. 11ff.
[98] Eustathius (*Od.* 310.33ff., *ad* Hom. *Od.* VIII 367) may imply that Empedocles used the myth of the
union of Aphrodite and Ares as an allegory for friendship; and since there is no stage within the
cosmic cycle itself at which Love and Strife unite, the likeliest location for that piece of symbol-
ism would indeed be his proem. However, Eustathius' words may mean no more than that some
allegorists proposed an Empedoclean interpretation of the myth; cf. Heraclit. *Alleg. Hom.* 69.8,
and Buffière (1956), pp. 168–72.

By this stage, it should be noted, I am no longer suggesting direct translation or line-by-line imitation of Empedocles' proem on Lucretius' part, but the deployment of the same sequence of themes as occurred in it, for increasingly Epicurean purposes.

I 50–61. The next section of Lucretius' proem is a programmatic address to Memmius. He asks Memmius to give him his full attention – perhaps an echo of the passage that contained Empedocles' surviving line 'Listen to me, Pausanias, son of wise Anchiteus' (B1). He then proceeds to outline the content of the poem. He will explain to Memmius the character of the heaven and the gods, and the elements (56–7)

> unde omnis natura creet res auctet alatque
> quove eadem rursum natura perempta resolvat.
>
> . . . from which nature creates, increases, and nurtures all things,
> and into which that same nature once more resolves them when
> they are destroyed.

After this he spends four lines naming his cosmic first principles (*genitalia corpora, semina rerum*, etc.).[99]

This dual process, whereby things combine and are once more dissolved into their constituents, bears a strong formal resemblance to Empedocles' own programmatic description in B17, a passage that is explicitly attested by Simplicius as coming from the opening of the physical poem.[100] Not only do we have Simplicius' attestation to that effect, but the new papyrus find includes a fragment which at its beginning coincides with lines 31–5 of B17 and then continues it for another 34 lines. Thanks to a line number (Γ = 300) preserved in the margin at the end of the new fragment, we can now say that the opening couplet of fragment 17 was probably lines 233–4 of the poem:

> δίπλ' ἐρέω· τοτὲ μὲν γὰρ ἓν ηὐξήθη μόνον εἶναι
> ἐκ πλεόνων, τοτὲ δ' αὖ διέφυ πλέον' ἐξ ἑνὸς εἶναι.
>
> I will tell a double tale. For at one time there grew to be just one
> thing from many, and at another it grew apart once more to be
> many out of one.

The symmetrical two-way nature of the process is emphasised repeatedly in similarly balanced antitheses for a further fifteen lines,[101] after

---

[99] See further, Ch. 2, §3; Ch. 7, §§3 and 6.
[100] Simplicius, *In Phys.* 161.14–15; see preamble to B17 in Diels/Kranz.
[101] In the new fragment which continues the passage there appear to be further returns to much

which Empedocles, like Lucretius, proceeds to name the cosmic principles underlying the process – the four elements, plus Love and Strife.
Empedocles' repetitiveness, a device for emphasising the eternality of
his cosmic cycle, is understandably not reproduced by Lucretius. But in
other respects the formal parallelism of the two programmatic passages
is striking.

It begins to look highly plausible that Empedocles' proem to *On nature*,
having opened with a hymn to Aphrodite, then continued with a programmatic address to Pausanias, of which B17 formed a part. Such a
structure would, naturally enough, mimic the opening of Hesiod's *Works
and days*, where a short hymn to Zeus is immediately followed by a personal address to Perses.

Given our new knowledge of Empedocles' line numbering, this
hypothesis would mean that the hymn to Aphrodite and the personal
address to Pausanias occupied around 230 lines.[102] Is this implausibly
long? I do not think so. Empedocles is a wordy and repetitive writer, as
the new fragments amply confirm. And we have no way of guessing how
much personal detail was included in the address to Pausanias (the
Hesiodic model would have permitted plenty).[103]

1.62–79. Lucretius' next section is his praise of Epicurus' intellectual
achievement.[104] At a time when mankind was wretchedly oppressed by
religion, a certain Greek became the first (*primum Graius homo*, 66) to stand
up against its tyranny. Such were his mental powers that he was able to
break through the 'flaming walls of the world' and traverse with his intellect the measureless universe. By reporting back to us the laws that bind
and limit natural processes, he has broken the power of religion.

Once more there is a clear Empedoclean model, B129, almost certainly referring to Pythagoras:

the same two-way description of change, as well as a brief preview of the beginning of the cycle,
to be resumed in earnest in B35.

[102] The numbering was not a system of textual citation but the scribe's way of keeping count of
the number of lines he was due to be paid for. It is therefore (I understand from Drs. Martin
and Primavesi) possible that his numeration included the title – in which case the number of
lines preceding B17 would be slightly reduced. Hence I have rounded my figure down to 'around
230 lines'.

[103] Full discussion of the opening part of the poem and its possible contents must await publication of the new fragments in Martin/Primavesi (1998).

[104] I am unpersuaded by the proposal of Edelstein (1940) that the reference is a general one to the
Presocratic physical tradition. The proems to books III, V and VI supply ample evidence of
Lucretius' belief that Epicurus was the first to make the crucial breakthrough, scientific as well
as moral.

There was among them a man of extraordinary knowledge, possessing a vast treasury of understanding, and master of every kind of wise deed. For when he reached out with all his understanding he easily saw everything there is, over ten and twenty human generations.

As Furley has pointed out,[105] the Lucretian passage unmistakably recalls the Empedoclean. Both men are great historical figures, too august to be named. And both are praised for their intellectual achievement in breaking through the boundaries of ordinary human experience – Pythagoras for his recollection of his former incarnations,[106] Epicurus for his grasp of the nature of the infinite universe beyond our own world.

Doctrinally, it should be noticed, Lucretius and Empedocles are veering ever further apart. Epicurus' discoveries, which secured his victory over religion, are taking the place of an Empedoclean religious doctrine that is anathema to Lucretius, the doctrine of transmigration.

1 80–101. There follows Lucretius' direct attack on the evils of religion, illustrated with the example of Agamemnon's sacrifice of his own daughter Iphigeneia.

Furley is right to point out the clear reminiscence of Empedocles B137, in which Empedocles attacks the sin of animal slaughter with the example of a father unwittingly sacrificing his own son, who has transmigrated into the body of an ox. There is no detailed linguistic imitation, but the close functional parallelism of the two pathetic scenes of sacrifice should leave little doubt that the one passage is written with the other in mind. (Lucretius' description does not, incidentally, appear to be directly modelled on any of the accounts of Iphigeneia's sacrifice extant in Greek tragedy.)

That B137 came from Empedocles' physical poem, and not from the *Katharmoi*, was until recently a highly unorthodox proposal. Now, however, we have the new papyrus fragments from the opening book of the physical poem, and they include B139, where the speaker expresses his regret that he did not perish before his wicked complicity in the slaughter and consumption of animals. So close is the thematic link between B137 and B139 that they have regularly been assumed to derive from a single original context. That context can now be identified as book I of the physical poem, and very probably its proem.[107]

---

[105] Furley (1970). See also Burkert (1972), p. 137; Hardie (1986), p. 39 n.17.
[106] For the tradition of Pythagoras' multiple incarnations, see Burkert (1972), pp. 137ff.
[107] It would be unwise, in the present transitional state of Empedoclean scholarship, to insist that B139 itself came from the proem. The work of Martin and Primavesi, based on its admittedly

I 102–35. Lucretius continues with a warning to Memmius not to be confused by superstitious tales, such as those about the survival and transmigration of the soul.

Why did he choose to include the topic of transmigration in his proem? In view of all the Empedoclean echoes we have already witnessed, it can hardly be a coincidence that Empedocles likewise outlined his beliefs about transmigration in his proem. It is here that I can at last call upon the findings of §§2–3 of this chapter, in which I defended the attribution of B115, Empedocles' explanation of his doctrine of transmigration, to the proem of his *On nature*. If I am right, and Lucretius' attack on transmigration is an intended counterpart to Empedocles' exposition of the doctrine at the corresponding point in his own proem, he has now moved yet further in distancing himself philosophically from his principal literary model. Where previously we saw him adapting themes from Empedocles' proem to his Epicurean philosophy, he is now presenting his own matching passage not as an adaptation of Empedocles but as a direct antidote to his teachings.

In the course of making this point, Lucretius names Ennius as the author of just the kind of confusion that he is condemning. Somehow Ennius managed to believe both in transmigration and in the sojourn of departed souls in Hades. The latter is an explicit reference to the dream in which Ennius, in his own proem to the *Annales*, had described meeting the shade of Homer. However, Lucretius allows, Ennius must be given his due as the great innovator who brought Greek poetry to the medium of the Latin language: '. . . our own Ennius, the first to bring down from lovely Helicon the enduringly-leaved crown which was to achieve glory throughout the Italian peoples'.

Here we should note Lucretius' concern with literary pedigree, and specifically with Ennius' pioneering role in the task which he is himself now engaged in, that of re-creating for Latin readers the poetic genres of the Greeks. There is in fact little doubt that the dream passage in Ennius' own proem is being directly echoed in Lucretius' lines.[108] Lucretius is here distancing himself from Ennius' beliefs, while revering his poetry, in a way that pointedly parallels his treatment of

fragmentary context in the papyrus, is currently favouring a location later in the poem, but with the further inference that the daimon's original sin and subsequent fate must already have been described in the proem. Given that B115, which I have argued comes from the proem of the physical poem, ends up with Empedocles' declaration that he is himself one of the fallen daimons — 'I too am now one of these, a fugitive from the gods and a wanderer, who trust in raving Strife' (above p. 8) — the story of his own downfall could very naturally accompany it.

[108] See Skutsch (1985), pp. 12, 155, Clay (1983), p. 310 n. 48, Waszink (1950), pp. 224–5.

Empedocles.[109] Anyone who may doubt the appropriateness of my distinction between a 'literary' and a 'philosophical' debt to Empedocles should note that just such a distinction is operating here with regard to Ennius.

I 136–45. Finally we come to the closing section of Lucretius' proem, in which he stresses the magnitude of his poetic task – a task made harder, he says, by the deficiencies of the Latin language and the novelty of the subject matter. It is overwhelmingly tempting to correlate this with the group of fragments (B8–11, B15) in which Empedocles deplores the imprecision of ordinary language in speaking of things' being born and dying, where there is in reality only combination and separation, but adds that he will nevertheless follow the convention. The shared theme of how to cope with the deficiencies of one's own language[110] constitutes a strong link between the two passages. We have no explicit attribution of these fragments to Empedocles' proem, but B8 is at least cited by Simplicius as coming from the opening book of *On nature*; and even without the Lucretian parallel the proem has always seemed the likeliest location.

8. EMPEDOCLES' PROEM

A little earlier we arrived at the informed guess that Empedocles' proem to *On nature* opened with a hymn to Aphrodite, followed by a programmatic address to Pausanias. We can now, in the light of our subsequent findings, ask how it went on.

Lucretius' proem offers the following sequence of topics in its latter part (62–145):
(a) Epicurus' intellectual achievement and defeat of religion;
(b) the evils of religion;
(c) the folly of uncritically believing religious tales, such as those about transmigration;
(d) the magnitude of Lucretius' poetic task.
The thematic link between the first three is a perfectly satisfactory one, and the last is, if not directly connected, still an appropriate enough

---

[109] The point is redoubled if, as seems likely, Ennius' beliefs were themselves influenced by Empedocles: cf. Hardie (1986), pp. 17–22, 79–83.

[110] Empedocles does not in the surviving fragments specify that the deficiency is one of his own language, Greek, rather than of language as such. But his contemporary Anaxagoras (B17) makes the same point with explicit reference to Greek usage, and that was a natural enough way to understand Empedocles too.

topic to address in a proem. And yet there is something disquietingly specific, not to say arbitrary, about the third topic. Why go to such lengths to criticise the transmigration thesis in particular, when there are countless other offending doctrines? Is it merely in order to introduce a heavily qualified tribute to Ennius?[111] My preferred explanation has been that the choice and sequence of topics was in some measure dictated by a further consideration, Lucretius' desire to reproduce the thematic structure of Empedocles' proem. One incidental by-product has been the materials for a scissors-and-paste reconstruction of the latter part of Empedocles' own proem. Now stand back and look at the result. We have supplied Empedocles with the following fluent sequence of topics:

(a) Pythagoras' achievement in recalling past incarnations: an appeal to authority for the doctrine of transmigration;
(b) the evils of animal slaughter, illustrated by the unwitting sacrifice of a deceased and transmigrated son: the moral importance of the doctrine of transmigration;
(c) the origin and nature of transmigration itself;
(d) the folly of being misled by ordinary linguistic usage into supposing that anything literally dies.

This time the thematic coherence of the sequence (a)–(d) is extraordinary. It is much more tight-knit than the corresponding passage in Lucretius, and tells a complete story of its own, one thematically parallel to the Lucretian passage, yet utterly unlike it in detailed content. What is more, the denial of literal birth and death with which it ends not only gives a philosophical basis to the transmigration doctrine that precedes it, but also prepares the ground for the physical exposition to follow, which will likewise be founded on the Parmenidean tenet that nothing literally comes to be or perishes.[112]

This emergence of a reconstructed Empedoclean proem with a coherence and vitality of its own is an additional windfall, which lends

---

[111] I do not mean to deny that direct reaction to Ennius plays a significant part in this passage. My question concerns the overall thematic structure of the passage. I would tentatively add that, even if Lucretius were thought to be reacting to current philosophical trends (which I doubt – see Ch. 3), he would still be unlikely to feel impelled to pick transmigration as a target. To judge from the evidence of Cicero's *Tusculan disputations*, the current revival of interest in Plato's immortality doctrine played down reincarnation in favour of discarnate survival. Nor does transmigration appear to be an attested feature of first-century BC neo-Pythagoreanism (for which see Dillon (1977), pp. 117–21, and cf. Vander Waerdt (1985), esp. pp. 388–9).

[112] See especially B12. The Parmenidean tenet seems to be applied by Empedocles indiscriminately to the soul's survival and to the permanence of the elements: both equally are separated, not destroyed. How coherent this conflation is is another question. Cf. especially Kahn (1960).

welcome support to my hypothesis about Lucretius' proem, quite apart from what it promises to teach us about Empedocles himself.

9. CONCLUSION

The nature of my case has been essentially cumulative. Every main stage of Lucretius' proem has proved to correlate with an Empedoclean original. The first part reads as if it were closely imitating an Empedoclean hymn, while the remainder sustains a virtually unbroken series of thematic links with known or attested passages of Empedocles. Moreover, every one of those Empedoclean originals can plausibly be located in the proem of his *On nature*, either on independent evidence, or through its thematic coherence with passages that have already been located there.

Lucretius is the servant of two masters. Epicurus is the founder of his philosophy; Empedocles is the father of his genre. It is the unique task of Epicureanism's first poet to combine these two loyalties. And that task is what gives his proem its very distinctive character.

CHAPTER 2

Two languages, two worlds

1. LINGUISTIC POVERTY

In the preceding chapter, we met at the end of Lucretius' proem his famous apology on behalf of the Latin language (1 136–45), in which he laments the linguistic struggle that he faces (1 136–9):

> nec me animi fallit Graiorum obscura reperta
> difficile inlustrare Latinis versibus esse,
> multa novis verbis praesertim cum sit agendum
> propter egestatem linguae et rerum novitatem.

> Nor do I fail to appreciate that it is difficult to illuminate in Latin verse the dark discoveries of the Greeks, especially because much use must be made of new words, given the poverty of our language and the newness of the subject matter.

In §§2–7 of this chapter I shall be considering how he handles this task of Latinising the technical terms of Epicurean philosophy. In §§8–13 I shall turn to his own poetic use of Greek loan-words and idioms. The two practices will come out looking antithetical to each other. At the end I shall suggest how we are meant to interpret this antithesis. What may start out looking like an issue of linguistic mechanics will turn out, if I am right, to reveal a fundamental tension in Lucretius' evaluation of his own poetic and philosophical task.

2. THE TECHNICALITIES OF PHYSICS

By a 'technical term' I intend a single word or phrase, either specially coined or adapted from existing usage, and at least implicitly earmarked by the author as his standard and more or less invariable way of designating a specific item or concept within a discipline. Its sense must be recognisably different from, or at least recognisably more precise than, any distinct sense that the same term may bear in ordinary usage. While medicine and mathematics were disciplines which had long possessed technical vocabularies, philosophy had been slow to catch up, acquiring little technical terminology before Aristotle. Nevertheless, Hellenistic philosophies had become thoroughly technical in their terminology, and Epicureanism, despite its (misplaced) reputation as an ordinary-language philosophy, was very nearly as jargon-ridden as Stoicism. It might in fact plausibly be maintained that the atomistic tradition from which Epicureanism emerged had, in the hands of its fifth-century exponents, been the first philosophical movement to forge itself a technical vocabulary.

The Latinisation of technical Greek, at least in rhetorical treatises, was a familiar practice by the mid first century BC, when Lucretius wrote. But from Cicero's letters one may get the impression that when educated Romans were locked in philosophical discussion they preferred simply to pepper their Latin prose with the authentic Greek terms. It was not until more than a decade after Lucretius' death that Cicero composed his principal philosophical works, in which the Latin philosophical vocabulary was largely forged.

A full-scale study of Cicero's handling of this task is, as far as I know, yet to be written.[1] Among many things it might help teach us is just what is distinctive about Lucretius' own near-contemporary efforts to accommodate Epicureanism within the Latin language. For the present let Cicero speak for himself, as his cast of philosophical Romans muse on their task of Latinisation in the first book of the *Academica* (1 24–6):

'. . . But the combination of the two they called "body" and, as one might put it, "quality" [*qualitas*]. You *will* permit us occasionally to use unknown words when dealing with unfamiliar subject matter, just as is done by the Greeks, who have been dealing with these subjects for a long time.'

'We will,' replied Atticus. 'In fact it will even be permissible for you to use Greek words when you want, if you happen to find no Latin ones available.'

'Thanks, but I'll do my best to speak in Latin, except that I'll use words like "philosophy", "rhetoric", "physics" or "dialectic" [*philosophiam aut rhetoricam aut physicam aut dialecticam*] — words which along with many others are now habitually used as Latin ones. I have therefore named "qualities" the things which the Greeks call ποιότητες, a word which among the Greeks is itself not an everyday one but belongs to the philosophers. The same applies in many cases. None of the dialecticians' words are from public language: they use their own. And that is a common feature of virtually all disciplines: for new things either new names must be created, or metaphors must be drawn from other fields. If that

is the practice of the Greeks, who have already been engaged in these things for
so many centuries, how much more should it be allowed to us, who are now
trying to deal with these things for the first time.'

'Actually, Varro,' I said, 'it looks as if you will deserve well of your fellow
countrymen, if you are going to enrich them not only with facts, as you have
done, but also with words.'

'On your instigation then,' he said, 'we will venture to use new words if it
becomes necessary.'

Two features deserve particular attention. First, the simple transliteration
of Greek words was, as the speaker Varro acknowledges, a familiar
and accepted practice, albeit confined largely to the names of the disciplines themselves, such as 'dialectic' and 'rhetoric'.[2] Second, Cicero presents his colleagues as considering it highly commendable when
discussing philosophy in Latin to coin the necessary technical jargon, if
possible on the analogy of the Greek original, as in the proffered
example of *qualitas* for Greek ποιότης (pointedly reminding us of the
well-known passage in Plato, *Theaetetus* 182a, where the technical term
ποιότης is itself invented).

In both respects Lucretius offers a stark contrast. Take the names of
disciplines once more. The *DRN* is a poem about physics, what
Lucretius' own contemporaries were calling *physica*, yet nowhere in it
can that term or its cognates be found. Does Lucretius then have no
name for the physical science he is practising? One clear case in which
he does is at 1 148, where the proper Epicurean justification for the study
of physics is given: ignorant and superstitious fears are to be dispelled
by *naturae species ratioque*. The phrase captures quite closely Epicurus'
preferred term for physics, φυσιολογία, with *naturae* and *ratio* picking up
its constituents φύσις and λόγος respectively.[3] But in Lucretius' rendition it has lost all terminological technicality, and become a subtly
descriptive formula for the poem's theme. Read actively, *naturae species
ratioque* no doubt denotes the rational philosophical procedure of
'looking at nature and reasoning about it'. But at the same time the
Latin permits and even encourages the additional reading, 'the appearance and rationale of nature': such a rendition emphasises the power of
nature herself to confront us with the truth – a motif which Lucretius
will be turning to good use in the poem. No strand in this web of

---

[2] Cf. Cic. *Fin.* III 5. Weise (1882) remains a very valuable survey of Greek loan-words in Latin, but
disappointingly brief on philosophical vocabulary (including, p. 241, the *de natura deorum* (*sic*) of
Lucretius!).

[3] The link is confirmed by Cic. *ND* I 20, where the Epicurean Velleius speaks of *physiologiam, id est
naturae rationem*, an equivalence also repeated by his Stoic speaker at *Div.* I 90.

connotations goes beyond the potential significance of the one Greek word φυσιολογία.

3. ATOMIC VOCABULARY

Similarly with individual technical terms within his chosen discipline, Lucretius' constant practice is to render Greek technicality neither with Latin technicality nor with mere transliteration, but with a range of his own live metaphors. Take the case of 'atoms'.[4] Of the earlier Latin prose writers on Epicureanism, we know only that Amafinius had rendered the term *corpuscula*,[5] although Lucilius' reference to *atomus . . . Epicuri* (753 Marx) shows that simple transliteration had long been another available expedient. Cicero, for his part, actually shows a strong preference for this transliterated form, with occasional resort to *corpuscula*[6] or to his own probable coinage *individua*, 'indivisibles'. None of these is ideal. Transliteration of a term from within a discipline — as distinct from the name of the discipline itself — is a rare resort for Cicero, and savours of defeat. *Corpuscula* captures the minuteness of the atoms but not their all-important indivisibility. And *individua* suffers in Cicero's philosophical prose from having to stand in for too many different Greek originals: he had already, in his paraphrase of Plato's *Timaeus* (21, 25, 27), used it to represent ἀμέριστος, ἀμερής and ἄσχιστος, all terms with importantly different technical connotations both from each other and from 'atom'.

Lucretius introduces his own set of terms for atoms in the proem to book I, 54–61, more than 400 lines before his first proof of their existence:[7] *rerum primordia, materies, genitalia corpora, semina rerum, corpora prima.* Unlike *corpuscula*, all these concentrate not on the smallness of atoms but on their role as the primitive starting-points from which other entities are built up. In introducing them, he places the chief emphasis on their dynamic generative powers, already indicated in the procreative implications of *materies* (a derivative of *mater*), *genitalia* and *semina*. These implications he then exploits in his first set of arguments, those against generation *ex nihilo*, in the course of which he seeks to persuade us that the biological regularities which are evident at the macroscopic level depend on fixed *materies* or *semina* at the microscopic level. (I shall be examining the strategy in detail in Chapter 7, §3.) The metrically conve-

---

[4] For the main evidence on Latin atomic vocabulary, cf. Reiley (1909), pp. 35–66.
[5] Cicero, *Ac.* 1 6.   [6] *ND* 1 66 7, 11 94, *Ac.* 1 6, *Tusc.* 1 22.
[7] For the role of this passage, cf. pp. 28–9 above, and pp. 194, 201 below, where the lines are quoted in full.

nient transliteration *atomi* never so much as puts in an appearance. But *corpuscula* does crop up as an occasional variant in later books, especially where their generative powers are not at issue.[8] So does *elementa*, 'letters', a convenient equivalent for στοιχεῖα ('elements' but also more specifically 'letters'), which helps to reinforce Lucretius' favoured analogy between atomic rearrangement and alphabetic realignment.[9] Hence it tends to occur in contexts where the *ordering* of atoms is in focus.[10]

4. *SIMULACRA*

A similar but more cautious metaphorical diversification of a single original Greek term is illustrated in book IV by Lucretius' range of renditions for εἴδωλα, 'images', the thin films of atoms which stream off bodies and cause vision. Lucilius, once again, had simply transliterated the word as *idola* (753 Marx). Cicero and his Epicurean correspondent Cassius, discussing the topic in 45 BC,[11] agreed to be appalled at the Roman Epicurean Catius for his translation of εἴδωλα as *spectra*. *Spectrum* is otherwise unattested in Latin before the seventeenth century (when it seems to mean 'appearance' or 'aspect'). It probably represents Catius' attempt to invent an off-the-peg jargon for Latin Epicureanism. I have no idea what connotations it conveyed to a Roman ear, but Cicero and Cassius seem to have found them comic.

Lucretius, at any rate, is considerably more subtle. He conveys εἴδωλον with a range of words which collectively capture the idea, already present in the Greek, of a painted or sculpted image preserving the surface features of its subject. His most regular term for this is *simulacrum*, but he also commonly uses *imago*, with the occasional further variants *effigies* and *figura*. (All four renditions were to enjoy at least some success with later Latin writers on Epicureanism.)[12]

By an extraordinary stroke of luck, the text of book IV preserves side by side Lucretius' earlier and later versions of the introductory lines in which his range of terms is sketched.[13] (The significance of this for Lucretius' change of plan during the composition of the poem will be

---

[8] II 153, 529, IV 199, 899, VI 1063. At IV 899 it is specifically their smallness that he wishes to emphasise with the diminutive.   [9] I 196-8, 907-14, II 688-94, 1013-22. See pp. 190-1 below.

[10] E.g. II 393, 463, IV 941, VI 1009.   [11] *Fam.* XV 16.1, 19.1.

[12] *Simulacrum*, Vitruvius VI 2.3, Gellius V 16.3; *imago*, Cicero, e.g. *ND* I 114, and often; *effigies*, Cicero, *ND* I 110; *figura*, Seneca, *NQ* I 5.1, Quintilian, *Inst.* X 2.15.

[13] The matter is lucidly explained by Smith (1975), p. 280, who sets out the text properly, as does Bailey (1947) I 364. The OCT of Bailey (1922) must be avoided at all costs: there he disastrously follows Marullus in a wholesale re-ordering of the lines. For further discussion, see pp. 137-8 below.

fully discussed in Chapter 5.) In the earlier version (45–53), the existence of εἴδωλα is first broached with the words (49–53)

> nunc agere incipiam tibi, quod vementer ad has res
> attinet, esse ea quae rerum simulacra vocamus,   50
> *quae quasi membranae vel cortex nominitandast,*
> quod speciem ac formam similem gerit eius imago
> cuiuscumque cluet de corpore fusa vagari.

> I shall now begin to deal with what is closely relevant to this: that
> there are what we call images of things, which are to be termed
> 'like membranes or bark', because the image bears a shape and
> form similar to those of whatever thing's body we say it has been
> shed from and travelled.

He thereby recruits, in addition to the family of artistic metaphors, the biological vocabulary of 'membranes' and 'bark' as helping to convey the ready detachability of these ultra-fine surface-layers of bodies. In the event, neither of the biological terms is brought into play in this role anywhere in book IV.[14] And that must be why, when for other reasons he came to rewrite the proem, Lucretius edited them out, limiting his vocabulary for εἴδωλα exclusively to the iconic imagery.[15]

In the rewritten passage (26–44) the existence of εἴδωλα is broached in language which starts out identical to the first version, but then departs significantly from it (29–32):

> nunc agere incipiam tibi, quod vementer ad has res
> attinet, esse ea quae rerum simulacra vocamus,
> quae quasi membranae *summo de corpore rerum*
> *dereptae volitant ultroque citroque per auras . . .*

> I shall now begin to deal with what is closely relevant to this: that
> there are what we call images of things, which, like membranes
> snatched from the outermost part of things' bodies, fly hither
> and thither through the air . . .

'Membranes' here is no longer part of the designated vocabulary for εἴδωλα, but forms instead the basis of an extended simile, designed to convey one specific aspect, the detachability and volatility of these atomic films. As for the other biological term 'bark', a clumsily inapposite name for a light and volatile surface layer of atoms, this has now been

---

[14] On *cortex*, see below. *Membranae* occurs once, at IV 95, but only in the descriptive phrase *tenuis summi membrana coloris*, where it is not left to fend for itself.

[15] *Effigiae* and *figurae* are in fact used only twice and three times respectively in the remainder of the book. *Imago* (most commonly singular, for metrical reasons) is used some seventeen times. Curiously, it does not occur in the revised version of the proem.

deleted. It does however put in an appearance at the end of the rewritten passage, in the company of the preferred sculptural imagery (42–3):

> dico igitur rerum effigias tenuisque figuras
> mittier ab rebus summo de cortice eorum.

> I say, therefore, that things' effigies and tenuous figures are
> despatched from them off their outermost bark.

I see no justification for the standard emendation of *cortice* to *corpore*.[16]
Lucretius has in his revised version rightly seen that 'bark' most
appropriately conveys the idea of the stable outer part of an object, *from*
which the εἴδωλα flow.[17]

It might seem pointless to wonder what motivated Lucretius' original
abortive attempt to introduce the pair of biological terms. But as it
happens the question can be answered with a surprising degree of
confidence. Alexander of Aphrodisias, in attacking the Epicurean
theory of vision by *simulacra*, asks why, if *simulacra* are as volatile as the
proponents assert they are, windy conditions are not sufficient to prevent
our seeing things.[18] In describing the images' volatility, he quotes the
actual words of the theory's proponents: ἐκ φλοιωδῶν καὶ ὑμενωδῶν ὡς
φασιν, '[consisting][19] of "bark-like and membrane-like" stuffs, as they
put it'. Once we place this Greek phrase alongside Lucretius IV 51, it
becomes scarcely deniable that he has quite simply *translated* it.[20] His *quae
quasi membranae vel cortex nominitandast* announces that 'membrane-like'
and 'bark-like' are appropriate descriptions to use of the *simulacra*.
Although there is a little evidence that the Epicureans did sometimes also
call the visual images 'barks' or 'membranes',[21] it seems clear that on this

---

[16] Here I am in agreement with Godwin (1986), pp. 94–5. Bailey (1947), who comments *ad loc.* that
cortice cannot be right because *cortex* designates for Lucretius the εἴδωλον, is overlooking the fact
that that was only in the now discarded version of the proem to book IV.

[17] Epicurus himself in the context of images uses ὁ ἐξώτατος χιτών (24.19.1–3 Arr.²), possibly as
a name for the fixed outer layer — although the text is too fragmentary to rule out the alternative that he means the image itself.

[18] *De anima mantissa* 135.24–6, εἰ δέ ἐστιν εὔκολος αὐτῶν ἡ κίνησις, ἐκ φλοιωδῶν καὶ ὑμενωδῶν
ὡς φασιν, καὶ πᾶσα ῥοπὴ ἱκανὴ παρασῦραι αὐτά, ἔδει μὴ ὁρᾶν τοὺς κατὰ τὸν ἄνεμον
βλέποντας. For discussion of the passage, see Avotins (1980).

[19] See Avotins (1980), p. 438 n. 40, for discussion as to whether a participle such as πεποιημένων
has fallen out here. Given the Lucretian parallel, I am at least confident that the phrase describes
the composition of the *simulacra* themselves, not (a possibility considered sympathetically by
Avotins) some external agent which moves them.

[20] The Alexander passage is cited for comparison with the Lucretius line by Lackenbacher (1910),
p. 229, and Ferrari (1937), p. 193, but I have not yet found anyone who notices the actual relation
in which it stands to Lucretius' own wording.

[21] For ὑμένες see Diogenes of Oenoanda 10 v 3 Smith; φλοίους is one available MS reading at
Plutarch, *Non posse* 1106A.

occasion Lucretius' *quasi* is added in order to capture the adjectival force of the -ώδης termination: not membranes and barks, but membrane-like and bark-like.

The conclusion from this must be that Lucretius, at least while working on his first draft (see Chapter 5), was ready in principle simply to draw his imagery from the technical terminology of Greek Epicurean prose, but that such borrowings survived into subsequent drafts only if they could prove their independent worth in the context of Latin poetic imagery. In this particular case, the technical force of the original Greek adjectives was to specify and illuminate one particular property of the images, their detachability, by exploiting the analogy of tree bark, reptile sloughs and the like.[22] Lucretius evidently found that this aspect did not, in the event, repay emphasis in the main body of book IV, where exploitation of it would have tended to fall between two stools, not as effective as the iconic imagery for capturing the extraordinarily accurate representational powers of the images, and positively detracting from his attempts to convey their all-important high velocity. In short, while the sculptural imagery survived, the biological imagery failed the test and was edited out.

This tantalising vestige of Lucretius' first draft, with its failed attempt to translate φλοιώδης and ὑμενώδης, suggests that at that early stage he was more hopeful of finding simple Latin translations of at least some Greek technical terms than he appears to be in anything else that now survives of the poem. Thus the policy which I am describing in this section should be seen as one evolved only during the writing process. Lucretius' initial conception of his linguistic task may have been significantly closer to the one I have described in Cicero. The policy at which he eventually arrived is well illustrated by the revised proem to book IV. Rather than follow Catius in supplying a Latin technical terminology for εἴδωλα,[23] he seeks to embody the notion in a set of live metaphors which will complement each other in focusing on the cardinal feature of εἴδωλα, their power to preserve a portrait-like resemblance to the object emitting them, even over a considerable distance travelled. Their detachability and volatility will be conveyed in other ways, by both simile and argument,[24] without being allowed to dilute or obfuscate the dominant metaphor of portraiture.

---

[22] See IV 57-62 for further examples.

[23] In this same context of *simulacra*, Clay (1983), p. 20, aptly points out how Epicurus' technical term ὁ ἐξωστικὸς τρόπος (*Nat.* II, 24.43.3, 44.1 Arr.²) has become in Lucretius (IV 193-4) the descriptive *parvola causa . . . procul e tergo quae provehat atque propellat.*   [24] IV 54-216.

5. PROSE AND VERSE CONTRASTED

Those familiar with Cicero's philosophical works may at this stage retort that there is nothing unique about Lucretius' search for a mutually complementary set of terms corresponding to a single Greek term. A similar-looking process can be glimpsed in Cicero's own forging of a philosophical vocabulary, where he often introduces a Greek term with a whole bevy of Latin equivalents. The Stoic term for infallible cognition, κατάληψις, literally 'grasping', provides a good illustration. Its use in rhetorical theory may have earned it Latinisation at an earlier date, since already in his youthful *De inventione* Cicero uses *perceptio* in a way probably intended to correspond to κατάληψις.[25] Yet still in the second book of the *Academica* his spokesman Lucullus can be found tinkering with the rendition of it, and listing a range of alternatives: . . . '*cognitio*' *aut* '*perceptio*' *aut (si verbum e verbo volumus)* '*comprehensio*', *quam* κατάληψιν *illi vocant . . .*' (*Ac.* II 17, cf. 18, 31).

Normally in Cicero this little fanfare would herald the first introduction of a term. But we are already here in the second book of the *Academica*, and it is certain that κατάληψις had already featured in book I.[26] What Cicero in fact turns out on closer inspection to be doing here is not creating but *enlarging* his stock of Latin terms for it, adding *comprehensio* to the terms *perceptio* and *cognitio* which he had been using up to now (in the *Academica*, that is, and also in the *De finibus*, composed contemporaneously with it). And one can see why. Both *perceptio* and *cognitio* were too widely and loosely used within the ordinary Latin cognitive vocabulary to capture the very special flavour of Stoic κατάληψις, whereas *comprehensio* and its cognates were barely yet familiar in a cognitive sense, so that the usage could still retain a suitably technical ring.[27]

Curiously enough Cicero too, just like Lucretius in book IV, can here be watched in the act of refining his vocabulary. Our version of book II comes from the *Academica priora*, Cicero's first edition. In his revised edition, the *Academica posteriora*, from which part of book I survives, *comprehensio* is heralded as the single correct translation right from the start (*Ac.* I 41):

' . . . When that impression was discerned in its own right, Zeno called it *comprehendibile*. Will you accept this?'

'Yes,' he replied. 'How else *could* you express καταληπτόν?'

---

[25] *Inv.* I 9, 36.   [26] *Ac.* II 28 indicates that Hortensius had already used it in book I.
[27] For the various cognate forms of *comprehensio* in Cicero, see Lévy (1992).

'But when it had already been received and endorsed, he called it *comprehensio*, like things grasped with the hand . . .'

This exclusive use of *comprehensio* for κατάληψις seems thereafter to become canonical in what survives of the revised book I, and was undoubtedly continued in the lost books II–IV of the revised version.[28] It enables Cicero to let it stand in contrast, as a term of art, with the less technical 'knowledge' vocabulary – *scire*, *cognoscere* and *percipere* – which in the ensuing chapters he puts into the mouths of pre-Stoic philosophers.[29]

Consequently, it would be quite misleading to assimilate the practices of Lucretius and Cicero when each sets about establishing a group of alternative or complementary Latin terms for a single Greek original. Cicero does it only as a step towards what will, if all goes well,[30] prove to be their eventual whittling down to a single technical term. For Lucretius, on the other hand, the range of alternative terms is no stopgap or compromise, but is intrinsically desirable. By means of it, he seeks to capture the Greek original, not by substituting a Latin technical term for a Greek one, but by keeping in play a whole set of mutually complementary live metaphors.[31] The policy is one not of finding a technical terminology, but of avoiding one.

In pursuing such a policy, Lucretius is doing no more than observing the traditional practice of his genre, the hexameter poem on physics.[32] The proper comparison to make is not with Cicero, but with Empedocles, whom, as I sought to show in Chapter 1, Lucretius reveres as the founder of his genre. Empedocles has no technical vocabulary for the six primary entities in his physics – the four elements plus the two powers Love and Strife – but deploys for each a varied set of evocative metaphors and allegorical names: thus the element water is represented not only by the word 'water' (ὕδωρ), but also by 'rain' (ὄμβρος), 'sea'

[28] It clearly suits his purposes well in a technical epistemological context like the *Academica*. Elsewhere he may have continued to feel uncomfortable with it, as at *Fin.* III 17.

[29] See e.g. I 44.

[30] Hence *Fin.* III 15, where Cato remarks *equidem soleo etiam, quod uno Graeci, si aliter non possum, idem pluribus verbis exponere*. On this passage, cf. Powell (1995a), pp. 292–4.

[31] Here and elsewhere I stress 'live' metaphors because it is not my aim to contrast the metaphorical, as such, with the literal. (I agree with Lloyd (1987), chapter 4, that this is usually a misleading or at least unenlightening antithesis, especially as most philosophical technical terms are themselves metaphors.) Rather, I am singling out those metaphors which actively work on the reader by exploiting the power of imagery.

[32] It is well recognised that the variety of vocabulary in philosophical verse is partly dictated by metrical constraints: a word which works well in one place may be inadmissible in another grammatical case or at another point in the hexameter. However, metre alone would not have prevented Lucretius from managing exclusively with, e.g., *effigies* and *atomi* throughout, had he preferred to do so.

(θάλασσα, πόντος), and 'Nestis', probably a Sicilian cult name for Persephone, who was especially associated with springs.[33]

At II 644–60, commenting on the cult of the 'earth mother', Lucretius licenses the potentially misleading vocabulary, so long as the associated false beliefs are absent. Likewise Empedocles himself, as we noted in Chapter 1,[34] had declared his readiness to continue using a philosophically misleading mode of speech, once his readers had been alerted to the implicit error. Ordinary talk of 'birth', 'death' and the like, he had observed, misdescribes what in reality is simply mixture and separation; but, he had added, he would himself go along with the convention.[35] His contemporary Anaxagoras had likewise noted that the conventional language of birth and death is misleading,[36] but he, being a prose writer, had faced no difficulty in simply acting on this insight and editing such language out of his treatise, replacing it with that of mixture and separation. This contrast neatly illustrates the differing strategies which typically separate scientific exposition in verse from that in prose. Lucretius' avoidance of terminological technicality, in the tradition of Empedocles, is another symptom of that difference.

However, a little new light can now be thrown on the findings of Chapter 1. There we witnessed the emergence of Lucretius' poem from his synthesis of two very different intellectual backgrounds, with Epicurus supplying the message, Empedocles the medium. But we are now in a position to see that the exact division of labour between the two had to be carefully negotiated. What we have recognised (above pp. 41–2) as Lucretius' attempt, in the early stages of his work, to Latinise Epicurus' technical terms φλοιώδης and ὑμενώδης suggests that the more Empedoclean approach to philosophical vocabulary was not straightforwardly Lucretius' first choice. His move away from Epicurean-style technical terminology towards Empedoclean informality and variety was gradual, hard won in the light of experience.

Lucretius himself likes to remind us that his poetic task is an excitingly new one. The point is emphasised, not just in the lines from the proem to book 1 with which this chapter opened, but also in his celebrated poetic manifesto at I 921–50, where he is a bold explorer in the untrodden terrain of the Muses. It may be significant that he chose to repeat this manifesto as the opening of the book IV proem,[37] the very place

---

[33] See Kingsley (1995), ch. 22.   [34] See p. 32 above.   [35] Empedocles B8–9.

[36] Anaxagoras B17.

[37] IV 1–25. See Gale (1994b), who argues effectively that these lines were intended by Lucretius to open book IV, and are not the product of editorial meddling by others.

where we have also witnessed his shift towards a more robustly
Empedoclean treatment of technical concepts. The findings of this
chapter may help us to appreciate Lucretius' reasons for his passionate
sense of being a pioneer. It is not simply that no one had previously
written philosophical verse in Latin[38] (although that is undoubtedly the
point made in the proem to book 1). It is also that the versification of
Epicureanism, a philosophy with a highly developed technical vocabulary, makes new demands on the poet quite unlike any faced even by the
founder of the genre, Empedocles.

6. DISTORTED REASONING

I do not mean to deny that any word in Lucretius ever has a technical
sense assigned to it, although interestingly enough the most prominent
cases are ones where the Greek original *lacked* such a term. (I am thinking here of *coniunctum* for 'permanent property' at 1 449ff.,[39] and the
animus/*anima* distinction set out in book III.) But what we have already
seen, the conversion of Greek technicality into flexible Latin metaphors,
is a far more pervasive feature of his poetry.

One very satisfying case, which was first detected by Myles
Burnyeat,[40] is Lucretius' rendition at IV 472 of the exclusively
Epicurean technical term for a thesis which 'refutes itself', περικάτω
τρέπεται. Scepticism, the claim to know nothing, is dismissed as self-
refuting, but Lucretius conveys the dry technicality of περικάτω
τρέπεται with a picture of the sceptic as an acrobat or contortionist (IV
469–72):

> denique nil sciri siquis putat, id quoque nescit
> an sciri possit, quoniam nil scire fatetur.
> hunc igitur contra mittam contendere causam,
> *qui capite ipse suo in statuit vestigia sese.*

> If someone thinks that nothing is known, he doesn't even know
> whether *that* can be known, since he admits that he knows
> nothing. I therefore decline to argue my case against this person
> who *has stood with his own head pressed into his footprints.*

[38] I discount Sallustius (see Ch. 1, §1), whose poem, whatever its content may have been, was presumably not yet published when Lucretius was writing.
[39] That *coniunctum* does not, as commonly supposed, translate the single Greek word συμβεβηκός
is argued in Long/Sedley (1987) §7, and more fully in Sedley (1988). As for *eventum* in the same
passage, it is introduced as already a familiar Latin usage (458).
[40] Burnyeat (1978). On the philosophical significance of this passage, see Ch. 3, §8.

The sceptic's confusion is reinforced in the last line with the Lucretian device which David West[41] has christened 'syntactical onomatopoeia': intellectual contortion is symbolised by contorted grammar, with the proper order *statuit in* reversed in defiance of basic syntax. I am inclined to resist the normalising emendation of *suo* to *sua*, adopted by most editors since Lachmann. That substitutes a regular Lucretian type of grammatical inversion – *sua in* for *in sua*[42] – for a highly irregular one. But irregularity may be exactly what he intends. Anyone who objects that the irregularity is *too* harsh for Lucretius to have perpetrated should consider my next example.

At IV 822–57, Lucretius rejects another topsy-turvy piece of thinking – the teleologist's mistake of supposing that, because a human bodily part serves a function, that function must have been conceived prior to the part's coming to exist. In Lucretius' view, a thing must already exist before any thoughts about its function can even be entertained. Teleology is back-to-front reasoning; or, as he puts it (IV 832–3):

> cetera de genere hoc inter quaecumque pretantur
> omnia perversa praepostera sunt ratione.

> All such explanations which they offer are back to front, due to
> distorted reasoning.

What was in his Greek original? My guess is that what he found there was a description of teleological reasoning as διάστροφος, 'distorted'. This term, which translates literally into Lucretius' word *perversa*, is one which, according to Sextus Empiricus,[43] Epicurus used for opinion which imposes a distorted construal on primary empirical data. But once again Lucretius has backed up the accusation with syntactical ono-matopoeia. The distortion is attributed to 'back-to-front' (*praepostera*) thinking, which in turn is conveyed by the reversal of linguistic elements contained in the tmesis *inter quaecumque pretantur*. Tmesis is a common Lucretian device, and one of his favourite forms of syntactical ono-matopoeia, usually given prominence by its positioning at a line end. Most commonly the line will contain an unseparated compound of prefix plus verb stem, followed by a second compound verb with that

[41] West (1975), p. 96.
[42] For a list of postponed prepositions in Lucretius, see Bailey (1947), I 107.
[43] SE *M* VII 209; for the authenticity of the Epicurean terminology in *M* VII 206–10, see Sedley (1992), pp. 44–55, and cf. Gigante (1981), pp. 118–48. For the philosophical significance of διαστροφή and its cognates, see Grilli (1963).

same prefix, but this time separated in tmesis. According to the context, this movement from the conjoined to the separated can equally effectively convey the overlapping ideas of mixture, fusion, penetration, containment, alternation and entanglement (e.g. II 154, *sed complexa meant inter se conque globata*),[44] or, on the contrary, that of separation (e.g. I 651, *disiectis disque supatis*).[45] But our present line, IV 832, offers one of only two Lucretian tmeses in which the bare verb stem, left exposed by separation from its prefix, is not a Latin word at all.[46] The teleological reversal cannot be contemplated, Lucretius' message runs: it produces nonsense.

7. THE PRICE OF FAILURE

In all these Lucretian strategies for the conversion of Greek technicality into Latin imagery, one invariable rule is observed: never transliterate the Greek term. There are, in fact, only two significant breaches of that rule,[47] and they both speak eloquently in its favour. A leading contender for the title of Lucretius' worst line (at least when taken at face value) is I 830. Lucretius' apology for it runs as follows (I 830–2):

> *nunc et Anaxagorae scrutemur homoeomerian*
> *quam Grai memorant nec nostra dicere lingua*
> *concedit nobis patrii sermonis egestas.*

> Now let us also take a look at Anaxagoras' *homoiomereia* – as the Greeks call it, but which the poverty of our native language prevents us from saying in our own tongue.

The ungainliness conveys a point about the unacceptable consequences of resorting to mere transliteration of the Greek. Anaxagoras' horrible word is glaringly not at home in the Latin language; and that in turn foreshadows the fact, which Lucretius satirically develops in the sequel, that the concept underlying it is equally unwelcome.[48]

---

[44] II 154, 394, III 262, 343, 484, IV 203, 332, 562, 887 (*inque gredi* helps make the mind sound like a passenger in the body), 1149, 1250, V 1268, VI 394, 456, 570, 1264 (higgledy-piggledy).

[45] I 318, 452, 651, II 1104 (separation from culpability?), III 233, 860, IV 247, 388, 948, V 287, 299, 1374, VI 332. The only tmeses which are (to my eye) not obviously syntactically onomatopoeic are IV 713 and V 883. One special case is III 878 (tmesis with reversal, to convey the idea of something left over).

[46] For the other, see the brilliant article of Hinds (1987), who observes that *seiungi seque gregari* at I 452 is thus used to convey the idea of a fixed property (*coniunctum*), like the heat of fire, whose loss its possessor cannot survive.

[47] I do not count *prester* (VI 424), which although in a way technical is not a philosophically controversial term.

[48] Cf. Wardy (1988), an article which illuminatingly explores the ideological basis for Lucretius' targeting of Anaxagoras; esp. p. 126, 'Accordingly, the suggestion of 1.830 is that Anaxagorean philosophy is in a number of senses untranslatable', an idea which Wardy develops in terms of the analogy between elements and alphabetic letters.

This link between the alienness of a word and the alienness of the concept it expresses is virtually explicit in the other passage where bare transliteration is resorted to. Early in book III the old Greek theory that soul is a harmony or attunement of the bodily elements is dismissed (III 98–135). In Lucretius' discussion of it the Greek word ἁρμονία is simply transliterated, not translated. This is not in itself surprising, since ἁρμονία is as resistant to rendition into Latin as it is into English. Even Cicero, in his paraphrase of Plato's *Timaeus* (27), while attempting the translation *concentio* for ἁρμονία, is sufficiently uneasy about it to take the step, uncharacteristic in this work, of supplying the Greek word too. Elsewhere Cicero's own preference with regard to ἁρμονία is for simply transliterating it.[49] But more is at stake for Lucretius: the word's undisguised alienness to the Latin language is symptomatic of the concept's irrelevance (III 130–5):

> quapropter quoniam est animi natura reperta 130
> atque animae quasi pars hominis, redde harmoniai
> nomen, ad organicos alto delatum Heliconi,
> sive aliunde ipsi porro traxere et in illam
> transtulerunt, proprio quae tum res nomine egebat.
> quidquid id est, habeant. 135

> So, since the nature of mind and spirit has been found to be like a part of the human being, give back the name of *harmonia*, whether it was brought down to the musicians from high Helicon, or whether they themselves drew it from some other source and transferred it to what previously lacked a name of its own. Whatever it is, let them keep it.

An alien concept deserves an alien name. By the same token, Lucretius' habitual practice has made clear, philosophically welcome concepts must make themselves at home in the language too.

8. BAILEY'S COMPLAINT

Now I come to the great Lucretian anomaly. Although Lucretius studiously avoids using transliterated Greek *terminology*, his whole poem is nevertheless knee-deep in Greek loan words.

These Greek words have been usefully catalogued by Bailey,[50] who concludes that

---

[49] E.g. *Rep.* II 69, *Tusc.* I 41. Even Lucretius himself once outside book III uses the transliterated *harmoniae* at IV 1248, where he may feel that his need for the musical metaphor leaves him no option.
[50] Bailey (1947) I 138–9.

(a) in some cases Lucretius' hand has been forced by the unavailability
     of a suitable Latin word;
(b) in many other cases, where a perfectly good Latin word is at his dis-
     posal, he is using Greek out of virtual 'caprice';
(c) in one extreme case, IV 1160–9, where sixteen Greek words occur in
     the space of ten lines, it is impossible to resist the conclusion that
     Lucretius is translating a Greek original.

It is hard to think of a more implausible set of explanations. With
regard to (a), what we have already seen of Lucretius' handling of
philosophical terminology should put us on our guard against ever
assuming too readily that he has been forced to resort to Greek by the
lack of a Latin word.[51] As for (c), Bailey's explanation implies a very poor
opinion of Lucretius' skills as a translator, and one totally negated by a
passage like III 18–22, where we know that Lucretius is following a Greek
original, the Homeric description of Olympus.[52] But in the remainder
of this chapter I want to concentrate on (b), the kind of cases where
Bailey thought the intrusion of Greek merely gratuitous. It seems to me
that there are remarkably few genuine cases that fit this description (see
the appendix to this chapter). I shall start by quoting Bailey's catalogue
in full,[53] since I aim to deal with every word on his list:

Many Greek words Lucretius seems to have used almost from caprice, sometimes when there was a good Latin word which he could have employed instead:
anademata iv. 1129, *baratre* iii. 955, *barathrum* vi. 606, *chorea* ii. 635, *durateus* (= *ligneus*)
i. 476, *gigas* iv. 136, v. 117, *lampas* ii. 25 etc. (5 times), *lychni* v. 295, *mitrae* iv. 1129,
scaphiis vi. 1046, *sceptra* iii. 1036, v. 1137, *scymni* (= *catuli* already used in the same
line) v. 1036, *thalassina* iv. 1127, *thyrso* i. 923.

9. EVOKING GREECE

Most of the Greek words attributed by Bailey to Lucretian 'caprice' do
not occur in isolation. They tend to turn up in droves. And again and
again this concentration of Greek words in a passage is exploited for a
specific effect – to conjure up for Lucretius' readers a Greek or an otherwise exotic context. When Greece joined the European Common
Market, *The Times* celebrated with a competition for the reader's poem
with the largest number of Greek-derived words. This is pretty much

---

[51] However, see n. 49 (p. 49) on *harmoniae* at IV 1248, and n. 47 (p. 48) on *prester* at VI 424.
[52] *Od.* VI 42–6. See the notes on Lucretius *ad loc.* in Kenney (1971), and notice especially *immubilus* (21)
for the Homeric ἀνέφελος, an apparent Lucretian coinage designed to capture the special flavour
of the original, but decidedly not a transliteration. (Cf. Seele (1995), p. 27, who contrasts Cicero's
sine nubibus when translating the same word from Aratus.)   [53] Bailey (1947) I 139.

what Lucretius is up to too: when he uses a whole convoy of Greek words, he is usually quite simply trying to make us think of Greece.

'Greek words' here should be interpreted broadly. It naturally includes Greek proper names as well as common nouns and adjectives. Moreover, it can be extended to include Greek linguistic idioms, such as the formation of compound adjectives, not native to the Latin language.[54] These points are well illustrated by 1 464–82, the wonderful description of the Trojan war. In the space of five lines, 473–7, we have not only six Greek names, but also the quasi-Greek compound adjective *Graiugenarum*:

> numquam *Tyndaridis* forma conflatus amore
> ignis, *Alexandri Phrygio* sub pectore gliscens,
> clara accendisset saevi certamina belli,   475
> nec clam *durateus Troianis Pergama* partu
> inflammasset equos nocturno *Graiugenarum*.

> never would that flame kindled deep in Alexander's Phrygian heart and fanned with love by the beauty of Tyndareus' daughter have ignited the shining battles of savage war, nor would that wooden horse by giving birth to its Grecian offspring at dead of night have stealthily set fire to the Trojans' Pergama.

Especially telling is the authentic Homeric adjective *durateus* used of the 'Wooden' Horse (where, as Bailey ruefully points out, there was the perfectly good Latin word *ligneus* available). And in this already Greek context it is legitimate to regard the archaic Latin nominative *equos*, with its Greek-like termination, as yet another linguistic detail contributing to the same cumulative effect. (It should therefore not, with the majority of editors, be normalised to *equus*.)[55]

The argumentative context of this description is Lucretius' discussion of the metaphysical problem how facts about the past maintain their present existence: what is there in existence now for them to be properties of? It therefore serves his purpose to present his example, the Trojan war, as a remote one. The epic ring of the Greek helps locate it in a context far removed from present-day Rome. And this brings me to a general observation: that the creation of a Greek context tends, in Lucretius' hands, to emphasise the remote and the exotic.

---

[54] On compound adjectives, cf. pp. 24–5 above.
[55] As J. N. Adams points out to me, the retention of the old *-os* termination is not particularly unusual in a noun whose stem ends in *-u* (to avoid the collocation *uu*). Nevertheless, it may be judged to acquire a Hellenising significance when contained, as here, within a broader Hellenising context.

10. MAGNETS IN SAMOTHRACE

Bailey's list of gratuitous Greek imports includes *scaphiis*, 'basins', at VI 1046. The word was a common enough one in Latin by Lucretius' day to pass unnoticed. Nevertheless, since it occurs here in a Greek context, flanked by Greek proper names, it does deserve consideration. It comes in the course of a long and involved discussion of the magnet, and at this point Lucretius is describing the phenomenon of magnetic repulsion (VI 1044–6):

> exultare etiam Samothracia ferrea vidi
> et ramenta simul ferri furere intus ahenis
> in scaphiis, lapis hic Magnes cum subditus esset.

> I have even seen Samothracian iron objects dance, and iron filings all simultaneously go crazy in bronze basins (*scaphiis*), when this Magnesian stone was placed underneath.

What are these Samothracian *ferrea*? Iron rings, the editors usually say. But I doubt it. There were rings called 'Samothracian', but they seem to have been a combination of iron and gold: on one report, gold rings with an iron 'head'; on another account, iron rings plated or decorated with gold.[56] It seems unlikely that either of these is meant. The neuter *ferrea* cannot easily imply the masculine complement *anuli* or *anelli*.[57] Besides, someone displaying the powers of a magnet would not be likely to use objects containing gold as well as iron, since the weight of the gold would reduce their responsiveness to the magnetism. Finally, both types of ring clearly had a predominantly gold exterior, and would not very naturally be known as 'iron' rings. (It would only be if you wanted to cause offence that you would be likely to refer to someone's gold-plated ring as their 'iron ring'.)

Ferrea must mean just what it appears to mean, namely 'iron objects'. But why, then, are they called 'Samothracian'? There is only one plausible answer: Lucretius is describing a display he once witnessed *in Samothrace*. Line 1044 means 'I have even seen the ironware of Samothrace dance'. The natural magnet or lodestone, variously called the Magnesian stone and the Heracleian stone,[58] was as the names suggest predominantly associated with Magnesia or Heracleia (there was some disagreement whether this was the Heracleia in Lydia or the one in Pontus). But according to one variant tradition the magnet was

---

[56] For the evidence, see Lewis (1959), 130, 1213.
[57] For similar doubts, see Godwin (1991), *ad loc.*
[58] For an engrossing discussion of ancient views on the lodestone, see Wallace (1996). The ancient testimonia are collected in Radl (1988).

first found in Samothrace, and was named after the city of Heracleia on that island.[59] If there had actually been a Heracleia in Samothrace, this association of the Heracleian stone with the island might have been dismissed as a simple error of geography, the confusion of one Heracleia with another. But Samothracian Heracleia seems to be a fiction. Hence a better explanation for the origin of this variant tradition may be that lodestones were indeed found on Samothrace, and that this led to a misconception regarding the location of the Heracleia in question.

The Lucretian passage, if I have interpreted it correctly, now stands in strong confirmation of that hypothesis. This use of a first-person eye witness account is a rarity in Lucretius,[60] and confirms that, exceptionally, he is recounting to us an exhibition of the powers of the magnet which he had seen when himself on the island of Samothrace – whether from a vendor, or in a religious ritual, or in other circumstances is impossible to guess. The seething iron filings cannot in fact have been the product of magnetic repulsion, as Lucretius thinks they were.[61] Their movement must have been produced by magnetic attraction – moving a lodestone around beneath the bronze bowl to make them alternately stand on end and lie flat again. But Lucretius' mistake makes slightly better sense if he had also witnessed genuine magnetic repulsion, of which the 'dancing' iron objects may therefore represent an authentic case.[62]

But how likely is it that Lucretius had been to Samothrace? A picture of Lucretius the seasoned Aegean tourist does not carry conviction, and should become still less plausible when we proceed to explore his wary attitude to things Greek. Nor is he, of all people, very likely to have gone on a religious pilgrimage to the celebrated Kabiric mysteries held there.[63] However, there is no obligation to see this visit as motivated by

---

[59] *Etymologicum magnum, s.v.* Μαγνῆτις = Lewis (1959), T20.

[60] The only other cases, I believe, are IV 577, recalling his own experience of multiple echoes, and (if this counts) IV 769, recalling his dreams. Given how sparing he is with them, I would take these autopsy claims seriously. When he has not witnessed something in person, Lucretius is ready to admit it: cf. his indication at I 727 (quoted p. 12 above) that he has never been to Sicily, and similarly V 663, VI 756, 848–9.   [61] See Wallace (1996), p. 184.

[62] The trouble is that artificial magnets have made knowledge of natural lodestones a rarity today. The fullest and most authoritative account of the powers of the lodestone is Gilbert (1600). He seems to acknowledge repulsion only between two lodestones, not between a lodestone and previously magnetised iron. My tentative guess is that what Lucretius actually saw 'dance' were pieces of lodestone shaped into rods with their poles at the tips. Lodestone being iron ore, these could easily have been mistaken by Lucretius for iron rods. It remains possible, alternatively, that this trick too was done with magnetic attraction (thus Wallace (1996), p. 184).

[63] There is reason to think that some Romans did go to Samothrace for the mysteries, possibly including one with Epicurean links. See Bloch (1940), esp. n. 18. For Samothrace in relation to the Roman tourist circuit, see Casson (1974), pp. 243, 261.

either tourism or religious zeal. Samothrace, lying just off the coast of
Thrace, was a natural point of anchorage for anyone on a sea voyage
between Europe and Asia. Acts of the Apostles 16.11 describes how St
Paul put in there for the night when sailing from the Troad to
Macedonia.[64] Ovid changed ships there on his way to exile in Tomi.[65]
Any Roman sent on a tour of duty to an Asian province might well stop
off there on the outward or homeward journey. One plausible such
journey would be – but here I am entering the realms of fantasy – a tour
of duty to Bithynia, where Lucretius' patron Memmius was propraetor
in 57 BC.

At all events, the use of the Greek word *scaphiis* at VI 1046 can now
hardly be called gratuitous. It is part of the window-dressing for
Lucretius' brief excursion into an exotic world – his report of tricks with
magnets in Greek bronze vessels, witnessed in person on this distant
Aegean island.

II. THE FAMILIAR AND THE EXOTIC

Nor are the remote and the exotic by any means always viewed with
sympathy or approval. In book IV, for example (1123–30, 1160–9), Greek
vocabulary piles up to describe the absurd luxuries and euphemistic epi-
thets which deluded lovers, blinded to the realities of life, bestow on the
objects of their affections. (These lines, incidentally, feature prominently
in Bailey's list of gratuitously introduced Greek words, and include the
ones which he thought must be translated from a Greek original.) And
book II has another build-up of Greek words and names in the frenetic
description of the worship of Cybele (600–43),[66] a cult whose theological implications we are immediately urged to shun. Just as they are culturally remote,[67] so too they are, as Lucretius puts it (II 645), 'far removed
from true reasoning'.[68]

This shunning of the exotic can be felt in the important ethical proem

[64] Although Samothrace was said to be ill-provided with harbours (Pliny, *NH* IV. 12.73), it certainly
had at least one (Livy XLV 6.3).
[65] Ovid, *Tristia* I 10.19–22. My thanks to Ted Kenney for this piece of information.
[66] As well as the Greek proper names in the passage, note *tympana* and *cymbala* (618), *chorea* (635),
and the compound adjectives at 601, 619, 627 and 632.
[67] This is emphasised by Lucretius' specific indications (600, 629) that he is giving us a *Greek* portrayal of Cybele.
[68] Elsewhere, much the same sense of cultural remoteness is conveyed by the Greek triplet *harmo-
niai, organicos* and *Heliconi* at III 131–2, quoted and discussed above, p. 49.

to book II, at lines 20–61. The simple idyllic Epicurean lifestyle is eulogised in pure pastoral Latin. Greek words and formations creep in only when Lucretius is describing the pointless luxuries with which it stands in contrast (*lampadas igniferas* and *citharae* in 24–8, where 24–5 themselves recall the well-known Homeric description of Phaeacian opulence at *Odyssey* VII 100–2).

One less hostile use of Greek is book III's quasi-heroic parade of the great men who, for all their greatness, proved mortal (III 1024–44) – *Scipiadas* (note the Greek termination),[69] the companions of the *Heliconiades*, i.e. the poets, including Homer, who out of all of them was the one who won the *sceptra* (1038), Democritus, and even Epicurus – whose actual Greek name appears nowhere but here in the entire poem. What is evoked this time is not alienness or remoteness, but the larger-than-life heroism of Homeric (as well as Ennian) epic, in a parade of the dead also reminiscent of the Homeric *Nekuia*.[70]

Homer's own canonisation in this list does reflect a recognition on Lucretius' part of Greek superiority in both music and poetry. This emerges from the key Greek terms and forms which highlight his own celebrated poetic manifesto at I 921–50: his poetic ambitions have struck his heart with a *thyrsus* (I 923), inspiring him to expound his philosophy 'with sweet-talking Pierian song' (*suaviloquenti | carmine Pierio*, I 945–6). We should perhaps also detect an implicit contrast of Roman and Greek noises at II 410–13:

> ne tu forte putes serrae stridentis acerbum
> horrorem constare elementis levibus aeque
> *ac musaea mele, per chordas organici quae*
> mobilibus digitis expergefacta figurant.

> So you must not think that the harsh grating of a shrieking saw consists of elements as smooth as those constituting the musical melodies which the instrumentalists with nimble fingers arouse and form on their strings.

---

[69] It is true that, for metrical reasons, *Scipiadas* becomes the standard verse name for Scipio (although *Africanus* was available as an alternative, and is used as such by Martial). Likewise, for that matter, some of the Greek loan words which I am considering were fairly common in Latin. This, however, does not alter the power of such words to help evoke Greekness *when they occur in the company of other Graecisms*.

[70] 1025 is Ennian (see fr. 137 Skutsch), followed immediately by the Iliadic line 1026 (cf. *Il.* XXI 107). The thematic link with the *Nekuia* is already set up by the preceding lines, 980–1012, on myths of torture in Hades. For the dense series of further echoes of Greek literature in this passage, see Segal (1990), esp. pp. 177–8.

The almost pure Greek third line contrasts with the pure Latin which precedes. Where Greece has given us sublime music, Rome's more characteristic noise is the shrieking sawblades of a workshop.[71]

Sudden switches of vocabulary have this power to transport us instantly to and fro between the Greek and the Roman worlds. They can be used not only to praise Greek superiority, and to marginalise what Lucretius shuns as alien, but also, on the contrary, to universalise a concept. In book v (1028–90), Lucretius argues for the natural origin of language partly by appeal to the way that all animals alike from infancy instinctively know their innate powers (v 1034–8):

> cornua nata prius vitulo quam frontibus extent,
> illis iratus petit atque infestus inurget;   1035
> *at catuli pantherarum scymnique leonum*
> unguibus ac pedibus iam tum morsuque repugnant
> vix etiam cum sunt dentes unguesque creati.

> The calf angrily butts and charges with his incipient horns before they have even protruded from his forehead. Panther whelps and lion cubs already fight with claws, paws and biting at an age when their teeth and claws have barely appeared.

Scymni (1036), the Greek *vox propria* for lion cubs, occurs in Latin literature only here. Bailey objected to it on the ground that there was a perfectly good Latin word for cubs available, *catuli*, and one which Lucretius could hardly have overlooked since he used it in the very same line! But this once again misses the point. The butting calf, a familiar sight in the Italian countryside, is described in pure Latin. The young panthers and lions, on the other hand, those exotic inhabitants of the eastern Mediterranean and beyond, belong to another world. The switch to that other world is made instantaneously with the consecutive Greek-derived words *pantherarum scymnique* in line 1036. Lucretius neatly gets across the point that this instinctive use of innate powers is the same the whole world over, even though the nature of the powers themselves may vary from region to region. Likewise, he is arguing, human beings the world over naturally express themselves in language, even though the actual sounds produced differ according to region.

It is worth looking out for a comparable universality in the account of disease with which the whole poem closes (vi 1090–1286). Initially, Lucretius emphasises how widely diseases differ from one region of the

---

[71] Cf. II 500–6, Lucretius' catalogue of qualitative extremes, where Graecisms indicate the exotic character of the finest dyes (500–1) and of the most sublime music (505).

world to another (VI 1103–18). The diversity is brought home mainly by the deployment of geographical names, although the exotic character of the Egyptian elephantiasis disease is further emphasised by its Greek name, *elephas* (1114). When Lucretius turns to his long closing description of the Athenian plague, however, there is no attempt to bring out its exotic character by the use of Greek, despite the ready availability of suitable vocabulary in the Thucydides text which he is following.[72] The thorny problem of Lucretius' purpose in closing with the plague passage must be deferred until Chapter 5. Here I shall simply observe that the linguistic pattern I have described confirms that its lessons, whatever they are, are meant to be universal ones.

12. THE SWALLOW AND THE SWAN

I hope that these examples have succeeded in demonstrating the wide-ranging evocative powers of strategically placed Greek names, idioms and loan words in Lucretius' poem. If I am right, something unexpected has emerged. Despite the proclaimed Greek origins of both his poetic medium and its message, Lucretius is very far from being a philhellene or Helleniser. Although the Greeks are acknowledged to outshine the Romans both artistically and philosophically, Greekness for him frequently symbolises the culturally remote, the morally dangerous, and the philosophically obscure. Seen in this light, the wholesale Latinisation of Greek philosophical terminology which I discussed in §§1–7 of this chapter will need careful interpretation. We can now see that Lucretius' concern is not the philosophical spoon-feeding of disadvantaged Roman readers linguistically incapable of savouring the Epicurean gospels in their original Greek. On the contrary, his readers' familiarity with the Greek language, as with Greek literature, is assumed from the outset, and is systematically exploited. Nor on the other hand is he transporting his Roman readers to Athens. He is importing to Rome from Athens its single most precious product, which, as the proem to book VI eloquently declares, is Epicurus' philosophy.

It is certainly no part of his strategy to play down Epicurus' Greekness. Right from the proem to book I, Epicurus has been labelled the great Greek discoverer (*primum Graius homo* . . ., I 66).[73] And in the

---

[72] For Lucretius' use of medical vocabulary, see Langslow (1998).

[73] As Farrell (1991), pp. 34–5, n. 17, points out, *Graius homo* echoes Ennius' application of the same phrase to Pyrrhus, thus implicitly bracketing Epicurus and Pyrrhus as formidable Greek invaders of Italy.

proem to book III not only is Epicurus hailed as the 'glory of the Greek race' (*o Graiae gentis decus*, III 3), but his Greekness is brought out with the same linguistic device that I have been documenting. Lucretius professes himself Epicurus' imitator, not his rival (III 6–8):

> quid enim contendat hirundo
> cycnis, aut quidnam tremulis facere artubus haedi
> consimile in cursu possint et fortis equi vis.
>
> For how should a swallow compete with swans, or what would kids, with their trembling limbs, be able to do in a race to compare with the powerful strength of a horse?

The familiar pattern emerges once again. Lucretius is the swallow, or the kid, described in his own langage, Latin. Epicurus is the swan, or the horse. The swan is so named in Greek: the Greek *cycnus* became common enough in Latin, but this may well be its earliest occurrence;[74] and at all events, the native Latin word *olor* was available to Lucretius as an alternative. Even the dative form of *cycnis* imports a further Graecism, the indigenous Latin construction after verbs of contending being *cum* plus ablative.[75] What is more, *fortis equi vis*, although Latin, honours the horse with the Greek idiom, familiar from epic, whereby a hero is periphrastically called not 'x' but 'the (mighty) strength of x', e.g. *Iliad* XXIII 720 κρατερὴ . . . ἲς Ὀδυσῆος (where ἲς is cognate with Lucretius' *vis*).[76]

So at this crucial juncture Lucretius is not only emphasising Epicurus' Greekness, but even acknowledging that the Romans are, philosophically, the poor relations.[77] The question 'How can a Lucretius compete with an Epicurus?' turns out to carry the subtext 'How can a Roman philosopher compete with a Greek philosopher?'

13. THE RESOLUTION

What are we to make of these contradictions? Lucretius considers Greek culture artistically and philosophically superior, and yet at the same time deeply alien.[78] He floods his poem with Greek words, but scrupulously

[71] See André (1967), p. 65.
[75] I am grateful to Roland Mayer for pointing this out to me. He illuminatingly compares the device of using a Greek nominative-plus-infinitive construction at Catullus 4.1–2, where the purported speaker is designated by a Greek noun, *phaselus*.
[76] This Graecism is noted by Kenney (1971), *ad loc.*, and I owe to David West the further point that ἲς, rather than βία, is the Greek form directly echoed by Lucretius.
[77] For a further twist on the 'swan' theme, however, see pp. 140–1 below.
[78] To investigate how typical a Roman attitude this is would take me far beyond my present task. But it is safe to say that it was widespread: see e.g. Woolf (1994).

avoids them in the course of doctrinal exposition. Let me close with a suggested explanation of these anomalies.

Epicurus is a Greek, a voice from an alien culture to which Lucretius has no interest in acclimatising himself or his reader. Lucretius' mapping-out of the Greek and the Roman, effected by his strategic interweaving of Greek and Latin vocabulary, is a constant reminder of the gulf that divides the two worlds. But although Epicurus' world is alien, his philosophy is not. It directly addresses the universal moral needs of mankind, and to that extent it transcends all cultural barriers. Lucretius, we have seen, is constantly emphasising the barriers. It is precisely by drawing attention to the cultural divide between the Greek and the Roman, while making Epicurean philosophy nevertheless thoroughly at home in his own native language, that he proves to us its true universality.

APPENDIX

On p. 50 I quoted Bailey's list of 'capricious' Greek imports. In the ensuing discussion I have dealt with nearly all of them, arguing that they serve a strategic function within deliberately Hellenising contexts. In this appendix I shall deal with the handful of items left over from the same list: *baratre* III 955, *barathrum* VI 606, *gigas* IV 136, V 117, *lampas* II 79, V 402, 610, VI 1196, *lychni* V 295, *sceptra* V 1137.

I have no need to fight very hard for these. As I have emphasised, a Greek word in company with others is significant, but an isolated one may easily pass unnoticed. Some of these remaining Graecisms fall into the latter category: *lychni* at V 295, *sceptra* at V 1137, and *barathrum* at VI 606 are likely to be such cases. (However, another occurrence of *sceptra*, at V 1038, did prove to be a significant Graecism, above p. 55; and so, below, will another occurrence of *barathrum*.)

Gigas, used as by Lucretius to designate the Greek mythical beings of that name, is extremely common in Latin authors. What indigenous Latin word does Bailey think Lucretius might have used in its place?

Lampas is so widely used in Latin as to fall far short of the 'caprice' Bailey alleges. I happily concede that at V 610 and VI 1196 its Greek origins are simply irrelevant. On the other hand, we have already met one significantly Hellenising use of it at II 25 (above p. 55), and another can now be added: at V 402, *aeternam . . . lampada mundi* is the sun in the explicitly Greek context of the Phaethon myth, where it is flanked by two compound adjectives (399–400), two occurrences of the name Phaethon (397, 400), and an attribution of the whole story to the 'ancient Greek poets' (405). Finally, at II 79, animal species' swift transition from one generation to the next is compared to the handing on of a torch: *et quasi cursores vitai lampada tradunt*. This time for once there is no accumulation of Graecisms, but it has long been recognised by Lucretian editors that the reference is to a Greek institution, the torch race, to which Plato too (*Laws* 776b) compares the passage from generation to generation. The Greek word is, to say the very least, apposite.

This leaves just *baratre* at III 955, where an old man lamenting his imminent death is rebuked by a personified Nature:

> aufer abhinc lacrimas, baratre, et compesce querellas!

> Away with your tears, *baratre*, and curb your complaining.

Unfortunately this word is unattested. Just one item of evidence is cited, however, for the existence of a very similar Greek noun βάραθρος,[79] meaning someone who deserves to be hurled into the *barathrum*, the pit. Not surprisingly, many editors have preferred to emend, usually to *balatro*.[80]

It is, at least, surely no coincidence that the neuter noun *barathrum* occurs just eleven lines later in Lucretius' poem (an occurrence missed by Bailey), where, speaking now in his own voice, he endorses nature's rebuke by observing (III 966–7)

> nec quisquam in barathrum nec Tartara deditur atra:
> materies opus est ut crescant postera saecla.

> And no one is sent down to the pit of hell: their matter is needed,
> so that future generations may grow.

In the current context, then, *barathrum* is the pit of hell. So if *baratre* were retained and held to mean someone who deserves to be hurled into the *barathrum*, there would be a most surprising irony in Nature's addressing the whinging old man with this particular term of abuse. Hardly a productive way of conveying Lucretius' principal message, that there is no pit of hell to fear!

In seeking a better solution, it is worth first observing that *barathrum* in line 966 (quoted immediately above) may well be added to our list of significant Graecisms. After all, it is there in company with *Tartara*, and they jointly invoke that terrifying realm of punishment familiar from Greek myth and literature.

In seeking to make sense of the preceding *baratre* (955), we could do worse than take our lead from this line. The chances are surely that here too the original text referred directly to the pit of hell, the *barathrum*. What has bedevilled attempts to cure the corruption is the assumption that the word must be a vocative. Why not emend in the following way?

> aufer abhinc lacrimas, barathri et compesce querellas.

> Away with your weeping, and curb your complaining about the
> pit of hell.[81]

---

[79] Cited by the editors from Ammonius, *De diff. adf. voc.* 113.29, βάραθρος μὲν γὰρ ὁ βαράθρου ἄξιος ἄνθρωπος. LSJ note hesitantly that it may occur with this meaning at Lucian, *Pseudologista* 17, adding, however, that this could be the neuter noun *barathrum*. I take it that the latter assumption influenced Bockemüller's conjecture *barathrum*.

[80] Smith (1975), p. 262 reports that *balatro* had, before Heinsius, already been proposed by 'anonymous critics in Turnebus, *Adversaria* 20.26'. Other emendations proposed are *blatero* (Merrill) and *barathrum* (Bockemüller).

[81] *Querella* + objective genitive is cited in *OLD* (s.v.) from Cicero and Apuleius. If alternatively one chose to construe *barathri* with *lacrimas*, one might think of Virg. *Aen.* I 462, *sunt lacrimae rerum*.

(Since *baratre*, if retained, would be taken to stand for *barathre*, the emendation amounts to a further change of one letter only.) The proposal has one immediate advantage. It supplies a piece of information which is otherwise left unstated, that the old man – whose words were not actually quoted – has been complaining partly about the prospect of hell. And without an indication to that effect, one might be left wondering why Lucretius, at 966–7, should offer his rationalistic denial of hell as directly confirming Nature's rebuke.

CHAPTER 3

Lucretius the fundamentalist

I. PHILOSOPHY IN ITALY

Virtually no facts about Lucretius' life have been determined by modern scholarship, beyond a consensus that it was spent mainly if not entirely in Italy, and that it terminated in the 50s BC.[1] But for a Roman with philosophical leanings those two facts in themselves ought to speak volumes. He could hardly have chosen a better time to be alive. The last fifty years of the Roman Republic were a period of unsurpassed philosophical upheaval in the Graeco-Roman world. And for the first time ever the philosophical centre of gravity was shifting away from Athens, with Italy capturing more than its share of the action. The events of the Mithridatic War (91–86 BC) – in particular, by a curious historical irony, the regime of the Epicurean tyrant Aristion (88–86) – had driven many philosophers out of the city.[2] The Athenian schools were no longer guaranteed the status of international headquarters for their respective movements.[3] And in the resultant diaspora, many philosophers found their way to Italy. Here a ready-made audience awaited them, including plenty of Romans who had already trained at Athens in one or more of the philosophical schools.[4]

The leading figures of the Academy, Philo of Larissa and Antiochus of Ascalon, conducted their well advertised rift over the true nature of their Platonic legacy not in Athens but from bases in Rome and

[1] For a judicious survey of Lucretian biography, see Smith (1975), pp. ix–xxviii. I shall have nothing to add to it in this book, beyond my argument in Ch. 2, §10 that Lucretius must have been to Greece.
[2] See Ferrary (1988), pp. 435–86, Habicht (1995), esp. pp. 299–313, Dorandi (1997).
[3] This is well argued, with regard to the Academy, by Glucker (1978), esp. pp. 364ff.
[4] The philosophical engagement of influential Romans during the late Republic is well brought out by Rawson (1985) and Griffin (1989) and (1995). Jocelyn (1977) supplies further invaluable material, which does not on the whole seem to me to support his rather negative conclusions. I have myself tried, in Sedley (1997a), to demonstrate the crucial role that philosophy played in Caesar's assassination.

Alexandria respectively.[5] And both became important figures at Rome, where their influence on leading public figures was considerable. Among Lucretius' Roman contemporaries, Cicero became a follower of Philo's New Academy, while Brutus, Varro, Lucullus, M. Pupinius Piso and others attached themselves to Antiochus' Old Academy, which professed to have rescued the true philosophy of Plato from obfuscation and distortion at the hands of the Stoics. Although it is debated how much influence Antiochus and his pupils exerted on later philosophical developments,[6] there can be no doubt of their importance to their own contemporaries. Partly as a result, renewed study of Plato's own text was at this very time becoming the basis of a revitalised Platonism:[7] the Middle Platonist era was just getting under way.

Pythagoreanism was already in some sense a native Italian philosophy. Around this time it was enjoying an Italian renaissance, and was to exert considerable influence on the re-emerging Platonism. It had as its leading figure a Roman, Nigidius Figulus.

Posidonius, the most influential Stoic of the day, was especially active in Lucretius' own chosen domain, cosmology. Although he had chosen Rhodes as the main base for his own teaching, he visited Rome at least twice, and was an intimate acquaintance of Cicero and other eminent Romans. Stoicism certainly had a considerable impact on Roman thought in the late Republic, although card-carrying Roman Stoics at this date seem relatively few in number. The most celebrated of them all was of course Lucretius' contemporary the younger Cato.

Peripatetic philosophy too was gaining in influence. Manuscripts of Aristotle's school treatises – works largely unknown or ignored during the preceding two centuries[8] – had arrived in Rome along with Sulla's other booty from Athens, acquired during the Mithridatic War. Owing to recent work by Jonathan Barnes,[9] it can no longer be assumed that from these copies the Peripatetic philosopher Andronicus was to produce the first full edition of Aristotle's treatises. Nevertheless, it was at just this time, the mid first century BC, that Aristotle's *Categories* suddenly and spectacularly burst onto the scene, provoking a stampede of commentators, some favourable, others highly critical. At least one of the first generation of Aristotelian commentators, the Stoic

---

[5] On this dispute see e.g. Glucker (1978), Sedley (1981), Barnes (1989a).
[6] For doubts on this, see Glucker (1978), Barnes (1989a).
[7] On the reasons for the return to the study of ancient texts at this date, see Hadot (1987). That Brutus, as an Antiochean, relied on a close knowledge of Plato's text in 44 BC is argued in Sedley (1997a).   [8] See Sandbach (1985).
[9] The standard story is brilliantly demolished by Barnes (1997).

Athenodorus, a friend of Cicero and teacher of Octavian, was almost certainly working in Rome by the mid first century.[10] I find it hard to doubt that the rediscovery of the *Categories* is one which really did emerge from the war booty at Rome.[11] And it marked the beginning of the Aristotelian commentary tradition, which was to remain the dominant form of philosophical exposition for the rest of antiquity. Thus, although the exact timing is uncertain, it may well be that in the last decade of Lucretius' life, when he was working on the *De rerum natura*, the philosophical intelligentsia of Rome was already turning its attention to Aristotelian school texts.

The history of Aristotelian scholarship is admittedly a speculative matter. But there can be no doubt that Antiochus and others had in any case done much to rekindle interest in Peripatetic texts in Lucretius' lifetime.[12] There were a number of prominent Peripatetics in circulation, at least some of them based in Italy.[13] The Antiochean M. Puponius Piso had, even before studying with Antiochus, for many years kept the Peripatetic Staseas of Naples as his philosopher-in-residence at Tusculum.[14] Crassus, too, enjoyed the services of a resident Peripatetic.[15] And the leading Peripatetic of the day, Cratippus, although based in Athens, was well known to, and very highly regarded by, a number of Romans, Cicero included.[16]

Even Epicureanism had at least one major base in Italy. In the next section I shall have more to say about Philodemus' Epicurean school at Herculaneum, which was at its zenith in the mid first century BC when Lucretius was writing. It would not be at all surprising if Lucretius had had links with it, not only because he was himself an Epicurean, but also because in the next generation leading literary Romans like Virgil and his eventual executors Varius and Plotius Tucca were to maintain close contacts with it.[17] Influential Romans in Lucretius' day who were Epicureans included Cassius, later the assassin of Caesar, Cicero's friend Atticus, and L. Calpurnius Piso Caesoninus, the target of Cicero's *In*

---

[10] See Goulet (1989), 1 654–7, for the probable identity of Athenodorus the commentator with Athenodorus the teacher of Octavian.

[11] The *Categories* and *De interpretatione* appear in two versions of a list of Aristotelian works held to derive from a late third-century BC source (one in Diogenes Laertius v 26, the other in Hesychius), but it is generally agreed that they are a later interpolation there (Moraux (1951), pp. 131, 186–90, 313, Düring (1957), pp. 69, 90).

[12] Cf. Cicero's close study of Theophrastus and Dicaearchus in 60–59 BC (*Ad Att.* II 3.4, 16.3). The issue of Cicero's knowledge of the Peripatos is thoroughly explored in Fortenbaugh/Steinmetz (1989). [13] See Griffin (1989), p. 7. [14] Cic. *Fin.* v 8, *De or.* I 104. [15] Plut. *Crass.* 3.

[16] Plut. *Cic.* 24. [17] See Gigante/Capasso (1989).

Pisonem and patron of Philodemus. Even Caesar himself is widely suspected to have been an Epicurean.[18]

Cicero's philosophical dialogues, even if they are dramatic fictions, cannot be wholly fictitious in representing many others from Cicero's circle as committed exponents of current Greek philosophical systems.[19] Indeed, Cicero's correspondence with numerous contemporaries shows them, in general, to be remarkably well attuned to live philosophical issues and inter-school debates.[20]

Lucretius was extraordinarily lucky to find such a ready-made philosophical environment for the maturation of his own ideas. No previous era at Rome could compare with it. And it is doubtful whether any subsequent era could either: barely a generation after his death, Alexandria would largely eclipse Rome as a philosophical centre. But did Lucretius seize this unique opportunity? Does the *De rerum natura*, the most brilliant philosophical composition to survive from its period, reflect the highly charged philosophical atmosphere of mid first-century BC Italy?

Amazingly, it does not.

2. THE SCHOOL OF PHILODEMUS

The Epicurean library discovered at Herculaneum, near Naples, in the mid eighteenth century (see Ch. 4, §1 below), is almost certainly that from the school of Philodemus,[21] which seems to have flourished from the 80s BC until late in the century.[22] The school, although located in a Greek-speaking region, was close enough to Rome for its influence to be felt there. Cicero names its leading figures, Siro and Philodemus, as Epicurean *familiares* to whom he can turn when in need of advice on some point of doctrine.[23] And Philodemus' library itself attests the deep involvement of contemporary Epicureans in current philosophical controversies, debating, for instance, the proper philosophical attitudes to rhetoric, music and poetry, and concerned to meet Stoic and Peripatetic challenges on these and other issues.[24]

---

[18] For details of these and many other known and putative Roman Epicureans in the late Republic, see Castner (1988), who on pp. 83–6 judiciously sifts the evidence for counting Caesar among them.   [19] However, for a cautionary note on this point, see Griffin (1995), p. 325.

[20] This is admirably demonstrated by Griffin (1995).

[21] For a valuable synoptic survey of the library and modern work on it, see Gigante (1995). For some residual doubts about its ownership, see De Lacy (1993).

[22] For Philodemus' biography, and in particular the date and circumstances of his move to Italy from Athens, see Dorandi (1997).   [23] Cic. *Fin.* II 119.   [24] For a survey, see Asmis (1990).

There has been much debate about Lucretius' orthodoxy or hetero-
doxy as an Epicurean choosing to write poetry. Philodemus was himself
a poet, and his aesthetic writings offer important evidence for anyone
setting out to resolve the issue.[25] But the study of these texts has so far
yielded no good evidence of a direct influence of Philodemus on
Lucretius, or vice versa.[26]

Knut Kleve[27] has opened new avenues for speculation by arguing that
the fragments of a Latin text found in the Herculaneum library come from
a copy of the *DRN*. This is not the place to examine the evidence adduced
by Kleve. The fragments are very tiny, but he nevertheless builds quite an
impressive case. I limit myself here to Kleve's conclusion from his findings:
'Theories building on the assumption that Lucretius had no contact with
contemporary Epicureanism, suffer a serious setback.' I do not think that
this in any way follows. The books people have on their shelves, unless
these contain autograph dedications, can tell us nothing about their personal acquaintance with the authors of those books. It would only be if we
had reason to suppose that Lucretius' poem was unavailable for public
purchase in the first centuries BC and AD that anything could be inferred
about personal contact between him and the school at Herculaneum. And
since (as my arguments in Ch. 5 will confirm) there is excellent reason to
accept the ancient tradition that the poem was published posthumously,
the chances are that any copy in the library was obtained only at a time
when personal contact was no longer even possible.

Evidence of contact between Lucretius and Philodemus, then, if it is
to be found, would have to be sought in the content of their writings.
These unfortunately have for the most part too little common thematic
ground to be of much help.[28] But one (partially) surviving work of

---

[25] There are a number of important papers relating to this question in Obbink (1995).
[26] Milanese (1989), pp. 134–9, detects echoes of Philodemus' aesthetics (and a reaction to Stoic
aesthetics) at Lucr. I 641–4, but seems to me to be exaggerating some rather unremarkable resemblances.   [27] Kleve (1989).
[28] I consign to a footnote the problematic question of their views on the gods. Lucretius, in common
with Cicero, Philodemus and most modern interpreters, treats the Epicurean gods as actually
living beings. I myself believe (Long/Sedley (1987), §23), albeit controversially, that Epicurus
intended them primarily as thought-constructs, saying little to resolve the question whether there
were any such beings actually alive in the universe. However, he clearly spoke at length about
how we should *think of* the gods as being and living (including, perhaps, that we should think of
them as living outside our world, cf. Lucr. v 146–55), and the inference that these were objectively real gods may have been a natural one for readers to make. It is striking (cf. Long/Sedley
(1987), I 149) that Lucretius' indications of this assumption are evident only in his proems, universally agreed to be his own original compositions, while in the main body of book v (1161–225),
where I shall argue that he is following Epicurus' text closely, he provides some of the strongest
evidence for the thought-construct interpretation.

Philodemus which significantly overlaps with Lucretius' interests is his *On signs*.[29] This fascinating text is testimony to a highly sophisticated debate between Epicureans and Stoics on scientific inference – the very branch of philosophical methodology which underlies Lucretius' own poem. Philodemus is no innovator here. He is reporting, in more than one version, the arguments of Zeno of Sidon, the Epicurean school-head under whom he studied at Athens. In other words, this is above all a teaching text from Philodemus' own school,[30] illustrating exactly the kind of issues to which we would expect Lucretius to have been exposed if he had studied there.[31]

The debate achieved enough publicity to leave an unmistakable imprint on the Academic critique of Epicurean theology created by Cicero in *De natura deorum* I.[32] Yet when we turn to Lucretius, the contrast is a stark one. His methodological pronouncements on the rules of inference are confined to areas which we know to have been covered by Epicurus – above all, his very clear assertion of the principle of multiple explanations in books V and VI.[33] Although he naturally enough uses inductive and analogical arguments throughout the poem, there is no indication in these that he is concerned with resisting the challenges to their validity which Stoic critics had posed and Zeno set out to answer.[34] One very clear such case is the debate about the size of the sun. I shall deal with this in §7 of the present chapter.

Reverence for Epicurus was to be expected of any Epicurean, but Lucretius' reverence is idiosyncratic in two ways. Not only did it, as I have argued, lead him to ignore the contemporary philosophical environment. It also focused more narrowly on Epicurus himself than school practice in his day expected. As Philodemus' writings make clear, it was normal for contemporary Epicureans to assign virtually biblical status not to the writings of Epicurus alone, but jointly to those of the foursome known simply as οἱ ἄνδρες, 'the Great Men'. These infallible four were the

[29] See the edition of De Lacy (1978); also Sedley (1982), Barnes (1988), Long (1988a), Asmis (1996).
[30] For this characterisation, and related aspects of Philodemus' work, see Sedley (1989b), 103–17.
[31] *Sign.* itself is too late for Lucretius to have known it as a written text. On its date, see Long/Sedley (1987), II 263. [32] As shown by Auvray-Assayas (1992) and Asmis (1996).
[33] V 526–33, VI 703–11.
[34] Cf. the judicious remarks of Clay (1983), pp. 24–5. The best that Schmidt (1990), p. 69, can do to find a Lucretian echo of these innovations is to cite I 265–328, where 'Induktionsschlüsse vorliegen'. Actually there are no inductive arguments here, and only one analogical argument, but what really matters is that neither here nor anywhere else do we find Lucretius using Zenonian-style formulations of sign-inferences or taking account of the contentious issues about validity that featured in the recent debate. There is nothing in this passage that could not be directly echoing Epicurus.

founding figures of the school, Epicurus, Metrodorus, Hermarchus and Polyaenus,[35] and all four were treated as absolutely and equally authoritative. In this context, Lucretius stands out for his singular devotion to Epicurus himself, eloquently declared in the proem to book III (9–13):

> tu pater es, rerum inventor, tu patria nobis
> suppeditas praecepta, tuisque ex, inclute, chartis,   10
> floriferis ut apes in saltibus omnia libant,
> omnia nos itidem depascimur aurea dicta,
> aurea, perpetua semper dignissima vita.

> You are our father, the discoverer. You it is who supply us with a father's precepts. It is from your scrolls, illustrious one, that like bees sipping everything in flowery glades we feed on all your golden sayings – golden, and ever deserving of unending life.

Just as he here declares his exclusive dependence on Epicurus' own writings, so too throughout the poem he offers no hint of bowing to other Epicurean authorities.

3. THE LOCATION OF THE MIND

To illustrate my thesis in a less negative way, let me now focus on a debate which had been simmering for two and a half centuries. Both the main doctrinal schools of the Hellenistic era, the Stoic and the Epicurean, had been founded around 300 BC, at a time when medical opinion tended to favour the heart as the location of the rational mind. This was certainly the view of the great contemporary physician Praxagoras of Cos, later invoked as an authority on the issue by the Stoic Chrysippus.[36] The alternative of locating it in the head, although supported by the Pythagorean tradition and accepted by Plato in the *Timaeus*, was not endorsed by Aristotle or, in the next generation, by the first Stoics and Epicureans. Zeno of Citium, the founder of Stoicism, was so confident on the point that he even produced his own syllogism in confirmation:

Voice comes through the windpipe. If it were coming from the brain, it would not come through the windpipe. Where speech comes from is where voice also comes from. But speech comes from the mind. Therefore the mind is not in the brain.[37]

Now, such was the commitment in philosophical schools to the truth of the founder's word that subsequent Stoics could not simply disown this

---

[35] See Longo Auricchio (1978), Sedley (1989b).
[36] Galen, *On the doctrines of Hippocrates and Plato (PHP)* I 7.1 = *SVF* II 897.
[37] Galen, *PHP* II 5.8 = *SVF* I 148.

3. The location of the mind

argument and its implications.[38] Philosophical debate within schools was
presented as recovery and interpretation of the founder's true views, not
their replacement or revision. And Zeno's argument was too unambiguous in its formulation to be explained away or rendered harmless by
reinterpretation. That was most unfortunate. For within a generation of
Zeno's confident syllogism, Alexandrian physicians, operating with the
grisly insights vouchsafed by the human vivisections which they were
permitted to perform on prisoners from the local jail, had discovered the
nervous system and put it beyond doubt that the brain, not the heart, is
the true command centre.[39] Following these discoveries by Herophilus
and Erasistratus, there is no record of any further doubt within medical
opinion that, if there is any seat of reason,[40] it is located in the head.[41]
This left Stoic philosophers of subsequent generations looking as
stranded as religious zealots defending the Genesis account of the creation in the face of the Big Bang and Darwin. Not only did Chrysippus
defend the outdated Zenonian anatomy – earning himself and his arguments a merciless tirade of ridicule from Galen[42] – but even Posidonius,

---

[38] Sedley (1989b). The only exception was Zeno's early *Republic*, which some Stoics seem to have
discounted as pre-Stoic (Philodemus, *De Stoicis* ix xv, in Dorandi (1982)).

[39] See Herophilus frr. 63 6 in von Staden (1989).

[40] I add this qualification because it was open to Lucretius' near-contemporary Asclepiades (SE,
M vii 380, Aetius iv 2.8), for one, to deny that there is any localised *hēgemonikon*. It was long
assumed that Lucretius knew Asclepiades, who in the nineteenth century was frequently, on no
evidence at all, referred to as his 'master' (see Schrijvers (1976), p. 238). However, the new revision of his chronology (he was dead by 91 bc, see Rawson (1982)) no longer makes that a very
appetising guess. There is in any case not the slightest sign in Lucretius of reaction to
Asclepiades' idiosyncratic theories (on which see Vallance (1990)) – the *anarmoi onkoi*, the non-
localisation of the *hēgemonikon*, or any other in which he might have shown an interest. Pigeaud
(1981) explicates Lucretius' 'eclectic' physiology largely in terms of his agreements and disagreements with Asclepiades, but offers no evidence that Lucretius was actually aware of Asclepiades'
work. See also n. 51 (p. 72).

[41] See the wide range of doxographical material on this topic assembled and studied by Mansfeld
(1990), pp. 3092 108.

[42] Galen, *PHP*, esp. ii 5. Diogenes of Babylon is another Stoic reported as backing Zeno's thesis:
SVF iii Diog. 29, 33. In the latter (of which a more up-to-date text can be found in Henrichs
(1974), pp. 19 20, or in Obbink (1996), pp. 19 20), Diogenes attributes this same view correctly
to Chrysippus, but also speaks of 'some Stoics', to whom Chrysippus appears to have been reply-
ing, who had located the *hēgemonikon* in the head. Since these are probably pre-Chrysippean
(*contra* Mansfeld (1990), p. 3095 n. 145; the text does not make this explicit, but Mansfeld is definitely wrong to make them later than Diogenes of Babylon, since it is Diogenes who is quoting
them), I assume them to be first-generation Stoics, writing before Zeno's death, when school
orthodoxy first became established. The one genuinely anomalous text is Aetius iv 21.4, where
'the Stoics' are given the thesis that 'the *hēgemonikon* itself, like the world's, resides in our spher-
ical head'. This, a transparent import from Plato's *Timaeus*, is out of step not only with all the
other evidence for standard Stoicism, but even with the preceding sentence in Aetius' report,
which apparently assumes the Zenonian anatomy. (I am not clear why Mansfeld, *loc. cit.*, thinks
Cornutus an exception to the generalisation at Aetius iv 5.6 that 'all' Stoics located the
hēgemonikon in the region of the heart.)

despite incorporating within his Stoicism the tripartite division of the soul which had enabled Plato to separate the rational mind, in the head, from the 'spirited' part in the chest and the 'appetitive' part in the abdomen, could not follow Plato on this point, and had no choice but to locate all three soul-parts in the heart.[43]

Now it appears that the Epicureans faced the same problem. Among the books in Philodemus' library were several by Demetrius of Laconia, the eminent Epicurean of the late second and early first centuries BC. One of these (P.Herc. 1012) is an exegetical treatise on a series of cruces in foundational Epicurean texts,[44] and at one point in its fragments (cols. XLII–XLVII) Demetrius is clearly discussing a passage in which Epicurus had argued that the rational mind is in the chest. The state of the text leaves it quite unclear what concession, if any, Demetrius and his fellow-Epicureans are making to modern science. But Demetrius shows himself well aware of what he calls an 'argument used by many doctors to prove that reason is located in the head' (XLVII 7–11). And he mentions the expedient, adopted by some leading Epicureans, of positing a scribal error and emending Epicurus' text on the point (XLIV). Whether the object was to justify Epicurus' statement on the location of the mind, or to absolve him of having made it in the first place, is unclear. But the recognition by contemporary Epicureans of the current state of medical opinion and of the challenge it posed for them is not in doubt.

And where does Lucretius stand on this fascinating issue? The extraordinary truth is that he is so out of touch with his own school, and with modern science, as never to have even heard of the debate. Such is his reliance on Epicurus' own word that he not only repeats his founder's argument that the mind is in the chest,[45] but shows himself altogether unaware of the challenge to it that expert medical opinion now presents. How else can we explain the following argument, which he deploys on two separate occasions?

At III 784–97 he argues that the mind could not exist outside the body, and at V 128–41 that the cosmic masses like sea and earth could not themselves be animate. On both occasions the ground is the same. A mind cannot exist in just any physical location. Not only can it exist only in an organic body, but it cannot even exist in just any part of that body (III 788–93 = V 132–7):

---

[43] Galen, *PHP* VI 2.5 = Posidonius F146 Edelstein/Kidd (1989).
[44] See the edition by Puglia (1988).
[45] III 140–2. For Epicurus' own very similar argument, see scholion on *Ep. Hdt.* 66.

sic animi natura nequit sine corpore oriri
sola neque a nervis et sanguine longius esse.
quod si posset enim, multo prius ipsa animi vis   790
in capite aut umeris aut imis calcibus esse
posset et innasci quavis in parte soleret,
tandem in eodem homine atque in eodem vase manere.

Thus the mind's nature cannot exist in isolation, without a body,
nor be separated from sinews and blood. For if it could, much
sooner would the mind's power be able itself to exist *in the head
or the shoulders or the soles of the feet* – and to be born in any part you
like, while still remaining in the same person and the same con-
tainer.

The words which I have italicised are hardly those of someone in tune
with the contemporary debate. The rhetorical force of Lucretius' argument depends on the expectation that it will sound as silly to imagine
your mind in your head as in your foot.[46] He must be astonishingly out
of touch with current opinion on the matter.[47] It is as if an evangelical
missionary in twentieth-century Britain were to tell the public 'If you are
going to believe things like that, you might as well deny that God made
the world in six days.'

This last is the analogy which suggests the title of my chapter,
'Lucretius the fundamentalist'.[48] Lucretius cannot, in my view, be an
interacting member of any current philosophical circle. His inspiration
comes from the unmediated scriptures of the philosopher he reveres,
Epicurus himself. Like any fundamentalist, he does not expect the
numerous contributions made since the composition of his sacred

---

[46] Hence I am puzzled by the claim of Mansfeld (1990), p. 3149 that Lucretius' argument shows he
is aware of the alternative view that the mind is in the head. Note too that Lucretius does,
throughout the poem, consistently locate thought in the chest – although the brain is often ille-
gitimately smuggled in by his translators, and interpreters often falsely assume that 'mind'
implies 'head' for him (e.g. the influential suggestion of Kenney (1971), 76–7 that at III 15 *divina
mente coortam* is an implicit reference to the birth of Athena from the head of Zeus). The only
place where he might appear aware of the head's claims is at III 138, where the *animus* is said *caput
esse quasi et dominari in corpore toto*. However, I take it that here the metaphor of 'head' derives from
the word's common usage to designate the source of a river, as also at V 601.

[47] It is often thought (see esp. Gottschalk (1996)) that on another aspect of the soul, namely its
composition, Lucretius reflects developments postdating Epicurus, since to the three ingredients
(wind, heat and the unnamed substance) listed at *Ep. Hdt.* 63 he joins the doxographical tradition (cf. Aetius IV 3.11) in adding a fourth, air. My preferred guess would be that Epicurus' full
account in *Nat.* already listed the four, but that his summary in *Ep. Hdt.* subsumes wind and air
under the deliberately vague description προσεμφερέστατον δὲ πνεύματι, which avoids actually naming a component, no doubt because 'wind' and 'air' consist of the very same atoms,
albeit in different patterns of motion.

[48] My thanks to David West, who first suggested to me that 'fundamentalist' was the word I needed
to capture my view of Lucretius.

scriptures, either by his school or by its critics, to have added anything worth taking into account.

I recognise the paradox of speaking in these quasi-religious terms about a self-declared enemy of *religio*. But it is Lucretius himself who, in his proems to books III and V, declares the religious nature of his devotion: Epicurus, whose divinely conceived philosophy is Lucretius' own inspiration and guide, was himelf a god, indeed a god who eclipsed the traditional Olympian deities in the importance of his benefactions to mankind. Without exploring Lucretius' fundamentalism, we cannot hope to appreciate the full force of these religious declarations.

I do not mean to suggest that Lucretius was a recluse, either socially or intellectually. In every other respect he shows himself an acute observer of his own society, sensitive and subtle in argument and thoroughly versed in the literary traditions of both Italy and Greece, including Hellenistic as well as archaic Greek poetry.[49] Even Hellenistic intellectual trends, such as euhemeristic and other allegorical rationalisations of religion, have left their mark on him.[50] It is only in his hardcore scientific and philosophical beliefs that his fundamentalism shows itself.[51]

---

[49] See esp. Kenney (1970).   [50] See Gale (1994a), esp. pp. 26–30, 75–80.

[51] I here dissent, with some misgivings, from the important contributions of P. H. Schrijvers, who has been the most eloquent modern defender of Lucretius' familiarity with Hellenistic thought, especially scientific thought. But I shall take up — and with apologies for the extreme condensation — only the cases where he offers explicit evidence for his position, and also ignore those where the alleged debt (e.g. to Dicaearchus, Schrijvers (1994), (1996); to Palaephatus, Schrijvers (1983)), even if accepted, might in principle be mediated by Epicurus, as well as those where no direct debt is even claimed. (I have not, at the time of writing, seen a text of Schrijvers (1997).) (1) Schrijvers (1976), pp. 238–9, links Lucretius' accounts of hunger and nutrition (IV 858–69) to those of Asclepiades, who had similarly explained them in terms of the dilation and refilling of bodily ducts (πόροι). Against this (a) πόροι are already a widely used explanatory device in Epicurus (see Usener (1977), *s.v.*); (b) there is no record of Epicurus having a *different* account of hunger and nutrition from that in Lucretius (*contra* Solmsen (1953), p. 39 n. 19, Epicurus fr. 293 Usener, where absorption of food is a case of attraction of like to like analogous to magnetism, is fully consistent both with Lucr. IV 858–69 and — read in context — with VI 946–7; for the role of πόροι in Epicurus' theory of magnetism, see fr. 293 Usener, p. 209, l. 13 and p. 210, l. 22); (c) in the third century BC, Damoxenus' comic cook, a self-declared follower of Democritus and Epicurus, says τοιγαροῦν εἰς τοὺς πόρους | ὁ χυμὸς ὁμαλῶς πανταχοῦ συνίσταται (*ap.* Athenaeus 102B = Damoxenus fr. 2, 29–30 Kassel/Austin); (d) see n. 40 (p. 69) on Asclepiades' date; and (e) as Pigeaud (1981), p. 189 points out, the account of thirst with which this passage continues (IV 870–6) is very different from Asclepiades'. (2) In the 'Discussion' appended to Furley (1978), p. 31, Schrijvers cites Gellius XVII 11.11–13 as evidence that the expression τραχεῖα ἀρτηρία, apparently reflected in Lucretius' *asperiora . . . arteria* (IV 529), was introduced by Erasistratus, i.e. too late to be taken up by Epicurus; but Gellius does not say this as far as I can see, and Anon. Lond. VIII 29–30 is powerful evidence that the term is much older. (3) On Aenesidemus, see §8 below.

4. PHILOSOPHICAL OPPONENTS

This impression is amply confirmed when one turns to Lucretius' polemics.[52] Epicurus' own targets in his philosophical critiques had been above all the Presocratics – especially his chief forerunner Democritus, along with his own Democritean teacher Nausiphanes – and Plato.[53] The contemporary Stoic school had apparently achieved prominence too late to feature as a further target. Later Epicureans adopted Epicurus' enemies as their own, but added contemporary ones, above all the Stoics. Lucretius' contemporaries illustrate this point effectively. Cicero's Epicurean spokesman Velleius in book I of the *De natura deorum* criticises Platonic and Stoic theology in tandem,[54] and Philodemus' targets include not only the by now obscure Nausiphanes but also near-contemporary Peripatetics and Stoics.

Lucretius' most sustained polemic is at I 635–920, concerning the ultimate constituents of things. Here he criticises the monists, exemplified by Heraclitus, the four-element theorists, represented by Empedocles, and finally Anaxagoras. There is little doubt that this derives from Epicurus' own critique in books XIV and XV of his *On nature*.[55] None of the named philosophers presented, by any stretch of the imagination, a live philosophical challenge to the Epicureans in Lucretius' own day, but, as I have said, it was quite unexceptional for contemporary Epicureans to perpetuate Epicurus' own invectives in this way. Where Lucretius differs from his contemporaries is in the entire absence of a matching critique of Stoic physics.

Many editors have assumed that the Stoics would be included among the unnamed followers of Heraclitus' doctrine that everything consists of fire (I 635–7, 705–6).[56] In fact, though, they were committed exponents of the four-element theory, and would be much more likely, if they were implicitly present in Lucretius' list, to be included among Empedocles' unnamed followers in his four-element theory (I 714–15,

[52] For a general survey of these, see Kleve (1978).   [53] For Epicurus' polemics, see Sedley (1976a).
[54] Cic. *ND* I 18–23.   [55] See Ch. 4, §10.
[56] This would gratuitously presuppose a distortion of Stoic physics on Lucretius' part – one admittedly found in much of the modern literature, but in none of the ancient. In some contexts the Stoics did call fire 'the element *par excellence*', but meant by this that it was privileged above the other three elements in that *between* world-phases everything became fire, and hence that our world starts from fire (*SVF* II 403). No plausible reading of Stoic physics could make fire the sole constituent of the world. Rather, at least for Zeno and Cleanthes, the role of fire in the present cosmos was as an active force imbuing and controlling the world's material constituents. Cf. Long (1975–6), p. 140.

734–5).[57] But although the four elements did indeed play an important role in Stoic cosmology, not even they were viewed by the Epicureans as the Stoics' candidate for the primary constituents of things, which were rather, quite correctly, taken to be the two principles 'matter and god'. Diogenes of Oenoanda goes through just the same list of targets as Lucretius (differing only in that he assigns names to the 'water' and 'air' monists, left anonymous at *DRN* 1 707–9). But, significantly, he adds the Stoic principles at the end of it (6 1 10–11 9 Smith):

> Heraclitus of Ephesus said that fire is the element, Thales of Miletus water, Diogenes of Apollonia and Anaximenes air, Empedocles of Acragas fire, air, water and earth, Anaxagoras of Clazomenae the 'homoeomeries' of each thing, *and the Stoics matter and god.*

It is the absence of any such updating in Lucretius' list of targets that makes him an anomalous figure within the Epicurean tradition. No one genuinely concerned to combat Stoic physics could have failed to allude at some point in his book to these two principles, or for that matter to the ordering role of *pneuma* in the Stoic cosmos.

But do the Stoics *never* feature as targets for Lucretian polemic? Editors long assumed that they frequently do so feature. But more than thirty years ago David Furley, in a seminal if controversial article, worked systematically through these purported cases and brought highly persuasive arguments to bear against the necessary identification of any of the opponents as Stoics.[58]

The one systematic attempt to refute Furley's arguments has been made by Jürgen Schmidt.[59] In reply to Schmidt, I will content myself with the following observations. Much of his case rests on two passages of Lucretius which, as I will be trying to show in the next two sections, have in view not Stoic cosmology but a Platonist forerunner of it.[60] And a good

---

[57] Thus SE *PH* III 31 classes the Stoics as four-element theorists, while implicitly acknowledging that it might be more correct to call them matter–god dualists.   [58] Furley (1966).
[59] Schmidt (1990).
[60] I therefore take the same to be true of the critique of anthropocentric teleology at II 167–82 (discussed by Schmidt at pp. 152–60), which is presented (182) as a foretaste of the book V passage. I am also unpersuaded by the argument of De Lacy (1948), taken up by Schmidt, that Lucretius' replies to anthropocentric teleology at V 195–234 are dependent on Carneades' critique of Stoic cosmology. Even supposing that Carneades was the source of the objection at Cic. *Ac.* II 120 and Plutarch fr. 193 Sandbach (= Porphyry, *Abst.* III 20) that the world is too full of pests to have been made for human beings, it is such an easy objection to anthropocentrism that we need hardly doubt that Epicurus or Lucretius could have hit upon it independently. Besides, Lucretius' expansion of the objection *tanta stat praedita culpa* (II 181) at V 195–234 has a twist not found in the Academic tradition — that other species have a *better* claim than we do to be the true beneficiaries.

deal of what remains turns on Lucretius' interest in allegory: even if there is a Stoic influence here,[61] it is likely to be one which has come to him through Hellenistic literature and literary theory, not through an interest in Stoicism as such.[62] That leaves just two passages where it can be made to look plausible that Lucretius has a specifically Stoic target in mind.

5. CREATIONISM

One of these passages is v 156–234. Here Lucretius argues against those who maintain that the world was created by the gods for the sake of mankind, and that it will therefore last for ever. These are standardly taken to be the Stoics, on the ground that no one before them held that the world was created for the sake of man.

The thesis attacked is that the world was divinely created, and therefore will never be destroyed. But most Stoics held that the world *will* one day be destroyed, in the conflagration. Those few who dissented, principally Boethus and Panaetius, not unnaturally adopted the matching thesis that the world had no beginning either.[63] The asymmetrical thesis attacked by Lucretius – creation, but no destruction – was regularly seen as the idiosyncratic view of Plato's *Timaeus*.[64] This attribution was

---

[61] For some cautionary remarks about the extent of Stoic concern with 'allegory', see Long (1996b).

[62] Schmidt focuses on (a) Lucretius' critique of allegorical interpretations applied to the worship of Cybele (II 600–60), (b) his image of the Golden Chain at II 1153–6, and (c) his favourable comparison of Epicurus to Heracles in v 22–54. Of these (a) seems to me rather persuasive (Schmidt (1990), pp. 113–44). But (b) (pp. 144–51, following Ernout/Robin (1962), I 365, and other commentators) is very weak evidence for a specifically Stoic allusion. Allegorisation of the Golden Chain was extraordinarily widespread (see Lévêque (1959)), and went back at least to Plato (*Tht.* 153c–d). Lucretius' remark *haud, ut opinor, enim mortalia saecla superne | aurea de caelo demisit funis in arva* (II 1153–4) imagines the golden chain as a vehicle by which life might have descended to earth from heaven. It has nothing whatever to do with the Stoic allegorisation of the Golden Chain as the universal causal nexus, and it is doubtful whether it deserves the name 'allegory' at all. I am no more persuaded by (c) (pp. 161–2). It is frequently claimed that Heracles was a Stoic hero, but there is only limited truth in this. Down to the first century BC, Heracles the legendary benefactor of mankind (which is what Lucretius takes him to be) is no more prominent in Stoicism than outside it. Heracles the allegorised moral hero is a separate tradition, associated mainly with Prodicus and the Cynics, and apparently not absorbed into Stoicism until the first century AD (it is found in Seneca, Epictetus and Dio Chrysostom).

[63] See Philo, *Aet.* 76–88. I take it that οἱ περὶ τὸν Βοηθόν (78), whose argument specifically rejects cosmic generation as well as destruction, are the entire Stoic group singled out at 76 for their rejection of *ekpyrōsis*.

[64] E.g. Philo, *Aet.* 13–16; cf. *ib.* 17, where the one possible exception, and a feeble one, is that Hesiod might have held the Platonic view, because he describes the world's beginning but says nothing about its end. The one other exception known to me is at ps.-Plutarch, *Epit.* II 4.1–2, 330.15–331.3 Diels (1879), where in most versions the asymmetric *Tim.* thesis is attributed without discrimination to Pythagoras, Plato and the Stoics. But that an unwarranted conflation has occurred (cf. Diels, *ib.* introd., II–12) is clear from the parallel Stobaeus text, where the standard distinctions are observed.

accepted by, among others, the Epicureans, who expressly distinguished the Platonic from the Stoic position in this regard.[65] What is more, the *Timaeus* also contains the principal thesis attacked by Lucretius – that it is thanks to the benevolence of its creator that the world will never be destroyed (*Tim.* 32c).

The one element which the *Timaeus* does not supply is the specific thesis, so characteristic of Stoicism, that the world was created for the sake of mankind. While it would no doubt be a mistake to credit any such view to Plato,[66] it remains entirely possible that the *Timaeus* was being read in this way by Epicurus' day. At 30b–c Plato says that the world 'truly came to be (γενέσθαι) an ensouled and intelligent animal, owing to the god's providence (πρόνοιαν)'.[67] Divine 'providence' already has strongly anthropocentric connotations (e.g. prominently at Xenophon, *Mem.* IV 1), and any such impression could well have been strengthened by 39b–e, where there is a clear indication that the heavenly bodies were created for the sake of the human race. Could it be that in the Academy of the late fourth century, under Zeno's teacher Polemo, this anthropocentric reading of the *Timaeus* was already being taught, to become in due course a mainstay of Stoic cosmology?[68]

There is at least one clear parallel for such a development. Theophrastus (fr. 230 FHS&G) gave a paraphrase of the *Timaeus* which sounds uncannily like the Stoic twin physical principles, 'matter' and 'god': the world is analysable into a passive principle, 'matter', and an active causal principle 'which he attaches to the power of god and of the good'. It is hard to believe that this highly revisionist interpretation is one that Theophrastus had arrived at simply by his own reading of the *Timaeus*. He surely must be echoing a way in which that text was currently being expounded in Plato's own school[69] – a hypothesis which would also comfortably explain how the matter–god doctrine passed in due course into the Stoicism of Polemo's pupil Zeno.

In the current state of our evidence, the picture which I have just sketched of Platonist cosmology at the end of the fourth century cannot

---

[65] Cic. *ND* I 20.   [66] See Owen (1973), pp. 355–6.
[67] The problems of construing this sentence, discussed by Runia (1989), should not affect the present issue.
[68] It cannot, however, have been the position of Crantor, whose commentary on the *Timaeus* belongs to this period, since he rejected the genetic interpretation (Procl. *In Tim.* I 277.8), which this version of the anthropocentric reading assumes.
[69] There may conceivably be a parallel explanation for Theophrastus' curiously inaccurate summary of the *Timaeus* at *Sens.* 5–6, 83–6, on which see Long (1996b). He seems less faithful, in this doxographical context, than at *CP* VI 1.

be directly confirmed. But there is powerful indirect confirmation for it in the philosophy of Antiochus of Ascalon. Antiochus (see pp. 62–3 above) presented his views as a return to the 'Old Academy', meaning by this not so much the text of Plato as the philosophy of the Platonic school under Polemo[70] – its final phase of doctrinal Platonism before it fell into the hands of the sceptical New Academics. Now Cicero's *Academica* includes a good deal of information on Antiochus' 'Old Academic' physics.[71] It is a system which is manifestly based on the *Timaeus*,[72] yet so closely prefigures Stoicism that some have questionably supposed it to be nothing more than his retrojection of Stoic physics onto Platonism. In fact, however, it differs from Stoic cosmology in just the sort of ways one would have predicted for Polemo. For example, on the one hand it already contains the analysis of the world into an active 'power' and passive 'matter'. On the other hand, the passive principle is described in terms unmistakably echoing the 'receptacle' in the *Timaeus*; and the active 'power' differs from the Stoic one in that, although it constitutes the essence of an immanent god, it is not fully identified with that god, which is itself a further 'power', namely a 'quality' compounded out of the active power and passive matter.[73] This relation between god and the active principle seems entirely compatible with what we have just seen to be Theophrastus' description of the active principle as one which Plato 'attaches to the power of god and of the good', without any formal identification between the two.[74]

Significantly, this same account of early Platonist physics contains the main ingredients of the anthropocentric thesis attacked by Lucretius. First, 'Old Academic' physics holds that the world is governed for the good of mankind:[75] the world soul's most immediate concern is said to be the motions of the heavens (a central message of the *Timaeus*), but after that 'those things on earth which relate to mankind'. Second, there

---

[70] Cic. *Ac.* II 131, . . . *Polemonis, quem Antiochus probat maxime* . . . Cf. Barnes (1989a), p. 78. However, Barnes is wrong in adding 'Antiochus is also said to have converted to Stoicism.'

[71] *Ac.* I 24–9.   [72] See Dillon (1977), pp. 82–8, esp. 82–4.

[73] Cic. *Ac.* I 24, *qualitas* is compounded out of the active *vis* and passive matter; *ib.* 29: *quam vim [sc. qualitatem] animum esse dicunt mundi, eandemque esse mentem sapientiamque perfectam, quem deum appellant, omniumque rerum quae sint ei subiectae quasi prudentiam quandam, procurantem caelestia maxime, deinde in terris ea quae pertineant ad homines.* (Platonist 'quality' thus looks like an antecedent of Stoic *pneuma*.)

[74] Theophrastus fr. 230 FHS&G. The suspicion that the reading of the *Timaeus* in terms of only two principles, rather than three, is itself a sign of Antiochus' retrojection of Stoic physics onto the early Academy (e.g. Görler (1994), pp. 949–51) can be adequately countered by citing this same fragment of Theophrastus, which shows that such a reading of the *Timaeus* was already in circulation by Theophrastus' day. (I must reserve for another occasion my fuller reply to Görler and other proponents of the Stoicising interpretation.)

[75] See the end of the passage quoted in n. 73 above.

are clear signs of the asymmetric thesis – creation, but no destruction. On the one hand the cosmological thesis is so worded as to imply that the world had a beginning.[76] On the other hand it also, according to Cicero, declared the world soul to be everlasting[77] – on the ground that there is nothing strong enough to destroy it – and added that the world-order which it governs is likewise everlasting.[78] Hence the Academy of the late fourth century, at least as interpreted by Antiochus, was committed to the asymmetric view that the world was created but, contingently, will last for ever. This is not the retrojection of a Stoic thesis, and it is hard to imagine what might have led Antiochus to invent the attribution.

Antiochus thus provides indirect but extremely strong evidence that the thesis attacked by Lucretius is to be identified, not with the tenets of Stoicism, but with their Platonist antecedent in the school of Polemo – in other words, with the cosmology of Plato as it was being expounded in Epicurus' day by Plato's own school. This finding underlines the key role of Polemo's Academy in the emergence of Hellenistic philosophy[79] – a story still waiting to be told in full.

6. GEOCENTRISM

The second passage where Lucretius is widely held to have a Stoic target in his sights is 1 1052–1113. Here he criticises a geocentric theory, according to which: (a) things on all sides tend inwards towards the centre of the universe; (b) people walk upside down in the antipodes, where it is day when we have night, winter when we have summer, etc.; (c) while earth and water are centripetal, air and fire are actually centrifugal; (d) the upward motion of fire from the earth feeds the heavenly bodies, which are themselves fiery, and also (apparently: the text is deficient here) enables nutriment to travel up into the branches of trees.

Against the then universal assumption that these geocentrists are the Stoics, Furley pointed out that the recorded Stoic theory of cosmic arrangement appears to *answer* one or more of the criticisms levelled by

---

[76] *Ib.* 1 28, . . . *unum effectum esse mundum.* The attribution of this cosmology to Polemo is supported by the unavailability of any other leading figure in the early Academy to be its author. Polemo's predecessors Speusippus and Xenocrates, and his principal colleague Crantor, all rejected the literal interpretation of creation in the *Timaeus.*

[77] The main Platonic antecedent is *Tim.* 32b8 33b1. Although there the context strictly concerns the world body, it entails the same kind of indestructibility for the world soul too.

[78] Cic. *Ac.* 1 28 9.

[79] Unfortunately the direct evidence for Polemo, beyond his ethics, is very thin: see Gigante (1976), where fr. 121 (Aetius 1 7.29) is all that survives of his physics.

Lucretius – strong evidence that Lucretius' criticisms are derived from Epicurus, who will himself have been attacking some precursor of the Stoic doctrine. I do not think that Schmidt has seriously undermined Furley's case, or provided adequate grounds for his alternative proposal that Lucretius is drawing on more recent Academic attacks on Stoic cosmology.[80]

There is a very strong additional reason for supporting Furley's denial that the target is Stoic. It seems to have gone unremarked that one feature of the theory, item (d), is definitely not Stoic. There is abundant evidence that the Stoics held that the heavens are nourished by moisture evaporating from terrestrial waters, and not by fire.[81] Indeed, whereas the moisture theory is an old one, going back at least to Heraclitus[82] and criticised at length by Aristotle in the *Meteorologica*,[83] the idea that the heavenly bodies are nourished by terrestrial *fire* is very unusual. (That is a point to which I shall return in a moment.)

The fact is that we have no record of precisely this version of the theory being held by anybody at all (including the early Aristotle, to whom Furley suggests attributing it). But that is hardly surprising. In particular, we have virtually no evidence about the cosmology taught in the Academy between the death of Plato and the advent of Stoicism, but I have nevertheless argued in the previous section that at least one Lucretian argument in book v is in fact targeted at a Platonist development of ideas contained in Plato's *Timaeus*, one dating from the end of the fourth century. It is more than likely that the version of the geocentric theory attacked by Lucretius comes from that same stable.

The *Timaeus* contains most of the materials needed for such a theory to be worked out, including the paradoxical image of the antipodes.[84] And, much more important, it is to the *Timaeus* that we can trace the extremely unusual thesis about the nourishment of the stars: terrestrial fire travels upwards through attraction, according to Plato, heading off to join the main cosmic mass of fire in the heavens.[85] This surely lies

---

[80] Schmidt (1990), pp. 212–22. His assimilation of Lucretius' arguments to Academic ones which can be recovered from Plutarch relies on the assumption that Lucretius is trying to expose an internal inconsistency in the position he is attacking, one between universal centripetalism and the centrifugality of air and fire. But none of Lucretius' arguments turns on any such contradiction.
[81] Aetius II 20.4, 23.5, Arius Didymus fr. 33 Diels, Cic. *ND* II 40, 43, 83, 118, III 37, DL VII 145.
[82] Heraclitus: Aetius II 20.16 (see 22A12 DK). Thales: *ib.* I 3.1. Innumerable further references in Pease (1955–8), II 635–6. Cf. esp. Macrobius, *Sat.* I 23.2, who goes so far as to attribute it to *all* philosophers. [83] Ar. *Meteor.* II 2, 354b32–355a32. [84] *Tim.* 63a2–4.
[85] *Ib.* 63b2–4, c3–7. Compare Lucr. I 1090–1, *et solis flammam per caeli caerula pasci,* | *quod calor a medio fugiens se ibi conligat omnis* with *Tim.* 63b2–4, ἐν τῷ τοῦ παντὸς τόπῳ καθ' ὃν ἡ τοῦ πυρὸς εἴληχε μάλιστα φύσις, οὗ καὶ πλεῖστον ἂν ἠθροισμένον εἴη πρὸς ὃ φέρεται.

behind item (d) in the theory attacked by Lucretius. The Stoics in this
matter followed an old and widely favoured tradition about the nourishment of the heavens by moisture, while the geocentric theorists attacked
by Lucretius were following a much more unusual tradition, apparently
stemming from Plato.

There is a further Platonising ingredient in the thesis under attack,
again one that distinguishes it from Stoic cosmology. According to
Lucretius, the opponents make the matter constituting our world gather,
not around its own centre, but around the centre of space. That is why
he is able to object, (i) that in infinite space there is no centre (1 1068–72),
and (ii) that space has no causal properties which would allow its centre
to exercise such a role (1 1072–82). Now, as Furley has emphasised, this
was certainly not the Stoic position. From Zeno onwards, the Stoics
maintained that the finite mass of body within infinite space gathered
around its *own* centre. The alternative idea that space itself supplies the
centre around which matter gathers can be plausibly traced, once again,
to the *Timaeus* (which itself in this case had earlier antecedents).[86]

Here (62e12–63a2) we learn that — implicitly even if our world did not
exist — *any* symmetrical body placed at the centre would remain there,
because of its equidistance from the extremities. This passage certainly
invites the interpretation that space as such has a centre. Now it is true
that Lucretius' argument (i) is that *infinite* space can have no centre,
whereas Plato's 'centre' is said to be equidistant from the extremes, and
therefore can only be the centre of the finite space which our world
occupies. But this should not be an obstacle. It may well be, as Furley
maintains, that the infinity of space is a premise supplied by Lucretius,
not by the opponents. However, for anyone who feels that this excessively
weakens the *ad hominem* force of Lucretius' objection, it is worth pointing out that the *Timaeus* easily lends itself to the interpretation that space
is infinite.[87]

How else is a reader who possesses a clear notion of geometrical space
(which Plato himself may have lacked)[88] to make sense of Timaeus'
concession that the creator could if he had wanted have made more than
one world, even infinitely many (31a–b), so that it was by his choice that

---

[86] Plato, *Phaedo* 108e–109a (and see Kingsley (1995), esp. p. 89, for the proposal that this itself is of
   Pythagorean origin), and Anaximander A26 DK = Aristotle, *DC* 295b10–16 For doubts about the
   accuracy of this attribution to Anaximander, see Furley (1989b); Anaximander can in any case
   hardly be Lucretius' primary target, being most unlikely to have posited the antipodes.
[87] I am grateful to Hendrik Lorenz for impressing this point on me.
[88] However, it is worth noting that the Pythagorean tradition on which the *Timaeus* draws already
   contained the concept of 'void' outside the cosmos: 58B30 DK.

our world is neither endangered by, nor in need of, anything external to itself (*ib.* 33b–34a)? It would have been natural to read Plato not only as attaching some kind of causal power to the central place in our world, but also as making that world itself an occupant of infinite space. And there is in fact independent evidence, once more thanks to Cicero, that the existence of extra-cosmic space came to be formally acknowledged by early Platonist physics. In summarising the cosmology of the early Academy – which I argued in the last section to mean the Academy of Epicurus' contemporary Polemo – Cicero attributes to these Platonists the tenet that outside our world there is 'no part of matter and no body' (*Academica* 1 28): it is hard to avoid reading this as indicating that there is extra-cosmic space, empty of all matter.

Perhaps a less Platonic-sounding component of the thesis under attack is (c) the centrifugal motion of air and fire. According to Plato, these two elements are centrifugal only in the special sense that portions of them are attracted outwards to rejoin their main masses. Although this in itself may sound compatible with the position attributed to the opponents, it would hardly seem to justify Lucretius' objection, according to which these same elements would carry on into inter-cosmic space and lead to the world's dissolution. But Lucretius' objection here is one which has in any case caused puzzlement,[89] since for some reason he protests that on the opponents' view even the heavy elements earth and water would be likely to disperse, leading to the total disintegration of the cosmos. Can we solve both problems together? The beginning of his objection is lost in a lacuna (1094–1101), resuming at 1102–4 with the words

> ne volucri ritu flammarum moenia mundi
> diffugiant subito magnum per inane soluta,
> et ne cetera consimili ratione sequantur . . .

Perhaps, then, the sense of the lacuna should be filled out as follows:

> [. . . They say that air and fire travel away from the centre because each element is attracted to its own kind. But if this were so, there would be nothing to hold the four cosmic masses *to each other*, in which case there would be a danger] that the walls of the world will fly apart like winged flames through the great void, and that in a similar way the other parts will follow . . .

Who the geocentrist opponents are is not answerable with certainty, but there is a very reasonable chance that they are Platonists, working in

---

[89] See discussion in Furley (1966), p. 19.

the Academy in the late fourth century, and developing the cosmological picture sketched by Plato in the *Timaeus*. There may, for all I know, be further possibilities.[90] What seems relatively safe to say is that they are not the Stoics.

7. CONTEMPORARY STOICISM

Quite apart from the difficulties of demonstrating that Lucretius ever has the Stoics in mind as a target, there is a much greater problem facing anyone who wishes to see him as responding to the contemporary Stoic challenge. Posidonius was not only by far the most influential Stoic among Romans in Lucretius' own day, he was also, arguably, the most prominent cosmologist that the Stoic movement ever produced. Like Lucretius, he made it his leading ambition to understand the causal structure of the world. His work, some of it based on his own empirical research, is undoubtedly reflected in the eloquent speech made by Cicero's Stoic spokesman Balbus (*De natura deorum* II) in defence of the providentially structured Stoic world and, at the same time, in ridicule of the Epicureans' appeal to mere accident as the cause of cosmogony. Even if we discount Lucretius' total failure to allow for the vital contributions made to cosmology since the time of Epicurus by mathematical astronomers, how are we to explain his equal lack of concern to counter the contemporary challenge posed by Posidonius?[91] Let me select just two examples.

First, Posidonius followed a tradition, inaugurated in the fourth century BC by Eudoxus, of demonstrating the perfect mathematical regularity of the celestial orbits, aided by the construction of mechanical devices reproducing those orbits. Balbus regards such devices as powerful support for the Stoic rationally governed cosmos (Cicero, *De natura deorum* II 88):

Suppose someone were to bring to Scythia or Britain the armillary sphere recently built by our friend Posidonius, which revolution by revolution brings about in the sun, the moon and the five planets effects identical to those brought about day by day and night by night in the heavens. Who in those foreign lands would doubt that that sphere was a product of reason? And yet these people

---

[90] If Epicurus was here following Theophrastus, *Phys. op.*, the findings of Ch. 6 below will open the possibility that Theophrastus has himself here synthesised a theory representing the ideas of two or more philosophers (e.g. the Pythagoreans, Anaximander, Plato).

[91] For an appropriately sceptical response to the suggestion that Lucretius borrowed material in books V and VI from Posidonius, see Clay (1983), p. 26.

[the Epicureans] hesitate as to whether the world, from which all things come into being, is itself the product of some kind of accident or necessity or of a divine mind's reason. And they rate Archimedes' achievement in imitating the revolutions of the heavenly sphere higher than nature's in creating them – and that when the original is a vastly more brilliant creation than the copy.

Indeed, we possess one such device, possibly contemporary with Posidonius and Lucretius, in the Antikythera mechanism, fished up from the Aegean sea-bed in 1900.[92] Now Epicurus had himself already been familiar with similar mechanisms, constructed by the mathematical school which Eudoxus had founded at Cyzicus, and had made a point of attacking the observational principles on which they were based.[93] We will see in Chapter 5 (item (xxix) on Chart 2, p. 136 below) that Lucretius, when drawing his own material for book v from Epicurus, *On nature* xi, chose to omit the critique of these machines. A perfectly reasonable decision, no doubt, on aesthetic grounds (although there is plenty of heavy-duty technicality which he does retain in this part of his book), but hardly a sign of concern to combat the contemporary Stoic challenge.

Second, and closely related to this, is the debate about the sizes of the sun and the other heavenly bodies. Epicurus, notoriously, had maintained that these objects are as small as they appear.[94] The main purpose served by this widely ridiculed thesis seems to have been to exempt the heavenly bodies from the normal laws of optics, and thus to invalidate the astronomers' attempts to track and measure their orbits.[95] The ideological importance of this motive probably accounts for Epicurus' decision to state and defend the doctrine right at the beginning of his own account of celestial motion. As we will learn in Chapter 5, Lucretius, in a rare departure from the order established by Epicurus, moved the topic to a less emphatic position, late on in his own digest of Epicurean astronomy.[96] This tends to confirm the impression that he retained none of Epicurus' concern for combating mathematical astronomy, even in the face of the Posidonian challenge.

And the point can be strengthened. Lucretius' defence of the thesis that the heavenly bodies are as small as they look appears to be drawn from a set of optical arguments already sketched by Epicurus, based on two analogies with terrestrial objects: (a) terrestrial objects whose colour and outline are still sharp (as those of the moon are) are always near

---

[92] See the brilliant reconstruction by Price (1975).
[93] See Ch. 4, p. 119–20, 130 below, and Sedley (1976b).
[94] Sedley (1976b), pp. 48–53; Barnes (1989b).   [95] Sedley *ib.*
[96] On the possible reasons for this transposition, see n. 35, p. 153 below.

enough for us to see their true size;[97] (b) when terrestrial fires are seen at
a distance (presumably he means especially at night) their size barely
seems to change as the distance increases.[98]

But the debate had moved on since Epicurus' time. The Stoics of the
late second century BC reported in Philodemus, *On signs*[99] had argued
energetically against the Epicurean thesis, alleging that it violated the
Epicureans' own reliance on analogy with familiar objects. For example,
they constructed an argument mimicking the sign-inferences the
Epicureans themselves now favoured:[100]

Familiar objects which appear slowly from behind things which screen them do
so either because they are moving slowly or because they are very large.
Therefore the sun too, since it appears slowly, must have one of these two
reasons applying to it. It presumably does not move slowly, since it completes
the journey from east to west in twelve hours, a huge distance. [Therefore it is
very large.]

The response of Philodemus' teacher Zeno had been to de-emphasise
the analogy with terrestrial fires, and to focus instead on defending the
possibility that in this respect the heavenly bodies are unique. He was
able to point out that such uniqueness could itself be defended analog-
ically, by a comparison with other unique items such as the magnet.[101]
In Lucretius' own day Posidonius had continued the onslaught against
the Epicureans in a monograph devoted to the topic,[102] bequeathing
much material for the later Stoic cosmologist Cleomedes to use in his
own attack on the same Epicurean position.[103]

Lucretius appears blissfully unaware of the entire debate raging
around him. At no point is his defence of the Epicurean tenet adjusted
to resist any known element in the Stoic critique, and he makes no use
of the new generation of Epicurean counter-arguments preserved by

---

[97] v 575–84; Epicurus, *On nature* xi, quoted in scholion on *Ep. Pyth.* 91.
[98] Lucr. v 585–91; Epicurus, *Ep. Pyth.* 91.
[99] For the identification of the opponents as Stoics, see Sedley (1982); the alternative thesis that
they are Academics is defended by Asmis (1996).   [100] Philodemus, *Sign.* IX 38–X 16.
[101] *Ib.* IX 18–38.   [102] Posidonius F8, 18, 19, 114–16 Edelstein/Kidd.
[103] Cleomedes, *De motu circulari* I 1. For a helpful survey of the debate, see Romeo (1979). Her article
is an edition of P.Herc. 1013, a work conjecturally attributed to Demetrius of Laconia, the fragments of which argue the Epicurean side in this very same debate, and which she takes to be a
reply to Posidonius. This last point may be right (see, however, Barnes (1989b), p. 34 n. 30), but
she is clearly wrong to take the whole book to have been on the size of the sun. Its closing column
makes it explicit that it was a defence of the reliability of the senses against their critics, and
there is therefore no reason why the debate about the sun should have been anything more than
one in a series of examples discussed. (This weakens her argument on p. 18, derived from
Philippson, for dating the book after that of Posidonius.)

Philodemus.[104] That would be most surprising either if he had had a serious interest in combating contemporary Stoic cosmology, or if, as often assumed, he had enjoyed significant philosophical interaction with the Epicurean school of Philodemus.

8. SCEPTICISM

We have already met in Chapter 2 (p. 46 above) Lucretius' celebrated rebuttal of scepticism as self-refuting (IV 469–72):

If someone thinks that nothing is known, he doesn't even know whether *that* can be known, since he admits that he knows nothing. I therefore decline to argue my case against this person who has stood with his own head pressed into his footprints.

It used to be widely assumed that this argument is directly derived from Epicurus. I shall argue in favour of the assumption, and hence against the recently more favoured view that it represents a later phase of Epicureanism, postdating Epicurus himself.[105]

Much debate has been expended on the question whether we are here dealing with 'Socratic' scepticism, in which one claims to *know* that one knows nothing,[106] or with the more refined scepticism commonly associated with Metrodorus of Chios (mid fourth century BC) and Arcesilaus (Epicurus' younger contemporary), according to which we know literally nothing, not even the very fact that we know nothing.[107] For convenience I will call these, respectively, 'non-reflexive' and 'reflexive' scepticism.

Actually neither kind seems at all likely to be the target of Lucretius' criticism. His argument assumes, on the contrary, that the sceptic has not stated any position on whether he does or does not know the truth of his sceptical claim. The inference that he must admit to not knowing

---

[104] Kleve (1978), p. 68, suggests that II 522–68 is Lucretius' 'counterpart' to the Epicurean debate with the Stoics about uniqueness recorded in Philodemus, *On signs*. But he does not succeed in showing any significant resemblance.   [105] Notably Vander Waerdt (1989), Schrijvers (1992).

[106] 'Socratic' scepticism is favoured as Lucretius' target by Schrijvers (1992), p. 128, who identifies it with the scepticism of the New Academy. This is a slightly misleading conflation. The image of the New Academy from the first century BC onwards was as holding ἀκαταληψία ('unknowability') as a *dogma*, but not as claiming to know it. Hence the best that Antiochus could do to find an inconsistency in their position was to complain that they *ought* to claim to know it (Cic. *Ac.* II 29).

[107] 70B1 DK. On Metrodorus' scepticism, see Brunschwig (1996). Metrodorus has been named as the target by Bailey (1947) and Ernout/Robin (1962), *ad loc.*, and by Burnyeat (1978). The proposal is rejected by Boyancé (1963), p. 194 n. 1, Vander Waerdt (1989), and Schrijvers (1992), pp. 127–8. (In Sedley (1983), p. 33, I argue the target to be the entire fourth-century tradition of Democritean scepticism, including Metrodorus, but without explicit reference to his 'reflexive' version of scepticism – which I shall argue below to be largely a later retrojection.)

whether it is true is the Epicurean's own triumphant move, which we are not meant to understand as having been anticipated by the sceptic. Hence this self-refutation argument is most likely to be one which was constructed before the reflexive and non-reflexive versions of scepticism had been explicitly formulated and differentiated.

Consequently, there is not the slightest reason why Lucretius' self-refutation argument should not have been first devised by Epicurus,[108] and at least some reason why it should not postdate him. It is quite doubtful whether what we think of as either the 'Socratic' or the 'Metrodoran' version of scepticism had actually been formulated by the last decade of the fourth century, when Epicurus was writing the books of his *On nature* which I shall argue to be Lucretius' source text (see Ch. 5). 'I know that I know nothing' is not attributed to Socrates by Plato, Xenophon or Aristotle. This non-reflexive sceptical dictum is first known to have been fathered on Socrates by Arcesilaus, i.e. well into the third century BC, in the same breath in which Arcesilaus himself opted for the reflexive alternative.[109] As for Metrodorus, he probably did not write 'We know nothing, not even the actual fact that we know nothing', but rather, as Cicero reports him, 'I say that we do not know whether we know anything or not . . .'[110] – a version which does not even appear to be fully sceptical, let alone vulnerable to the self-refutation argument.

On the other hand, the simple unrefined denial that anything is known was endemic in the atomist tradition to which Epicurus had aligned himself, from Democritus onwards.[111] Democritus himself, whatever his final position may have been on the question, had for example written: 'This argument too shows that in reality we know

---

[108] The main objection of Vander Waerdt (1989), founded on the lack of explicit evidence that Epicurus did formulate this argument, carries very little weight, given that considerably less than one per cent of his writings has survived. Vander Waerdt himself is not proposing any explicit alternative to Epicurus' authorship, which he rejects in indirect support of his main goal — to transfer from Epicurus to Colotes ownership of the pragmatic argument against scepticism which follows in Lucretius' text. Let me therefore add that he comes up with no positive reason for denying Epicurus the latter either.

[109] Cic. *Ac.* I 45: *itaque Arcesilas negabat esse quidquam quod sciri posset, ne illud quidem ipsum quod Socrates sibi reliquisset*. See further, Long (1988b), pp. 157–9, for Arcesilaus' role in inventing the sceptical Socrates.

[110] Cic. *Ac.* II 73 = 70B1 DK. In favour of the Ciceronian version, see Brunschwig (1996), and Sedley (1992a), p. 27, where I also argue that the explicitly reflexive version of his dictum was probably transmitted by Aenesidemus (I do not mean to imply that he was necessarily its inventor, and my argument below will imply that it is likely to have Hellenistic antecedents).

[111] There are even signs of scepticism in Epicurus' own reviled teacher Nausiphanes: 75B4 DK = Sen. *Ep.* 88.43. I leave Pyrrho out of account, since there is no reason to think the Epicureans ever considered him a sceptic: on this see Vander Waerdt (1989), pp. 325–6.

nothing about anything . . .'[112] It seems to have been only after Epicurus' intervention that sceptics started to take a firm position on whether their scepticism was reflexive or not. And it may well have been Epicurus' self-refutation argument that forced the issue into the open. It was at that stage, it seems, that Socrates and Metrodorus were, with hindsight, reinterpreted as belonging to one or the other camp.[113]

Once the issue of reflexivity was in the open, the self-refutation argument lost its bite. If a sceptic has already told you whether or not he claims to *know* that he knows nothing, it becomes pointless to draw your own inferences on the matter. Instead, the main area of probing in Hellenistic debate about scepticism was whether the sceptic's position is internally coherent or not. Reflexive and non-reflexive scepticism were each defended as coherent by some, denounced as incoherent by others.[114] Self-refutation arguments as such by no means go out of fashion in this period or after,[115] yet the self-refutation argument against scepticism never puts in a reappearance – except, that is, in Lucretius. There is therefore excellent reason to see Lucretius' anti-sceptical argument as one dating back to Epicurus, rather than as reflecting the debates of his own time.

Once we see that the self-refutaton argument is a throwback, echoing Epicurus' own original contribution to the debate, it becomes hard not to view in the same light the remainder of the anti-sceptical argument at IV 469–521. The overall structure is:

S1 A self-refutation argument: the sceptic's thesis undermines his own commitment to it, in that he cannot claim to know whether it is true (469–72).

[112] Democritus B7 DK. I can see no force in the objection of Vander Waerdt (1989), pp. 238–9, that the challenge of 'atomist scepticism' did not require the self-refutation argument as a reply but simply a revision of the theory of perception. (a) The revision of perceptual theory could only be enforced if its alternative, scepticism, had first been shown to be untenable; (b) Democritus deployed more than one argument for scepticism, as the opening of B7 proves, and the sequel to that opening (ἀλλ' ἐπιρυσμίη ἑκάστοισιν ἡ δόξις) is most plausibly interpreted as itself relying not on a perceptual premise but on a broader metaphysical one, the identity of all belief with physical rearrangement; (c) by Epicurus' day there were non-atomist versions of scepticism too, e.g. that of Gorgias.

[113] Once the question of reflexivity was addressed to Socrates, Plato, *Apol.* 21b4–5 must have seemed quite sufficient to Arcesilaus and others to reveal him as a non-reflexive sceptic. Needless to say, though, that goes well beyond what, in context, he is actually saying there.

[114] Reflexive scepticism is coherent according to Arcesilaus and Carneades (Cic. *Ac.* I 45, II 8) but incoherent according to Antiochus (*ib.* II 29). Non-reflexive scepticism is coherent according to Antipater but incoherent according to Carneades (*ib.* II 28). For a satisfying reconstruction of Antipater's defence of it, see Burnyeat (1997).

[115] This is fully documented and explored in Burnyeat (1976).

s2(a) An argument questioning the sceptic's access to the conceptions needed to make his case coherently. By denying himself cognitive access to conceptual distinctions like 'true/false' (*notitiam veri . . . falsique,* 476) and 'certain/uncertain', the sceptic cannot claim to grasp the dependent notion of knowledge either, or, therefore, to understand the terms in which he formulates his own scepticism (473–7).

s2(b) The conception of 'true' in fact comes from the senses, which must themselves be irrefutable (478–99).

s3 A pragmatic argument: scepticism is unlivable in practice (500–21).

This sequence employs a type of argumentative strategy used by Epicurus himself in *On nature* xxv, in a digression where he criticises determinism:[116]

d1 A self-refutation argument: the determinist's thesis undermines his own defence of it, since he must admit that he is compelled to defend it, regardless of its merits (Long/Sedley (1987), 20c5–7).

d2 An argument based on the conception (*prolēpsis,* = *notitia?*) involved: the determinist may supply a new *name,* 'necessity', for what we have previously called personal agency, but he fails to change the accompanying conception (20c8–12).

d3 A pragmatic argument: if the determinist took his own doctrine seriously, he would find life unlivable (20c13–14).

Details inevitably differ as between the two arguments, but it is hard to doubt their shared authorship. Furthermore, both play the same overall role in the strategies of their respective books. Lucretius first sets out in book iv his positive doctrine of vision and its reliability, and only then rejects the opposing sceptical viewpoint as self-undermining. Likewise Epicurus, after first setting out his own positive account of human agency as autonomous, goes on, in what he explicitly labels a 'digression', to expose the self-defeating character of its alternative, determinism. These considerations, added to the preceding evidence that at least **s1** must be a throwback to Epicurus, seem to me more than enough to establish that Lucretius' entire anti-sceptical digression

---

[116] I argue this fully in Sedley (1983), pp. 18–31. The text and translation can be found there, or, more accessibly, in Long/Sedley (1987), 20c, to whose section-numbering I refer for convenience.

at IV 469–521 originated with Epicurus as a single integrated argument.[117]

I have saved until last the strongest case known to me for allowing Lucretius a philosophical source more recent than Epicurus. In an outstanding article,[118] P. H. Schrijvers has demonstrated the large amount of Lucretian material on illusions, especially in the section of book IV leading up to his critique of scepticism, that is also to be found in the ten Pyrrhonist Tropes, those massive compilations of evidence for perceptual relativity on which Aenesidemus' revival of Pyrrhonism was founded. Given that both Aenesidemus and Lucretius were working in the first century BC, it may seem very reasonable of Schrijvers to posit a direct borrowing from the former by the latter.

However, the picture is not quite so simple. For one thing, Aenesidemus' dates are uncertain, and it has recently been argued that his revival of Pyrrhonism occurred in the 40s BC, well after Lucretius' death.[119] That dating is controversial,[120] but the fact remains that even Cicero, writing in 45, has not heard of this Pyrrhonist revival.[121] That shifts the onus of proof onto anyone who wants Lucretius, ten or more years earlier, to be in direct touch with it. But no such hypothesis is necessary. As Schrijvers acknowledges, there is a good deal of material in the Tropes which we know to have been traditional, some of it even going back as far as Heraclitus. While it is perfectly true that many of the examples common to Lucretius and the Tropes cannot be traced

---

[117] See Vander Waerdt (1989) pp. 239–42 (also nn. 108, 112 above (pp. 86, 87)) for opposition to my thesis. I have dealt with most of his individual points in what precedes, and I would add that his consideration (a) in note 46, 'the targets of these passages are very different, the former being directed against the ethical determinist and the latter against the skeptic', is an *ignoratio elenchi*, since I only claim structural analogy between the two arguments, not identity. Lévy (1997) implicitly accepts that **s1** and **s3** may well go back to Epicurus, but argues that **s2** reflects first-century debate between Antiochus and the New Academy, comparing Cic. *Ac.* II 29. I agree that there are interesting analogies between Lucretius' argument, concerning the sceptic's non-access to the *conceptions* of true and false, and that of Antiochus, about the sceptic's lack of a *criterion* of true and false; but they are not nearly enough to show that Lucretius' argument cannot predate Antiochus'. Its absence from Colotes' third-century polemical work reported in Plut. *Adv. Col.*, pointed out by Lévy, proves nothing. Colotes' work, as indicated by its title *The impossibility of even living according to the doctrines of other philosophers*, as a matter of policy invoked exclusively the pragmatic arguments against scepticism: its silence about non-pragmatic arguments can therefore tell us nothing about their unavailability to him.   [118] Schrijvers (1992).

[119] Caizzi (1992).

[120] The reply by Mansfeld (1995) does not directly address the question of date, but its conclusions implicitly threaten Caizzi's late dating of Aenesidemus. For further replies which do question her dating, see Görler (1994), pp. 983–4, Lévy (1997).   [121] Cic. *Tusc.* V 85.

back to the fourth century or earlier, there is no reason in principle why they should not already have been in the tradition early enough for Epicurus to have borrowed them,[122] or even, in some cases, to have introduced them.[123]

If the preceding run of my argument had lent any credence to the idea that Lucretius had his finger on the philosophical pulse of his own day, it would be easy to adopt Schrijvers' explanation as the most economical. But if my general argument is right, for Lucretius to have borrowed directly from Aenesidemus would be so contrary to his usual *modus operandi* that to assume that he did so, when our hand is not forced, would be in reality a false economy.

9. BEROSUS

If the question is posed, who (apart from Epicurus) is the latest philosopher or scientist to whom Lucretius unambiguously refers, the answer must be Berosus, the Babylonian historian, astrologer and astronomer. The idiosyncratic theory about the moon which Lucretius considers sympathetically at v 720–30 – that it has one bright hemisphere, and rotates – is there called 'the Babylonian doctrine of the Chaldaeans'; and our sources inform us that the Babylonian in question was Berosus.[124] Now Berosus' biography is problematic (it is not even universally agreed that the astronomer and the historian were the same person). His work the *Babyloniaca* was dedicated to Antiochus I Soter, who reigned from 281 to 262, although he had been co-regent from 294. But this must have been late in Berosus' life, since he is reported to have called himself a contemporary of Alexander the Great. There is no good reason to think

---

[122] I do not see why this should not apply equally to the example of the lion fearing the cock (IV 710–21). Even if Schrijvers is right (*art. cit.* p. 129, following Wellmann) that such 'sympathies and antipathies' were first anthologised as such by Bolos in the late third century BC, it does not follow that the example itself 'est clairement à dater dans une période plus récente du scepticisme aussi bien que de l'épicurisme'. Schrijvers also argues (pp. 129–30) that the anomalous positioning of this topic within book IV is a sign that Lucretius is drawing on his own knowledge; against this, in Ch. 5 I shall be arguing that anomalous grouping of topics is a pervasive feature of book IV, reflecting its unrevised state. For important further negative arguments regarding Schrijvers' case, see Lévy (1997). Lévy's positive arguments for his own preferred alternative, that Lucretius drew the material from recent Academic debate, seem to me no better supported. His suggestion that the dialectical character of the anti-sceptical arguments is more characteristic of late than of early Epicureanism is contradicted by the evidence, discussed above, of Epicurus' own anti-determinist argument, and even Cic. *Fin.* 1.31, which he cites in his support (n. 28), goes back to Epicurus' own arguments in my view (Sedley (1996), pp. 323ff.).

[123] For evidence that the illusion described at Lucr. IV 404–13, that the sun is setting on a nearby hill, is Epicurus' own contribution, reported from personal experience, see p. 130 below.

[124] Aetius II 25.12, 28.1, 29.2; Cleomedes II 4.

that his astronomical theories were to be found in his historical treatise *Babyloniaca*,[125] or, even supposing that they were, that he had never aired them before writing this very late work.[126] There is, in short, no obstacle to assuming that his theory about the moon could have been familiar to Epicurus at the end of the fourth century, or even for that matter to readers a quarter of a century earlier.

But that is where the door closes. If one looks in Lucretius' poem for comparably clear references to the astronomical or other scientific theories of the third century and after – such as those of Aristarchus (whose heliocentric theory was a talking-point among the third-century BC Stoics), Eratosthenes, Archimedes and Hipparchus – one looks in vain.[127] And the same applies to the philosophical innovations of the same period.

10. FUNDAMENTALISM

The position that I am defending can at this stage afford a little relaxation. Even if it were in the future to turn out, in one or two isolated cases, that Lucretius was aware of some philosophical or scientific development which demonstrably postdated Epicurus, that would not alter the general picture. Some such snippet of information could have reached him through his non-philosophical reading, through a chance encounter, or even through marginal scholia in the copy of Epicurus which he consulted.[128] It would still be his *lack* of such contact, and his preference for the unmediated arguments of Epicurus, that predominantly characterised the content of his poem.

Thirty years ago, Furley's own attempted explanation of the phenomenon which he had discovered – Lucretius' lack of interest in Stoicism – was that Stoic physics was little more than a down-market version of Aristotelian physics, too unimportant to occupy Lucretius' time. Such an explanation would be unlikely to be put forward today, when the power, originality and contemporary influence of Stoic physics are widely acknowledged, while it is Aristotle's importance to Hellenistic

[125] On this see Kuhrt (1987), esp. pp. 36–44; for Berosus' life and work, see also the article by J. Campos Daroca, *s.v.* in Goulet (1989–), II 95–104.
[126] The argument of Runia (1997), pp. 101–2, that Berosus' theory is too late to have been reflected in *Nat.* XI rests on the supposition that it first appeared in the *Babyloniaca*.
[127] On this see Furley (1978), pp. 4–5.
[128] There are marginal scholia in the papyrus of book XIV of Epicurus, *On nature* (on which see Leone (1984)). There are also scholia incorporated into the versions of Epicurus' shorter writings that have been preserved in DL X.

philosophers that has become increasingly controversial.[129] Nevertheless, I believe that the conclusion which Furley's explanation was trying
to make sense of is itself correct, and is of the utmost importance for the
understanding of Lucretius' intellectual position. Once again it reveals
Lucretius as an Epicurean fundamentalist, uninterested in pursuing the
history of philosophy beyond the zenith it had reached when the
Epicurean gospels were written.

It is important to emphasise that my claims in this chapter in no way
exclude the possibility, indeed the likelihood, that those of Lucretius'
Roman readers who were better acquainted than he was with Stoicism
construed his poem as having anti-Stoic dimensions – much as, in later
centuries, many were to read it as anti-Christian. My thesis is one about
the motivating forces of Lucretius' project as he himself conceived,
researched and realised it. Contemporary philosophical and scientific
debate played no part in this, and we seriously misconceive the character of his enterprise if we assume otherwise.[130]

Nor should this kind of fundamentalism, with its accompanying deaf-
ness towards contemporary opponents, be thought historically incredible, as it very often is.[131] One partial parallel can be found in the Sceptic
writer Sextus Empiricus. Although himself almost certainly working in
the second century AD,[132] Sextus in his philosophical critiques shows virtually no interest in, or even knowledge of, contemporary developments
and concerns, which were in fact dominated by Peripatetics and
Platonists. None of his philosophical targets, either named or unnamed,
can plausibly be dated later than the first century BC. Significantly, the
first century BC was when his school's foundational literature had been
largely written, by its re-founder Aenesidemus. Evidently for Sextus, as
for Lucretius, the list of his school's philosophical targets had been

---

[129] The rehabilitation of Stoic physics was largely the work of Sambursky (1959), while the new
challenge to Aristotle's Hellenistic influence has come from Sandbach (1985).
[130] It has been impossible to deal here with all the innumerable studies of Lucretius that have
detected Stoic allusions. In many of those with which I am acquainted attention is drawn to
features which I would happily agree might have an at least partly Stoic reference *if* it were
already established that Lucretius is conscious of the Stoic challenge, but which do not themselves constitute evidence for such a consciousness. Long (1997) is an outstanding example of
such a study.
[131] E.g. Kleve (1978), although his even-handed assessment of the evidence does not point firmly
either way, surprisingly concludes (p. 71) that it is 'improbable that Lucretius should have felt
himself bound exclusively to present the polemics from the time of Epicurus', and that 'we
can confidently use Lucretius as a source for the general philosophical situation of his own
time'.
[132] See House (1980), who allows, however, that Sextus might even be dated to the early third
century.

definitively drawn up, and did not need extending. Plenty of further examples of this same phenomenon could be added.[133]

If this should still sound historically implausible, some modern analogies may help. Think of Christian preachers who see no need to inform themselves about Islam or any other post-Christian faith. Think of the Marxist who is content to remain altogether unversed in post-Marxian political theory. Think even of traditional literary critics who are content, and may actually prefer, to know nothing of contemporary critical theories. Ignorance of the current alternatives may signal no more than total confidence in one's own chosen ideology.

That Lucretius, unlike Philodemus and his associates, never consulted Epicurean texts other than those by Epicurus himself – either those written by the other three authoritative founders, or those of the many later Epicurean writers of whom we know – is of course incapable of demonstration. But I believe that such a hypothesis has every chance of being correct. It is strongly supported by his formal declaration of loyalty to Epicurus alone, and by his imperviousness to later developments inside and outside the school. Even more than that, it makes the best sense of his poem's contents. As I shall argue in the next two chapters, his sole philosophical source and inspiration from early in book I until late in book VI is Epicurus' great physical treatise, *On nature.*

---

[133] Although Diogenes of Oenoanda (second cent. AD) does, as we have seen (p. 74 above), know about the Stoics, he shows no acquaintance with the Platonism and Peripateticism which by his day were even more dominant: cf. his notorious mistake about the Peripatetics in fr. 5 Smith. Cleomedes (datable between the second and fourth centuries AD) is still locked into Posidonius' debate with the Epicureans, and shows little if any awareness of more contemporary issues, or even of Hellenistic astronomy (cf. Goulet (1980), p. 5: 'Le système planétaire de Cléomède ignore apparemment les développements de l'astronomie grecque depuis le IIIᵉ siècle avant J.C. et répète pour l'essentiel la cosmologie du stoïcisme ancien'). Or again, take Calcidius, of whom Dillon (1977), pp. 401–8, shows that although he probably wrote in the fourth century AD he is philosophically living in the second.

CHAPTER 4

Epicurus, On nature

I. THE DISCOVERY

The cataclysmic eruption of Vesuvius in AD 79 buried the town of Herculaneum in a torrent of boiling mud. Streams of lava from subsequent eruptions increased its depth to some hundred feet below the surface. Not surprisingly, the teams of excavators assigned to the site from 1709 onwards by the Bourbon rulers of Naples did not consider uncovering the buildings from above, but chose instead to plunder their contents by means of underground tunnels. The most spectacular discovery was made during the 1750s – a vast suburban villa containing an art collection of unrivalled magnificence. The excavation of the villa proceeded, room by room, over a period of many years. Towards the end of the second year, workmen excavating the *tablinum* began to happen upon black lumps which they mistook for charcoal. Many they threw away or took home to kindle their fires, and it was only when the fragments of one which had been dropped were seen to contain writing that they were recognised as rolls of papyrus.

The *tablinum* was a pleasant room looking out onto the garden on one side and onto a portico on the other, with a mosaic floor and, down the centre, a row of eight bronze busts. The papyrus scrolls were found strewn around the room, together with a few wax tablets. But over the next few years papyri were found in four more rooms of the villa, in one of which the excavators found some 250 scrolls, and three busts of Epicurean philosophers. Another room was plainly set out as a library, with 337 Greek scrolls arranged on shelves along the walls and in an inlaid wooden cupboard placed in the middle, as well as a bundle of eighteen Latin scrolls in a box.

This was the first discovery of papyri in modern times, and still one of only two major Greek papyrus finds ever made outside Egypt (the Derveni papyrus being the other).

The papyri were brittle, and the action of damp had tended to weld the layers together. They were, moreover, in a carbonised condition – a fact which enabled them to survive centuries of burial, but which also further impeded their legibility. Naturally the outer parts of the rolls, containing the beginnings of the books, had suffered most, while the centres were sometimes comparatively undamaged. The first reaction was to separate the layers by splitting the rolls along their length; but this turned out to reveal only isolated groups of letters, and certainly no intelligible text. Hundreds were destroyed in this way.

The next stages of the story can best be told by quoting a letter from a 'learned Gentleman of Naples' to Monsignor Cerati, of Pisa, dated 25 February 1755:[1]

At length signor Assemani . . . proposed to the king to send for one father Antonio, a writer at the Vatican, as the only man in the world, who could undertake this difficult affair.

This Father Antonio was Antonio Piaggio, who was to become the most important figure in the early history of the Herculaneum papyri. He was summoned, and in early 1754 he set to work on one of the worst preserved rolls, using a technique which was not to be superseded for the next two centuries:

It is incredible to imagine what this man contrived and executed. He made a machine, with which (by means of certain threads, which being gummed, stuck to the back part of the papyrus, where there was no writing), he begins, by degrees, to pull, while with a sort of engraver's instrument he loosens one leaf from the other (which is the most difficult part of all), and then makes a sort of lining to the back of the papyrus, with exceeding thin leaves of onion (if I mistake not [he did – it was the strips of beaten oxgut known as 'goldbeaters' skin']), and with some spirituous liquor, with which he wets the papyrus, by little and little he unfolds it. All this labour cannot be well comprehended without seeing. With patience superior to what a man can imagine, this good father has unrolled a pretty large piece of papyrus, the worst preserved, by way of trial . . . The worst is, the work takes up so much time, that a small quantity of writing requires five or six days to unroll, so that a whole year is already consumed about half this roll.

What Piaggio had done was to construct a case in which the roll could be hung up by silk threads attached to its outer edge, its main bulk resting on an adjustable platform. Through gradual tightening of the threads over a period of months, even years, the papyrus was allowed to unroll

---

[1] From Comparetti/De Petra (1883), pp. 245–6, quoting an English translation by John Locke of the letter, published in *Philosophical Transactions* 49 (London 1756).

under its own weight, while the layers were gently eased apart with a variety of instruments and the verso of the papyrus was strengthened by gluing on a backing of goldbeaters' skin. Whenever a sizeable section – say two feet in length – had been unrolled, it could be cut off and glued to a sheet of card.

As Piaggio's work proceeded with agonising slowness, excitement mounted in the learned circles of Europe. There were expectations of a second Renaissance. Surely the lost poetry of Sappho, or some exquisite play by Menander, was about to come to light. These expectations turned to bafflement and disappointment when rumours started to emerge from Piaggio's workshop at Portici that the first columns deciphered contained a Greek prose text in which harmful effects of music were criticised. A flattering mention of 'Zeno' led to reports that the author was a Stoic. But when after nearly two years the unrolling was completed, the title given at the end turned out to be 'Philodemus, *On music*', and this Philodemus was soon identified as the Epicurean philosopher of that name, already known as the author of some attractive epigrams. The Zeno whom he praised was not the Stoic Zeno of Citium, but the Epicurean Zeno of Sidon, whose bust was among those found in the villa's library. It has since come to be generally accepted that the library was that of Philodemus' school (see Ch. 3, §2).

The next papyri opened proved to contain other works of Philodemus – on rhetoric, virtues and vices, and similar topics. Scholarly impatience mounted. It was even proposed, by no lesser a luminary than Winckelmann, that if any roll being opened appeared to have similar contents it should be immediately abandoned.

When Piaggio died in 1796, forty-four years of work had resulted in the opening of just eighteen rolls. In 1802 the Prince of Wales (later George IV) offered to finance the unrolling and transcribing of the papyri, and sent his chaplain John Hayter to organise the work at Portici. Hayter employed thirteen local draughtsmen who had already for some time been engaged in this work. Many Piaggio machines were built, and Hayter further speeded up the work by paying his men according to results, offering the sum of one *carlino* for every line of text unrolled and copied in facsimile. The effects of the system were only partially beneficial. Haste in copying, by draughtsmen ignorant of Greek, might have been expected to introduce errors, but thanks to Hayter's attentive supervision the standard of copying was in general very high. On the other hand, there seems little doubt that papyri were often unrolled too quickly. Piaggio's first attempt had been on a badly preserved roll, but by spending nearly two years on its unrolling he had succeeded in saving a remarkable proportion of the writing. Under Hayter it became common to spend only months, or even weeks, on each roll, because his method of payment undoubtedly made it more lucrative to abandon those portions whose fragility or adherence to other layers of papyrus demanded special skill and patience on the part of the unroller, and to save only those which could be quickly separated.

Hayter stayed for four years at Portici, until February 1806, when the impending French invasion of Naples drove him to take refuge in Palermo along with the Bourbons. He brought his facsimile copies back to Oxford, but most of the papyri remained in Naples, where work on them continued.

Since the beginning of the scroll was invariably lost or illegible, it was only when the unrollers reached the end that they could hope to identify the text they had been unravelling. (Fortunately it was standard ancient scribal practice to repeat the name of the book at the end.) During Hayter's four years, a substantial number of the papyri unrolled turned out to contain at the end the title

ΕΠΙΚΟΥΡΟΥ
ΠΕΡΙ ΦΥΣΕΩΣ

sometimes followed by a book number (II, XI, XIV, XV, XXVIII), by an indication of the book's length, and in two cases even by a date of composition. Later discoveries have identified a few extra pieces of these same rolls, a further copy of book XI, the number of one further book (XXV), and one further date. But the golden age for the recovery of Epicurus, *On nature* was undoubtedly Hayter's four years.

So began the modern partial rediscovery of Epicurus' great physics treatise, *On nature*. So formidable are the problems of deciphering these ravaged papyri that even today, after almost two centuries, we do not have adequate published editions of all of them.[2] Nevertheless, thanks

---

[2] There are modern editions, based on a proper autopsy of the papyri with binocular microscope, of books XIV (Leone (1984), XV (Millot (1977)), and XXVIII (Sedley (1973)). We are near to having the same for book XXV: so far there are Laursen (1987), (1988), (1992) and (1995), and further parts of the book in Sedley (1983) and Long/Sedley (1987), §20. Still awaited are adequate editions of books II and XI (for which we have Vogliano (1953) and (1940) respectively), each of which confronts editors with the irritating obstacle that some of the papyrus material is in the British Museum, the remainder in Naples. In the mean time, Arrighetti (1973) offers a comprehensive collection of the *Nat.* papyri, based on what were at the time the best available editions plus, in some cases, Arrighetti's own further readings. Wherever possible I shall include an Arrighetti reference (abbreviated as Arr.[2]) to each passage, placing it in square brackets when the current text differs significantly from his.

especially to the studies of Achille Vogliano between the wars, and to a resurgence of work on the Herculaneum papyri since the early 1970s,[3] we know a vast amount more about them than we did. Virtually none of these gains has filtered through into Lucretian studies.

2. THE PAPYRI

The library produced remnants of the following books from *On nature*:[4]

Book II: 2 copies (P.Herc. 1149/993; P.Herc. 1010)

Book XI: 2 copies (P.Herc. 1042; P.Herc. 154)

Book XIV: 1 copy (P.Herc. 1148)

Book XV: 1 copy (P.Herc. 1151)

Book XXV: 3 copies (P.Herc. 419/1634/697; P.Herc. 1420/1056; P.Herc. 1191)

Book XXVIII: 1 copy (P.Herc. 1479/1417)

4 further unidentified books (P.Herc. 1431; P.Herc. 989; P.Herc. 1413; P.Herc. 362)

One remarkable feature of these is that virtually all of them appear, on palaeographical grounds, already to have been of great antiquity when they were buried by Vesuvius in AD 79.[5] Compared to the papyri of Philodemus, they form a group which is distinguished by the early date of its scribal hands and orthography, nearly all of which can be plausibly located between the beginning and the end of the second century BC. Moreover, three of the scribal hands recur.[6] A single copyist is responsible for one of the two copies of book II (P.Herc. 993/1149), one of the three copies of book XXV (P.Herc. 1191), and the sole copy of book XXVIII.[7] Another scribe wrote a further copy of book XXV (P.Herc. 1420/1056) and P.Herc. 1039, a text which is too badly damaged to have

---

[3] This has followed from the creation of the Centro Internazionale per lo Studio dei Papiri Ercolanesi on the initiative of Marcello Gigante, to whom we also owe the inauguration of the journal *Cronache Ercolanesi* and the series of editions *La scuola di Epicuro*.

[4] The main catalogue, with a physical description of the papyri and comprehensive bibliography, is Gigante (1979), supplemented by Capasso (1989). A multiple number (e.g. 149/993) indicates a broken roll whose pieces were first catalogued separately, then reunited.

[5] Although the chronology of the Herculaneum papyri is a subject still in its infancy, the pioneering work of Guglielmo Cavallo has, I think, put this conclusion beyond serious doubt. See Cavallo (1983), esp. pp. 28–57. As regards age, the one clear exception among the *On nature* papyri is P.Herc. 362, which Cavallo implies may even have been written after Philodemus' lifetime (*ib.* pp. 55–6).   [6] Cavallo (1983), pp. 44–6.

[7] Cavallo adds to this list the unidentified book of *Nat.* contained in P.Herc. 1431, but I prefer to suspend judgement on that, since my notes on the handwriting of this book (taken in 1971, however, and not checked since) record a number of differences from the scribe of P.Herc. 1479/1417.

been identified, but which in the circumstances is likely also to contain some part of *On nature*. Finally, one and the same scribe wrote the surviving copies of both book xiv and book xv.

All this encourages the conclusion that these papyri of *On nature* formed part of a separate collection, acquired in Greece and brought to Italy by Philodemus. It has been plausibly (though unprovably) suggested that he inherited the book collection of his teacher Zeno.[8]

3. FAVOURITE BOOKS?

Since only a small fraction of the papyri were rescued and successfully unrolled, and yet this rich haul emerged, it is natural to assume that the library contained at the very least one complete set of *On nature*, a work which we know to have run to thirty-seven volumes (see §4). Indeed, given the recurrence of the same scribal hands, it is not unlikely that there were one or more complete sets each written by a single scribe.[9]

Yet there is something decidedly odd about the distribution. Why should the random process of recovery have given us so high a proportion of duplicate or even triplicate sets? Unfortunately the excavators kept no record of where individual papyri were found: if they had, it might have turned out that as a matter of library policy all the copies of each individual book – rather than all the volumes in a single complete set – were stored together, so that where one survived because fortuitously protected from damage the others had a better chance of surviving along with it.

However, I do not believe that this could be a sufficient explanation. For one thing, it can be no accident that books xiv and xv, both written by the same scribe, survived. And, although the assignment of numbers to individual scrolls belongs to Hayter's time,[10] and seems to have been largely random, it may be no accident that these two papyri received almost adjacent numbers (1148 and 1151). The combined proximity of their catalogue numbers and of their book numbers, plus their scribal uniformity, suggests that they survived together and were brought out and stored in the same batch. Even if the copies of book xiv and those of book xv are assumed to have been stored close to each other, so that they shared the same accidental protection and one of each survived, is it just coincidence that these two surviving copies should both be by the same scribe?

---

[8] On this proposal of Vogliano's, see Dorandi (1997).   [9] Cf. Cavallo (1983), p. 58.
[10] See Obbink (1996), p. 29 n.1.

A likelier explanation of the imbalance is that some books of *On nature* were especially treasured and collected. This is supported by the following fact. The scholia accidentally incorporated into our surviving texts of Epicurus' *Letter to Herodotus* and *Letter to Pythocles* (in book x of Diogenes Laertius) contain several citations of individual books of *On nature*.[11] These are: book I (two citations), book II (one citation), book XI (one citation),[12] book XII (two citations), and books XIV and XV (one joint-citation). This list largely coincides with that of books surviving among the Herculaneum papyri, and confirms the impression that these books were especially favoured by readers of Epicurus. Since in addition the Herculaneum papyri contain two citations of book XIII, one of them jointly with book XII,[13] we seem to be dealing with two favoured *groups* of books: I–II and XI–XV. Clearly also highly valued was book XXV, as is attested by the three copies preserved at Herculaneum: the fact that no scholia refer to it may simply reflect the fact that (as I shall argue in §12) its subject matter postdates the *Letter to Herodotus* and the *Letter to Pythocles*, leaving the scholiasts on those letters no opportunity to cite it.

There is even some reason to suppose that Epicurus had given his own blessing to this preferential treatment of certain books. His *Letter to Herodotus*, an epitome of his doctrines on physics, opens with the following admittedly rather difficult sentence (*Ep. Hdt.* 35):

> For those, Herodotus, who are unable to study closely the individual books[14] of our work *On nature* (ἕκαστα τῶν Περὶ φύσεως ἀναγεγραμμένων ἡμῖν), or even to peruse the more important books in the sequence (τὰς μείζους τῶν συντεταγμένων βίβλους), I have prepared an epitome of the entire system (ἐπιτομὴν τῆς ὅλης πραγματείας) . . .

Although it is not demonstrable that this is an explicit reference to *On nature*, rather than simply to 'what we have written on nature', there is every probability that it is. The form of citation closely resembles that

---

[11] These are conveniently collected in Epicurus frr. 73–91 Usener.

[12] *Ep. Pyth.* 91, where the scholion is followed immediately by Epicurus' own citation of what he says 'in the books *On nature*', certainly referring to the same passage in *Nat.* XI.

[13] Philodemus in *De pietate* twice cites book XII, along with a single citation of book XIII (frr. 84, 87–8 Usener = 27–8 Arr.² = Philodemus, *Piet.* 225–7, 523–4, 1050–1 Obbink (1996)): both XII and XIII dealt *inter alia* with the origins of religion. XII and XIII are also cited jointly in P.Herc. 1111, fr. 44.1–6 (= 19.5 Arr.², fr. 41 Usener, but now edited in an improved text with apparatus in Obbink (1996), pp. 300–1). Unfortunately the papyrus is lost and the putative title Περὶ φύσεως, if present, is corrupted in the facsimile to ΠΕΡΙΣΥΝ [. . . But the context leaves little doubt that the citation is of *Nat.*

[14] It is quite unproblematic that 'books' (i.e. βιβλία) should be neuter when, as here, the noun is unspecified, despite becoming feminine (βίβλους) in the following clause. Citations of *Nat.* (including Epicurus' own at *Ep. Pyth.* 91) vary between the two forms: cf. frr. 73–89 Usener.

used in book xxvIII of *On nature*, where Epicurus clearly has a specific text in mind: '. . . which we discuss in our work *On ambiguity*' (. . . ἅς λέγ[ο]μεν ἐν το[ῖ]ς Περὶ ἀμ[φ]ιβολίας ἡμῖν ἀναγεγραμμένοις).[15] If that supposition is granted, then Epicurus is distinguishing the awesome task of studying the entire *On nature* from the lesser one of reading its more important books. Implicitly, his readers already know which are the more important books. It may, then, have been Epicurus' explicit blessing that conferred preferential status on certain books in the sequence.

Even taken as a whole, *On nature* was by far Epicurus' most widely discussed work. It heads Diogenes Laertius' list of his 'best' works.[16] It was picked out for special attack by Epicurus' arch-enemy Timocrates.[17] It was cited repeatedly, as we shall see.[18] There is even reason to think that, such was this entire work's pre-eminence, Epicureans regularly referred to individual books of it simply by their number, without needing to name the work itself: thus 'book vI' was understood to mean 'book vI of *On nature*'. There are several such citations in the Herculaneum papyri, and at least one of them can be shown to refer to *On nature*. This is because we know from Philodemus, *On piety*[19] (225ff.) that in '*On nature* book xII' Epicurus spoke of the origins of religion, yet elsewhere (523–4), in a context where *On nature* is not still under discussion, and despite the fact that several works other than *On nature* have been cited in between, Philodemus refers to Epicurus' attack on the atheists simply 'in book xII', without naming the work. Since the atheists in question prominently included those who had attributed the origins of religion to human invention, there is every reason to suppose that this too refers to the account of the origin of religion in book xII

---

[15] *Nat.* xxvIII, 13 v 2 inf. vI 1 sup. Sedley (1973) = 31.14.26–15.1 Arr.². It hardly seems likely that this is a generic reference to a range of writings by Epicurus on ambiguity, and no editor (Vogliano and Arrighetti, as well as myself) has had any hesitation in supplying the capital letter. We have no independent citation of this work, but our surviving list of Epicurus' writings (DL x 27–8) is avowedly selective.   [16] DL x 27.   [17] *Ib.* 7.

[18] Obbink (1996), pp. 305, 472, is puzzled at how *few* citations of *Nat.* there are in the Herculaneum papyri outside *De pietate*, which he remarks contains 7 of the 10 citations. Actually this should be 7 out of *13*, if we add the apparent references to it from the *Life of Philonides* (see below). But in any case, no surprise is called for. We should not expect much reference to it in works on ethics and aesthetics, which predominate among the Herculaneum papyri. One might have expected it to be mentioned in Philodemus' *De signis*, but there are no citations of any early Epicurean works there, so its absence is again unremarkable. The 13 references to *Nat.* in the Herculaneum papyri comfortably beat those to any other work by Epicurus or anyone else. The nearest rivals are Epicurus' *On rhetoric* (6 citations), *On lives* (5 citations), and *Symposium* (4 citations) – see Delattre (1996). (I am discounting citations where the title is purely conjectural.)

[19] Text and notes in Obbink (1996).

of *On nature*,[20] and confirms the impression that citations by book
number alone were readily understood to refer to this treatise.[21]

Once this is accepted, a number of further citations in the
Herculaneum papyri can be recognised as probably referring to the
same work. The fragments of the biography of the second-century BC
Epicurean Philonides include a list of the notes he possessed from his
own studies under a series of teachers. These include notes he had taken
from one of his teachers on 'book VI', and from another 'on book I and
continuing to those on book [?]ty-three, with some omissions'.[22] This is
important evidence that *On nature* was a major focus of exegetical study
in the Epicurean school, yet another sign of its philosophical pre-eminence.

Why was *On nature* so formidable a text to read, yet so highly valued?
The two main factors are likely to have been its length and its style. We
will take these in turn in the next two sections.

4. LENGTH

That there were thirty-seven books of *On nature* is attested in three separate passages of Diogenes Laertius.[23] But how long was each book? Two
of the papyri, those of books XIV and XV, still preserve at the end a stichometric indicator. Book XIV contained 3,800 lines,[24] book XV probably
3,200.[25] By the ancient scribal convention these figures will indicate, not
the number of lines of writing in this actual copy, but a standardised

---

[20] See Obbink (1996), pp. 306, 351–2.

[21] On this see the very full discussion in Obbink (1996), pp. 304–6, cf. 477. One small disagreement:
he assumes too readily that the pattern was always to cite the work by title first, then by book
number alone thereafter. I do not think that the *Life of Philonides* passage (below; not taken into
account by Obbink) encourages this assumption.

[22] Anon. *Vita Philonidis* col. 7; text in Gallo (1980), p. 60. The context is uncertain (for a partly different interpretation see Gallo *ad loc.*), but it does at least seem probable to me that either the biographer or, more likely, a contemporary of Philonides whom he is quoting, is telling us about
Philonides' collection of notes, as evidence of his education. Thus: '. . . he makes it clear'
(διασα]φεῖ?) 'that he has heard [the lectures of . . .?]; while in book form he brings' (φέρει: precise
sense unclear, but surely not 'cites', as Gallo takes it) 'the following notes: two early sets, on the
lectures of Eudemus and on comments on book VI; about scientific modes of thought; on the
lectures of Artemon, starting with comments on book I and continuing to those on book [?]ty-
three, with some omissions; and on the classes of Dionysodorus'. The last book number seems
to be corrupt. Gallo reports the papyrus at lines 9–10 as πρὸς τὸ τρίτ[ον] καὶ Ι οισ[.]κοστον.
He emends this last word to <τρι>[α]κοστόν, to restore the reading which Crönert had originally misreported from the papyrus itself. I find this emendation rather harsh, and suppose it to
be at least as likely that the number underlying the apparent corruption was τρίτον καὶ εἰκοστόν,
'23rd'.   [23] DL x 7, 27, 30.   [24] See Leone (1984), pp. 22–3.

[25] See Millot (1977), p. 26, who alerts us to the possibility of a lost extra digit at the beginning or
end of the number.

measure of length whereby one 'line' means the equivalent of one hexameter line.[26] The average length of a hexameter line is thirty-six characters. Therefore, if one takes this measure strictly, the length of book xiv was approximately $3,800 \times 36 = 136,800$ letters, and the length of book xv was approximately $3,200 \times 36 = 115,200$ letters. Hence, although two books out of thirty-seven are not as good a sample as one would like, and although the length of a one-line unit is in principle capable of a fair degree of variation,[27] the best working hypothesis available to us is that the typical length of a book was around 125,000 letters. At an average of six letters per word, and allowing for the occasional blank space (Greek texts contain no spaces between words, except occasionally as punctuation marks), this would make a little over 20,000 words.

Then how large a written text were Epicurus' readers confronted by? As a rough unit of measure, we can take a page from the Oxford Classical Text of Thucydides. An average page of Thucydides contains around 1,400 letters. So a typical book of *On nature* would have filled some 90 pages of OCT . This is just a little longer than a normal book of Thucydides, whose book i, for example, is 88 pages long.[28]

This should give some idea of the monumental scale of Epicurus' *magnum opus*. We cannot assume that all its books were of equal length, but the book divisions of surviving prose works from antiquity do permit us to hypothesise *some* degree of uniformity in length. Assuming books xiv and xv to be not untypical, the treatise, if it survived intact, would fill nine or ten volumes of Oxford Classical Text. Even books i–xv, which I shall later be arguing to be Lucretius' source, would have comfortably filled four volumes.

---

[26] Cavallo (1983), pp. 20 2.

[27] In Philodemus, *De pietate* (Obbink (1996), pp. 62 3 n. 1), and in the second-century BC logical papyrus P.Par. 2 (Cavini et al. (1985), p. 130), the scribe uses marginal marks to divide the text into smaller sections of 20 of his own lines, and bigger sections of 200. Apparently then in both cases the scribe equated two of his lines with the standard unit of stichometric measure – a very approximative device, since in P.Par. 2 it produces a unit of roughly 36 letters, but in *Piet.* one of only around 30 letters. If the scribe of *Nat.* xiv and xv were following the same practice, his stichometric unit would be around 40 letters, since his lines average roughly 20 letters in length. However, there is no sign that he is keeping his own running total (a practice probably used for calculating the payment due), and the stichometric totals which he records are likely to be taken over from his archetype. Thus 36 letters per 'line' remains the best available hypothesis, but we should allow for an error of 10 per cent or even more.

[28] Since first writing this sentence I have learnt (from Obbink (1996), p. 71 n. 1) that according to Dionysius of Halicarnassus (*Thuc.* p. 339.14 16 U.R.) Thucydides 1 1 88 (a passage running to 51 pages in the Oxford Classical Text) was measured at 2,000 lines long. This permits the calculation that the whole book was measured at 3,450 lines long – just 50 lines less than the average of *Nat.* xiv and xv. That this fits my calculation quite so closely is no doubt accidental, but it nevertheless lends it very welcome confirmation.

5. STYLE

On nature was a lecture course. This is stated explicitly at the end of book XXVIII, where Epicurus announces:[29]

[ἱκ]ανῶ[ς] οὖν ἡμῖν ἠδολεσχήσθω ἐπὶ τοῦ παρόντος. καὶ ὑμεῖς [μ]υ[ρι]άκ[ις μνημο]νεύε[ι]μ π[ειρᾶ]σθε τὰ ἐμοί τε καὶ Μητρ[ο]δώρωι τῶιδε ν[εωστὶ εἰ]ρημένα. οἶμαι δ' ὑμῖν ὄ[γδο]ον καὶ εἰκοστὸν εἶδος ἀκ[ρο]άσεως τῆ[ς] ἑξῆς περαιν[ο]μένης τουτὶ ν[ῦ]ν ἠδολε[σ]χῆσθαι.

Well, let that be enough chat from us for the time being. And you others, try ten thousand times over to remember what Metrodorus here and I have just said.

I think I have now finished chatting to you this twenty-eighth instalment of our sequential lecture-course.

If any confirmation is needed that we are dealing with a lecture, the demonstrative reference to 'Metrodorus here' puts the matter beyond doubt.

How long was each lecture? We have already learnt (§4) that a typical length may have been around 20,000 words. If we imagine that a lecture in ancient Greek was delivered at even approximately the same rate, in words per minute, as a lecture in modern English, the delivery of each must have taken Epicurus some two and a half hours.

Aristotle's *Physics* was a lecture course too, according to its ancient title Φυσικὴ ἀκρόασις, but there is little if anything in its content to confirm that this was so. By contrast, even what little survives of Epicurus' *On nature* confirms its status as the written text of a lecture course. The second person plural, used for addressing his audience, is found not only in the above closure, but also in that of book XXV[30] (where unfortunately the remainder of the sentence is too fragmentary to be of use).

The informality implicit in the verb 'chat' (ἀδολεσχεῖν) at the end of book XXVIII may to some extent be explained by the specific content of the book. In what survives from its last part, Epicurus is at several points conducting a one-way conversation with his colleague Metrodorus, and what we have seen to be its closing words suggest that the whole book has been cast in this form. Here is a sample from an earlier passage in it:[31]

---

[29] *Nat.* XXVIII, 13 XIII 6 10 sup. Sedley (1973) [=31.22.6 10 Arr.²]. The strange termination of μνημο]νεύε[ι]μ reflects the scribe's regular way of modifying final ν before a labial.

[30] Laursen (1992), p. 146, lines 46, 48. For another second person plural earlier in the same book, see P.Herc. 1420, 6 III 7, in Laursen (1995), p. 92.

[31] *Nat.* XXVIII 13 IV 1 inf. V 12 sup. Sedley (1973) [=31.13.23 14.12 Arr.²]. ἔχειμ = ἔχειν (see n. 29 above), ἐγδεξ- = ἐκδεξ-, ἰθισμένων = εἰθισμένων.

ἀλλὰ γὰρ ἴσως οὐκ εὔκαιρόν ἐστ[ι ταῦ]τ[α] προφέροντα μηκύνει[ν· κ]αὶ μάλ'
ὀρθῶς [γε, ὦ] Μητρόδωρε· πάνυ γὰρ οἶμαί σε πολλὰ ἂν ἔχειμ
προε[ν]έγκασθαι ἃ ἐθεώρεις γελοίως [π]ώ[ς] τι[να]ς ἐγδεξαμένους καὶ
π[άν]τ[α] μᾶλλον ἢ τὸ νοούμενον κατὰ τὰς λέξεις, οὐκ ἔξω τῶν ἰθισμένων
λέξεων ἡμῶν χρωμένων οὐδὲ μετατιθέντων ὀνόματα ἐπὶ τῶμ φανε[ρ]ῶν.

But perhaps you'd say this isn't the right time to prolong the discussion by bring-
ing these up. Quite so, Metrodorus, because I'm sure you could bring up lots of
cases of words you've seen certain people taking in some ridiculous sense or
other, in fact in any sense rather than their actual linguistic meaning, whereas
our own usage does not go beyond ordinary language, nor do we change names
with regard to things which are evident.

Similarly, we will see later (p. 118) that at least one book of *On nature* is
likely to have taken the form of narrated dialogue.

But 'chat' is also a piece of self-deflation on Epicurus' part, perhaps
even a little reminiscent of that ultimate philosophical 'chatterer'
(ἀδολεσχής), Socrates. Thus elsewhere in *On nature* Epicurus describes
himself as 'babbling' (θρυλῶ) and even 'ranting' (ληρῶ).[32] This
informality brings with it yet another potentially endearing feature, a
disarming willingness to admit to mistakes. Book xxviii has a good deal
to say about past wrong views on language – some held by Metrodorus,
some by Epicurus himself, which he now openly recants, and some
jointly by the two of them.[33] A brief snippet (fragmentary at both ends)
which conveys this tone of self-criticism is the following:[34]

. . . that it is unclear whether we completely forgot this opinion and took the
standpoint opposed to ourselves, as many others have done in many cases, or
remembered it but . . .

It is hard to be sure whether the greater visibility of these human touches
in books xxv and xxviii represents a change of tone of the later books
(written years after the first, see §12), or simply reflects the fact that
significantly longer stretches from these two books survive than from the
earlier ones, enabling us the better to glimpse the range of Epicurus'
style. What little we have from the earlier books does sound less personal.
But even in them it is possible to witness a broader feature of which these

---

[32] *Nat.* xxv, 34.30.6 7 Arr.[2], καθάπερ πάλαι θρυλῶ; also the passage, from the same book, reported
in Laursen (1992), p. 145, l. 16, ὡσ[πε]ρ λ[η]ρῶ.

[33] Since Epicurus himself branded some of his early writings as mistaken, school orthodoxy had
no choice but to concur, as can be seen in Philodemus, *De Stoicis* xi 4–22 (in Dorandi (1982)), who
refers to these juvenilia as τὰ ἀρχαῖα or τὰ ἀρχαικά. Hence the *subscriptio* of book xxviii,]τῶν
ἀρχαίων [, may perhaps be filled out as '[Concerning] the early [works]' (Sedley (1989b), p. 107
n. 30), rather than '[From] the old [exemplars]' (Vogliano (1928), pp. 19 and 107, Sedley (1973),
pp. 56 and 79; some doubts in Cavallo (1983), p. 59). [34] *Nat.* xxviii, 12 v Sedley (1973), p. 45.

touches form a part. That is, Epicurus does not use the crabbed prose of his physical epitomes, or the contrived Gorgianic symmetries of his ethical epitome the *Letter to Menoeceus*. Rather, he affects what we may call the lecturing style. He tends towards being expansive, repetitive, and, at times, colloquial.[35]

A good example of this is his repeated use of the demonstrative to convey the notion of multiple choice. A crucial tenet defended in book xxv is our initial potentiality to develop in many alternative ways:[36]

ἀπ[ό] τε [τῆς πρ]ώτης ἀρχῆς σπέρμ[ατα ἡμῖν ἀ]γωγὰ τὰ μὲν εἰς τάδ[ε], τὰ δ᾽ εἰς τάδε, τὰ δ᾽ εἰς ἄμφω [ταῦ]τά [ἐ]στιν ἀεὶ [κα]ὶ πρά[ξ]εων [καὶ] διανοήσεων καὶ διαθέ[σε]ων καὶ πλεί[ω] καὶ ἐλάττω.

From the very outset we have seeds directing us some toward these, some towards those, and some towards both these and those, actions and thoughts and characters, in greater and smaller numbers.

Already in book xi the same mannerism can be witnessed. At one point he asks how mathematical astronomers can choose a privileged vantage point for taking measurements of risings and settings:[37]

τ[ί] γὰρ τὴν ἐν[θένδ]ε κ[α]ταστάθμησιν ἢ τὴν ἐνθένδε καταστάθμησιν ἢ τὴν ἐνθένδε ἢ τήν[δε] σε [π]οιεῖν δεῖ πισ[τοτέρ]αν καταστάθ[μησιν] τῶν ἀνα[τ]ολῶν [ἢ δ]ύσεων;

Why, after all, should you make the measurement from here, or the measurement from here, or the one from here, or this one, a more reliable measurement of risings or settings?

The heavy repetition is a quite unliterary feature, but one fully appropriate to the lecturing style. It is only too easy to imagine each repetition accompanied by a gesture.

Other human touches include disarmingly frank talk about other philosophers. Sometimes Epicurus shows exasperation, as when he says of Plato's reasoning about the interrelation of the elements in the *Timaeus*[38]

[35] The 'chat' in book xxviii even contains a totally non-literary usage, albeit one well attested in Ptolemaic papyri: ἐάν with the indicative (Sedley (1973), pp. 69–70).
[36] Text from Sedley (1983), p. 19 (= Long/Sedley (1987), 20c 1), but with the first word altered to accommodate the new reading of Laursen (1992), p. 151 n. 18. The importance of these 'seeds' is confirmed by a new reading of the following passage given in Laursen (1992), p. 145, l. 15. The same concept can be paralleled at Apuleius, *De Platone* 105, *hominem . . . habere semina quidem quaedam utrarumque rerum cum nascendi origine copulata*.
[37] *Nat.* xi, 1 iii 1 = [26.37.11–19 Arr.²]; text from Sedley (1976b), p. 31.
[38] *Nat.* xiv, xxxvii 12–17, Leone (1984), p. 61 = 29.2.12–17 Arr.². Leone, following Schmid (1936), takes this column to be a critique of *Tim.* 56c on elemental intertransformation. I think it is more likely to be focused on *Tim.* 31b–32c. But that issue is irrelevant to the point I am illustrating.

ἀλλὰ γὰρ καὶ τοῦτο γελοίως ἐκ τῆς φαντασίας ἀναλελόγισται, καὶ οὐκ
ἐπισταμένως τἀφανὲς διὰ τοῦ φαινομένου συλλογί[ζ]εσθαι.

But this too is a ridiculous piece of analogical reasoning from appearances,
showing ignorance of how to work out the non-evident by means of the evident.

At other times, though, his criticisms are couched in generous terms, as
where he regrets a lapse on the part of the early atomists when they
unwittingly implied universal determinism, but nevertheless describes
them as 'greatly excelling not only their predecessors but also, many
times over, their successors'.[39]

I have illustrated these human touches in the hope of capturing,
however fleetingly, the tone which must have given *On nature* such a
special place in the affections of Epicurus' followers. To read it, it seems,
conveyed a sense of joining Epicurus in his quest.

On the other side, it must be admitted that, to modern readers spoiled
by Lucretius, the main style of argument throughout the surviving fragments is likely to seem remarkably sparse, abstract, theoretical and
impersonal in tone. Physical theses are defended by regular appeal to the
usual Epicurean requirement that they be 'consistent with' or 'uncon-
tested by' phenomena, but there is no sign of Epicurus focusing his audience's minds, as Lucretius would have done, on familiar examples of the
analogous phenomena. To read these books was surely a demanding
task. When at the beginning of the *Letter to Herodotus* we saw Epicurus
speaking of those who were 'unable' to read them, he may have been
referring to their lack of the required intellectual stamina, not just lack
of time.

However, this impression must not be taken to extremes. It is easy to
be misled by the fragmentary state of these texts into overestimating
their original unreadability. Often our editions of them contain sen-
tences which appear to make little sense, but we must always remember
that (a) these sadly damaged texts are only as good as the fallible editors
who have restored them (myself included), and (b) we have fragments
only from the later parts of the books, often undoubtedly deploying allusions, concepts, terms and assumptions which were set up in the lost
earlier parts.

Graziano Arrighetti, although his work on the papyri of *On nature* has
done so much to further our synoptic understanding of them, and
although he has himself fully appreciated their importance as a show-
case for Epicurus' human side, has also promoted the idea that the work

---

[39] *Nat.* xxv, in Sedley (1983), p. 20 = Long/Sedley (1987), 20C13. For full text, see below p. 142.

as a whole lacked a formal structure.[40] He points out (as we shall also note in §12) that it was written in stages over many years, with a certain heterogeneity of styles, and argues that in it Epicurus was happy to return to a topic for a second time if his interest in it was rekindled by second thoughts or polemical needs. From this he concludes that the collected books of *On nature* did not constitute a single linear investigation, but served the Epicurean community as a record of the various phases in the evolution of Epicurus' philosophy.

Let us pause to try a small thought experiment. Imagine that in a parallel universe numerous small papyrus fragments of a large philosophical work have been discovered. Scholars trying to reconstruct the work are perplexed by the wide variety of topics and styles. Some fragments appear to discuss music, some metaphysics, some politics. Some contain high-flown mythological narrative, others are colloquial in style and take the form of rapid dialogue. Dating criteria show the first and last books probably to have been written years apart. And one topic occurs twice in widely separated books, the later discussion appearing to overturn the conclusions of the earlier one. The scholars naturally incline to the suspicion that this work lacks formal unity, that it is a compilation of a somewhat *ad hoc* character, ranging over several phases of the author's thought. But in this instance they are wrong. For the work which I have described is a literary and philosophical masterpiece of outstanding formal unity: Plato's *Republic*.

Our papyrus fragments and other testimonia do not compel us to expect any less of *On nature*. Returning to a subject already treated, for example, may be perfectly proper even within a single consecutively structured argument (just as it was proper for Plato to return to the subject of poetry once he had his psychology and metaphysics in place). Besides, the philosophical logbook described by Arrighetti would be a most unusual kind of work, and that fact is enough to place the onus of proof firmly on anyone who wishes to propose such a hypothesis.

A more direct obstacle to Arrighetti's view is the following. In the closing sentence of *On nature* xxviii (quoted p. 104 above), Epicurus describes the treatise as ἀκ[ρο]άσεως τῆ[ς] ἑξῆς περαιν[ο]μένης, 'our sequential lecture-course'. What does this description mean? The paral-

---

[40] Arrighetti (1973), appendixes 1 and 2, esp. pp. 715–17. Arrighetti's own main aim here is to explain the apparent structural incoherences of the *Letter to Herodotus* and the *Letter to Pythocles* by deriving them from the structural incoherence of their source text, *On nature*. In my view, what structural awkwardness the *Letter to Herodotus* displays is adequately explained by the process of abridgement; while that of the *Letter to Pythocles* is likely in addition to reflect its derivation from two or more different but possibly overlapping source texts (cf. §9 below).

lels for the expression ἑξῆς περαίνειν show that it does not simply signify 'accomplish in a series', but 'accomplish in a proper order'. In Plato's *Gorgias* Socrates explains to Gorgias the interrogative methodology he is adopting: 'not for your sake, but for the sake of the argument, so that it may proceed in such a way as to make it totally clear to us what we are talking about' (453c2–4); and referring back to this explanation shortly afterwards, he remarks (in Dodds' translation): 'For as I said (453c2), I am questioning you in order to get the argument carried through in a coherent way . . .' (τοῦ ἑξῆς ἕνεκα περαίνεσθαι τὸν λόγον, 454c1–2). This is strong evidence that what Epicurus is claiming for *On nature* is exactly the feature which Arrighetti denies it, structural coherence.[41] That finding is further confirmed by Epicurus' concern, in the closing sentence of book II (below p. 111), to stress the proper thematic continuity (again expressed by ἑξῆς) between this book and what follows it.

I do not mean to insist that before he set pen to papyrus Epicurus already had the entire work mapped out. How many writers *could* claim to do that? All I want to insist on is that he saw its sequence of topics, however and whenever decided upon, as forming a natural philosophical progression.

6. RECONSTRUCTING THE CONTENTS

So what was the work's structure? What is the 'proper order' in which Epicurus delivered his massive lecture series? It is important to remark that arguing in the right order – in particular, arguing in such a sequence as never to presuppose what is yet to be proved – is a cardinal feature of Epicurus' physical methodology, one to which we will turn in Chapter 7.[42] What I want to attempt for the present, however, is not so much a methodological defence of Epicurus' chosen sequence of topics, but the actual task of establishing what that sequence was. For this purpose I shall draw on nearly all the available evidence.[43] This includes of course the scholia and other secondary citations, as well as the papyrus fragments. And one crucial further guide will be the sequence of topics in the *Letter to Herodotus*, which, as we have seen, is almost certainly presenting itself as an epitome of *On nature*. Even the *Letter to Pythocles* will come to our rescue at one stage.

---

[41] Cf. also Plato, *Phlb.* 12b4–6.   [42] See also Ch. 5, §§4–7 below.
[43] There is a helpful succinct guide to the data on *Nat.* in Erler (1994), pp. 94–103. Cf. also Steckel (1968), cols. 601–11, and of course the texts in Arrighetti (1973), pp. 189–418, with commentary pp. 577–609.

Lucretius himself, however, had better stay in the background. The aim of this reconstruction is to be able, in the next chapter, to determine the relation of Lucretius' organisation of topics to that in *On nature*. To avoid circularity, therefore, *On nature* must be reconstructed so far as possible without Lucretius' help.[44] However, the occasional glance at Lucretius will prove unavoidable.

One restriction which can be fairly safely asserted at the outset is that *On nature* was a treatise on physics, and not, as has been suggested,[45] one covering the whole of Epicurus' philosophy. None of our evidence about it requires us to dismiss the obvious meaning of its title, confirmed by the following passage of Diogenes Laertius (x 29–30):

> It [Epicurus' philosophy] is divided into three parts: canonic, physics and ethics. Canonic covers the methodological approach to the system, and is found in the work entitled 'Canon'. Physics covers the entire study of nature, and is found in the thirty-seven books *On nature*, and summarised in the letters. Ethics covers the issues of choice and avoidance, and is found in the books *On lives*, in the letters, and in *On the end*. However, their practice is to class canonic with physics.

This very clearly announces that *On nature* was a work devoted to the physical part of the system, but that we should expect to find some treatment of epistemology ('canonic') there too — as indeed we do. Although there were undoubtedly ethical remarks in it,[46] and although a great deal of Epicurus' physics has ethical implications, there is no evidence that any book or substantial section of a book was devoted to ethical inquiry as such.

Readers who have limited stamina and are willing to take a certain amount on trust may wish to jump to §13. But the wary would be better advised to check my arguments in the intervening sections.

7. BOOKS I–IV

To reconstruct this first group, it is best to start at the very end of book II, which survives virtually intact:[47]

[44] An earlier version of the reconstruction which follows appeared in Sedley (1984), and is reproduced in Erler (1994), p. 95. But there I used Lucretius as a source for the reconstruction itself. On the present occasion I shall place Lucretius alongside the reconstruction of *Nat.* (Ch. 5, §2) only when it is virtually complete.   [45] Steckel (1968), col. 601, cf. 609.

[46] See §11 below for some ethically-related themes in the later books, and cf. DL x 119, where the dictum that the wise man will marry and have children is attributed to *On nature*. For the beginning of an ethical digression in a non-ethical book, cf. *Nat.* XXVIII, 13 VI 8 sup. ff. in Sedley (1973), p. 49. Cf. also n.90, p. 127 below.

[47] Vogliano (1953), pp. 92–3 = 24.50.17–51.8 Arr.² My text combines the letters preserved in both of the parallel papyri.

ἀ[ποδέ]δεικται οὖν ἡμ[ῖ]ν δὴ ὅτι ἔ[σ]τι[ν εἴ]δωλα, καὶ ὅτι τὴν γένεσιν
αὐτῶν [ἅ]μα νοήματι συμβέβηκεν ἀποτελεῖσθαι, καὶ ἔτι τὰς φο[ρ]ὰς
ἀνυπερβλήτους τοῖς τάχεσιν κεκτῆσθαι. τὰ δ' ἁρμόττοντα ἑξῆς τούτοις
ῥηθῆναι ἐν τοῖς μετὰ ταῦτα διέξιμεν.

Thus we have proved (a) that images (εἴδωλα) exist, (b) that they have the property of being generated as quick as thought, and (c) that they have motions
unsurpassed in speed. In what follows [or 'in the following books']⁴⁸ we will go
through the topics which belong in sequence after these ones.

Book II, then, or at least its final part, introduced the 'images' which
Epicurean physics postulates to explain vision and thought. In fact, we
have enough of the two papyri extant to be able to say that topic (c) occupies the last fourteen columns of P. Herc. 1149/993. That is, given the
column size in this particular copy, topic (c) ran to some 6,300 letters.
Hence, assuming that the book was comparable in length to book XIV
(see §4 above), (c) occupied less than one-twentieth of the book. How
long, then, was the whole account of images?

Actually, the account appears to have come in four parts. In addition
to the three which Epicurus lists in his summary, there was undoubtedly
also a proof of the *fineness* of the images, which must have been placed
between (a) and (b).⁴⁹ We may call this (a)*. To help us guess the total
length of the sequence (a), (a)*, (b), (c), we must fall back on our parallel
texts – not only the *Letter to Herodotus*, but also Lucretius (whom we may
invoke as attesting the relative *quantities* of Epicurean material on these
several topics, without any presupposition at this stage that *On nature* was
his direct source).

In Lucretius, (c) occupies 42 or more lines (IV 176–216, followed by a
lacuna of one or more lines); (b) occupies 34 or more lines (IV 143–75,
with a lacuna of at least one line); (a)* occupies 20 or more lines (IV
110–28, again including a lacuna); and finally (a) occupies 56 lines (IV
54–109). That is, in Lucretius (c) is *between a third and a quarter* of the whole
argument. In the *Letter to Herodotus* (46–8) (c) takes up 15 lines of von der
Muehll's text, (b) 10 lines, and (a) 7 lines. ((a)* is not treated separately

---

⁴⁸ Where Vogliano reports τοῖς from both papyri, Arrighetti prints ταῖς, but without signalling a
correction to Vogliano in his *ap. crit.* I therefore assume ταῖς to be merely a typographical error.
If the feminine had been correct, the reference would undoubtedly have been to 'books'
(βίβλοις). The neuter is less explicit. It could refer to books (βίβλίοις), or, more vaguely, to the
next discussion (cf. also n.68, p. 120 below).

⁴⁹ 24.35–6 Arr.² clearly marks the transition from (b) to (c). Epicurus' very first argument in (c) for
the images' high velocity (24.36–7) uses their fineness as a premise (see below p. 139). Therefore
the proofs of fineness must precede (b). But they can hardly precede (a). So they came between
(a) and (b). The reason why Epicurus does not list (a)* in his closing summary is simple: the fineness of images was needed, not as a conclusion in its own right, but as a premise for establishing their speed of generation and travel.

there, simply appearing as a premise in (c).) Thus in Epicurus' own summary of the same argument (c) is nearly *half* the argument.

These parallel texts suggest that in Epicurus' original exposition too, the arguments for the images' speed which make up (c) were a substantial part of the whole, and certainly not less than a quarter of it. So since, in *On nature* II, (c) has proved likely to be less than one-twentieth of the whole book, it is scarcely imaginable that the entire account of images with which the book ends occupied more than the last fifth of it.

This conclusion has required some tedious calculations, but it is of the utmost importance. Scholars have usually assumed from its closing words that book II as a whole was about images. We have now seen this to be almost inconceivable. And, by the same move, we have freed up the bulk of book II for other contents.

There is no problem about filling the space vacated. According to a scholion on *Letter to Herodotus* 73, Epicurus' description of time as a special kind of accidental property (σύμπτωμα) was also to be found 'in *On nature* book II, and in the *Great epitome*'. This has caused some consternation. The fact that the equivalent remark comes only late on in the Letter, combined with the assumption, now proved incorrect, that the whole of book II was about images, has led some to suspect that the book number in the scholion is corrupt.[30] This is unnecessary. The remark that time is a special kind of σύμπτωμα almost certainly first occurred at a point in *On nature* corresponding to *Letter to Herodotus* 40. There, having established the ontological dualism of body and void, Epicurus adds:

Over and above these nothing can be conceived, either by imagination or by analogy with what can be imagined, as things grasped in terms of complete natures, and not as what we call the 'accidents' (συμπτώματα) and properties (συμβεβηκότα) of these.

Now the manifestly parallel passage in Lucretius (I 430–82) argues against the independent existence, not only of 'accidents' and 'permanent properties', but also of time and of historical events. There need be little doubt, then, that the full text which *Letter to Herodotus* 40 is abridging had already included a preliminary analysis of time as a special kind of 'accident'. This early analysis of properties and time had a primarily negative motive – to eliminate them as contenders for independent existence. The more sophisticated account of them which is reflected at

---

[30] E.g. Arrighetti (1973), pp. 579–80, 650, Erler (1994), p. 96.

Letter to Herodotus 68–73 was presumably one which Epicurus was able to undertake only in a later book of *On nature*, once his metaphysics of atomic and phenomenal properties was in place. At *Letter to Herodotus* 40, atoms have not even yet entered the story. (This exemplifies the point made above, p. 108, that Epicurus may have had entirely legitimate reasons, within the constraints of his methodology, for returning to a topic for a second time.)

We are now in a position to list the contents of books I–II. Book I no doubt started with the methodological preliminaries echoed at *Letter to Herodotus* 37–8. The remainder of it was devoted to establishing the foundational principles summarised at *Letter to Herodotus* 38–40, giving us the full sequence:

BOOK I
(i) **methodological preliminaries;**
(ii) **nothing comes into being out of nothing;**
(iii) **nothing perishes into nothing;**
(iv) **the all never changes;**
(v) **the all consists of bodies and void;**
(vi) **of bodies, some are compounds, others the constituents of those compounds.**

Some confirmation is found in the fact that (v) is explicitly attributed to *On nature* I in a scholion on *Letter to Herodotus* 39. I have added (vi), from the end of *Letter to Herodotus* 40, because a scholion there attributes it to *On nature* book I. I shall return to this point in a moment. Finally, an unnumbered book of *On nature* refers back to something that has been said about 'collisions (κρούσεις) with each other', apparently in book I.[51] In the absence of further information, it is hard to know where to place this.

---

[51] Fr. 78 Usener = 36.24 Arr.², . . .] ἀναγκαῖόν τι αὐταῖς ὑπάρχειν κατὰ τὰ[ς] πρὸ[ς] ἀλλήλας κρούσεις, ὡς ἐν τῇ[ι] πρώτη[ι] γραφῆ[ι] εἴρητα[ι], οὐθὲν ἧττο[ν π]αρὰ τὰς [. . . That this expression might refer to 'book' I is suggested by Philodemus' usage at P.Herc. 1005, XVIII 6–12 (Angeli (1988), p. 182); see also Capasso (1981), p. 397 for Epicurean usage of γραφή. I do not see how Epicurus could possibly have reached the topic of specifically *atomic* collisions in book I: we should expect them first to occur in item (xi) below, which, as we shall see, must be well into book II. Possibly the feminine pronoun αὐταῖς refers not to atoms but to compounds (συγκρίσεις), whose collisions might have cropped up in the context of item (iii), (v) or (vi). Alternatively, Epicurus may be referring back to his first 'draft' of the current book (cf. *Nat.* XXVIII, 8 IV 9–10 in Sedley (1973), p. 41 for a possible reference to two drafts of the same book), to the first 'book' of the current section (i.e. group of books) of the treatise, or to the first 'section' (i.e. group of books) of the entire treatise. In the majority of cases, γραφή in Epicurean sources means 'writing' or 'piece of writing', rather than 'book' (see Capasso *loc. cit.*).

And that is all for book I, because the next item (*Letter to Herodotus* 40),
(vii) *nothing exists independently apart from bodies and void*
was (as we saw above when considering the topic of time) argued in book
II, presumably at the beginning of it. The sequence at *Letter to Herodotus*
40–1 implies that book II continued with the proof that
(viii) *the constituents of bodies (distinguished already in (vi)) are atomic.*
There is a small inconcinnity here, in that the Letter places (vi) after (vii).
However, there is no difficulty in assuming that (vi), the very basic division of bodies into compounds and constituents, did indeed first occur
in book I as part of the defence of (v), but that it was then re-invoked in
book II as a premise for (viii). It was in fact one of Epicurus' best-known
and most repeated dicta.[52]

If we take our lead from *Letter to Herodotus* 41–5, the full sequence for
book II can be filled out as follows:

BOOK II

**(vii)   nothing exists independently apart from bodies and
       void;**

**(viii) the constituents of bodies (distinguished already in (vi))
       are atomic;**

(ix)   the all is infinite;

**(x)   there are unimaginably, not infinitely, many atomic
       shapes;**

(xi)   atoms are in perpetual motion;

(xii)   there are infinitely many worlds;

(xiii) there are images, which are swiftly generated and fast.

Here (xiii) of course links up with the ending of book II as we have
already met it. Given our conclusion that (xiii) occupied one-fifth of the
book or less, there seems no obstacle to assuming that (vii)–(xii) fitted
snugly enough into the remaining four-fifths (or more).

Finally, we can look ahead into books III–IV. As we saw, at the end of
book II Epicurus promises to continue with themes consequent upon
those of the existence and speed of images. This makes it overwhelmingly likely that he proceeded with much the same sequence of topics as
in *Letter to Herodotus* 49–53, namely the functioning of vision and the
other individual senses, and of thought. The wording of his promise
leaves it uncertain whether he is referring to the following 'books', or

---

[52] The scholion on *Ep. Hdt.* 40 reports that it was repeated also in *Nat.* XIV and XV and in the *Great
epitome*; and in Philodemus, *Piet.* 37 41 (Obbink (1996), p. 108) it is quoted verbatim by critics of
Epicurus' theology.

more vaguely to 'what follows', the latter leaving open the possibility that the whole of this topic was contained within book III.[53] However, the tiny fragment of evidence that we have for book IV may support the expectation that the same topic continued there. It is a minute papyrus fragment, attributed to Philodemus, and containing an explicit citation of '*On nature* book IV', with the preceding words apparently including some form or cognate of μνήμη, 'memory'.[54] Memory would certainly be included under the rubric of 'thought', so in a small way this snippet encourages the assumption that psychological phenomena constituted the contents of books III and IV, and that thinking was dealt with after perception (although there is no separate treatment of thinking included in the *Letter to Herodotus*). This seems to justify the following tentative addition to our accumulating chart:

BOOKS III–IV
(xiv) vision, truth and falsity;
(xv)   the other senses;
(xvi) thought.

Before we leave this first group of books, a word of caution is needed. We have found an encouraging degree of fit between the overall sequence of topics in *On nature* and that in the *Letter to Herodotus*. But it cannot necessarily be traced down to the details of the individual sections. Although the treatment of images occurs in each work at the same point in the sequence, in the Letter Epicurus has undoubtedly adjusted the sequence of arguments *within* that section. Thus where *On nature* has

(a) existence of images,
(a)* their fineness,
(b) their speed of generation,
(c) their velocity,

the Letter (46–8) has the sequence

(a) existence of images
(c) their velocity – including (a)*, their fineness, merely as a premise,
(b) their speed of generation.

The suppression of (a)* as a separate item is insignificant, merely reflecting the obvious fact that epitomisation involves some abridgement. But the reversal of (b) and (c) is not insignificant. This small difference will, as it happens, be extremely useful to us in the next chapter.[55] But how is it to be accounted for? It may be that to produce

---

[53] See n. 48, p. 111 above.
[54] 25 Arr.[2] = fr. 80 Usener. The remaining restorations in the first two lines are sheer guesswork, and should be discounted.   [55] P. 141 below.

the epitome Epicurus worked his way through the books of *On nature*, selecting the principal topics for inclusion, but that when he settled on each topic he then wrote his digest of it largely from memory. Thus in cases where the precise order of arguments did not matter methodologically, some variations could have crept in. Neither of (b) and (c) seems to presuppose the other, so that they might easily and harmlessly be reversed. On the other hand, they do undoubtedly both presuppose (a) and (a)*, and both *On nature* and the *Letter to Herodotus* in their own way respect that fact.

8. BOOKS V–X

There is not much helpful evidence about these books, beyond the contents of *Letter to Herodotus* 54–73.[56] The best way forward, therefore, is to list the main topics in the sequence found there (chapter references to the Letter are added):

(xvii)   atoms lack secondary qualities (54–5);
(xviii) atomic dimensions (55–9);
(xix)   up and down (60);
(xx)   equal speed of atoms (61–2);
(xxi)   nature of the soul (63–5);
(xxii)   mortality of the soul (65–6);
(xxiii) soul is not incorporeal (66–7);
(xxiv)   metaphysics of properties and time (68–73).

I have already speculated (pp. 112–13 above), on Epicurus' motives in returning to the topic of properties and time, as he does in (xxiv). But why precisely here? The conjunction of (xxiii) and (xxiv) shows that it was the issue of incorporeality that provided him with a natural bridge from the topic of soul to that of properties. To call either the soul or properties 'incorporeals' is implicitly to endow them with *independent* incorporeal existence, and hence is an unwelcome step towards Platonism. The main object of (xxiv) is to say, in positive terms, what ontological status we can safely attribute to properties and time.

How far can we go in correlating topics (xvii)–(xxiv) to individual books of *On nature*? There are some obscure references to books VI (possibly) and VIII which might help us here. In *On piety* 1043–89, Philodemus, engaged in cataloguing references by the authoritative

---

[56] Starting the group V–X at *Ep. Hdt.* 54 assumes the correctness of my findings in §7, where the cognitive psychology of 49–53 is correlated with *Nat.* II–IV. Ending at 73 is based on the finding of §9 below that the closing part of *Ep. Hdt.* 73 corresponds to *Nat.* XI.

early Epicureans to the benefit and harm that can befall humans because of the gods, lists a number of relevant citations from Epicurus himself. These include a sadly fragmentary passage which Obbink restores as follows (1077–89):[57]

ὁμοί]ως καὶ [ἐν τῷ] ἕκτω[ι π]ερὶ [τοῦ δι]κάζεσ[θαι . . . . .]ουπ[.] . [.]και[
. . . .]στησδα[. . . . . κ]αὶ εὐόρκους [καὶ δι]καίους ταῖς ἀ[ρ]ίσταις
διαδόσε[σι] κινεῖσθαι καὶ παρ' αὐτοὺς καὶ παρ' ἐκείνους· [κ]αὶ
παρα[π]λησίως ἐν τῶι ὀγδόωι.

similarly in book vi[58] concerning adjudication (*6–8 words missing*) . . . and that those who are oath-keeping and just are moved by the best transmissions, which depend both on their own selves and on them [i.e. the gods]. And likewise in book viii.

It is risky to infer too much from these citations about the primary themes of books vi and viii,[59] since Philodemus is plundering them for his own current purpose alone, and may be drawing on parenthetical or even digressive remarks. Certainly we should not infer that theology was the main theme of these books. Philodemus implies merely that the gods – presumably meaning our mental attitude to them[60] – were there added to the 'self' as a second explanatory factor for certain kinds of behaviour. Nor can we be confident that 'adjudication' is the word associated with book vi (one alternative possibility would be εἰ]κάζεσ[θαι, 'being imaged' or 'being conjectured'). Nevertheless, the recurrence of the reported remarks in two almost juxtaposed books does suggest the presence of a thematic link, which would have to be in some sense a *psychological* one.

The remark about the best 'transmissions' (διαδόσεις) has no precise parallel in our surviving Greek Epicurean literature, but sounds very much like a technical reference to the transmission of motions within the soul.[61] Lucretius tells us that the fourth 'nameless' element in the soul

---

[57] Obbink (1996), pp. 180–1. My translation largely follows his.

[58] Obbink (1996), p. 477, hesitates before identifying this as a probable reference to *Nat.* vi. The identification is, however, much strengthened by the reference to *Nat.* vi merely as τὸ ἑκτόν in the biography of Philonides (above p. 102).

[59] It is hard to decide whether it is anything more than coincidence that books vi and viii are likewise coupled in the Life of Philonides: he wrote something in connexion with book viii (col. 13 inf., Gallo (1980)), and possessed a set of notes on book vi (see p. 102 above).

[60] For an excellent discussion of this question, see Obbink (1996), pp. 458–64.

[61] For a somewhat different interpretation, see Obbink (1996), pp. 477–8. It is certainly possible that, as Obbink proposes, the διαδόσεις represent the gods' causal influence on us (in which case, however, this is a non-technical use of the word, as at Epictetus, *Diss.* 1 12.6 and Marcus Aurelius 1 17.6, not helpfully explicated by reference to *Ep. Pyth.* 105–6). If so, the topic would still be psychological.

'transmits' motions through the body (III 245, 'sensiferos motus quae didit prima per artus'), and his verb 'didit' here sounds like a rendition of διαδίδωμι, the verb cognate with διάδοσις. The 'best' transmissions perhaps contrast with the excessive or insufficient sensitivity of those souls which have an unbalanced atomic composition, as described by Lucretius at III 288–322.

This makes it a tempting guess that all of items (xvii)–(xx), on atomic matters, were contained in book v, and that books VI–VIII were in their entirety about the soul.

What then about books IX and X? If we take at least the last topic, (xxiv) on the metaphysics of properties and time, to correspond to book x, it is worth asking whether P.Herc. 1413[62] may not be the remains of that book. Its last part – perhaps as many as 80 columns, which could easily be one-third of the whole – is about the metaphysical and epistemological status of time. Its scribal hand places it in the same palaeographical group as the bulk of the *On nature* papyri,[63] and since all the Herculaneum papyri from that group whose content has been identified have so far proved to be from *On nature*, it has long been recognised as probable that this is yet another book of the same work.

One remarkable feature of this text is that, at least in the surviving portion, it appears to take the form of a narrated dialogue. In view of what we have noted above (§5) about the stylistic heterogeneity of *On nature*, including the personal address to Metrodorus in book XXVIII, this fact should in no way discourage us from assigning the book to it.[64]

Suppose that this assignment is right. If we also bear in mind (a) that as much as the last third of the book in question is devoted to time, and (b) that the same topic, time, takes up slightly under one-third of the passage on the metaphysics of properties and time in the *Letter to Herodotus* (68–73), it becomes a plausible inference that the whole of topic (xxiv) occupied the whole of book x.

We now have the following distribution: book v on atoms, books VI–VIII on the soul, book x on metaphysics. What about book IX? I can see no easy way to decide whether it continued the discussion of soul, began that of metaphysics, or dealt with some further topic which has fallen out of our sources. However, given the close thematic link between (xxiii), 'Soul is not incorporeal', and (xxiv), the metaphysics of properties and time, it seems natural in the absence of counter-evidence to

---

[62] This text is 37 Arr.². See Arrighetti (1973), pp. 381–415 and 647–67, which is in fact the fullest and most up-to-date edition of it; *q.v.* for details of earlier editions (pp. 648–9), and for a defence of its provenance from *On nature* (p. 650).   [63] Cavallo (1983), p. 50.
[64] Thus too Arrighetti (1973), p. 630.

locate topic (xxiii) in book IX. I therefore propose the following assignment of topics to books:

BOOK V

(xvii)   **atoms lack secondary qualities;**
(xviii) **atomic dimensions;**
(xix)   **up and down;**
(xx)   **equal speed of atoms;**

BOOKS VI–VIII

(xxi)   **nature of the soul;**
(xxii)   **mortality of the soul;**

BOOK IX

(xxiii) **soul is not incorporeal;**

BOOK X

(xxiv)   **metaphysics of properties and time.**

9. BOOKS XI–XIII

We now move to cosmology. The best vantage point from which to start on this group is the last part of book XI. In the papyrus fragments, book XI concludes with the following trio of topics: the motions of the heavenly bodies; an attack on astronomical devices; and, finally, the stability of the earth. But a scholion (on *Letter to Pythocles* 91) also refers us to book XI for the doctrine that the sun and other heavenly bodies are as small as they appear (see Ch. 3, §7), and since this is also astronomical it is likely to belong not much before the surviving fragments on celestial motions. Thus we get:

   size of heavenly bodies;
   motions of heavenly bodies;
   attack on astronomical devices;
   stability of the earth.

The first three of these coincide exactly with the sequence of topics at chapters 91–3 of Epicurus' surviving epitome on cosmological, astronomical and meteorological matters, the *Letter to Pythocles*.[65] There, moreover,

---

[65] I have little to contribute to the issue of its authenticity (on which see esp. Bollack/Laks (1978), introduction; cf. also the illuminating remarks of Mansfeld (1994a), p. 29 n. 2), beyond the observation that the ancient doubts about its authenticity recorded by Philodemus (see Angeli (1988), pp. 176–7, with valuable commentary pp. 289–99) probably just reflect the later Epicureans' problems in establishing a fully consistent canon of texts by the school's founders (see Sedley (1989b), p. 106), and are unlikely to be motivated by impartial scholarly suspicions. Without this potentially misleading information from Philodemus, I doubt if any modern scholar would ever have questioned the Letter's authenticity. However, even for those who persist with such doubts, there should be no problem in regarding it as *somebody's* digest of Epicurus' writings on the same subject matter, which is all that matters for my own purposes here.

the denunciation of astronomical devices as the 'slavish contrivances of the astronomers' (τὰς ἀνδραποδώδεις ἀστρολόγων τεχνιτείας, *Ep. Pyth.* 93) echoes the wording of the equivalent passage in book xi, which likewise speaks of the astronomers' 'enslavements' ([ἀνδρα]ποδείας) to doctrine in the use of their instruments.[66] It starts to look extremely likely – as Arrighetti has already maintained[67] – that at least this early part of the *Letter to Pythocles* is epitomising *On nature* book xi.

The *Letter to Pythocles* itself merely claims to be summarising what Epicurus has said 'elsewhere' (ἐν ἄλλοις, 84).[68] Hence he may well be drawing on more than one source text, and it would be unwise to rush into correlating the whole of the Letter with *On nature.* But in its early part, at least, we seem to be on relatively safe ground in doing so. Since this letter (85) refers to the *Letter to Herodotus* and therefore postdates it, it is reasonable to take it to be filling a gap which the first letter had left in its exposition. This will be because the *Letter to Herodotus,* although dealing at some length with the same range of topics (76–82), does so in entirely general terms, stressing methodological, religious and ethical aspects, without actually supplying any specific explanations of phenomena. It is this gap that Pythocles, the recipient of the second letter, has apparently asked Epicurus to fill (*Ep. Pyth.* 84).

Now the preceding topics in the *Letter to Pythocles* appear to join those listed above in making a seamless whole, and it is at least a strong possibility that the entire opening sequence of the Letter reflects the same source. This assumption would allow us to add the two opening topics at *Ep. Pyth.* 88–90 before the above sequence, giving us the full sequence:

BOOK XI

(xxv)   **origin of our world;**
(xxvi)   **origin of heavenly bodies;**
(xxvii)   **size of heavenly bodies;**
(xxviii) **motions of heavenly bodies;**
(xxix)   **attack on astronomical devices;**
(xxx)   **stability of the earth.**

While it cannot be proved that this entire sequence, even if correctly reconstructed, fell entirely into book xi, it does not seem too much

[66] Text in Sedley (1976b), p. 32 [=26.38.8–9 Arr.²].   [67] Arrighetti (1973), esp. chart on p. 700.

[68] Jaap Mansfeld has pointed out to me that this plural is sometimes used even for a precise citation of a single text. In Aristotle (see numerous instances in Bonitz (1870), s.v. Ἀριστοτέλης) citations of specific passages in his own works standardly use the plural: ἐν ἄλλοις, ἐν ἑτέροις, ἐν τοῖς περί . . . etc. For Epicurus, cf. n. 12, p. 100 above. Hence 'elsewhere' is safer than 'in other works'.

material to fill one book, especially when one makes the comparison with what we learnt above (§7) about the contents of book II. Tentatively, then, we may adopt the above list as the probable main contents of book XI.

For book XII we have no papyrus remains, but several secondary citations. We may initially take these in the order in which Usener lists them as fragments, although omitting those where his attribution is purely conjectural:

fr. 82, scholion on *Letter to Herodotus* 74: in *On nature* XII, Epicurus describes and delimits the range of shapes other worlds may have.

fr. 83, scholion on *Letter to Pythocles* 96: in *On nature* XII, Epicurus gives various explanations of eclipses.

fr. 84, Philodemus, *De pietate* 225–31 Obbink: in *On nature* XII, Epicurus speaks of early mankind's formation of the concept of divinity.[69]

fr. 41 (cross-reference under fr. 85), anon. Epicurean treatise (P.Herc. 1111): some topic which Epicurus treated in his *On piety* he also discussed in *On nature* XII and XIII.[70]

fr. 87, Philodemus, *De pietate* 523–33 Obbink: in *On nature* XII, Epicurus criticises Prodicus, Diagoras and Critias (the standard list of atheists) as insane.[71]

To these we can add the closing sentence of book XI, as we have it in the papyrus:

ἐν δὲ τοῖς ἐχο[μέ]νοις ἔ[τ]ι περὶ τῶν [με]τεώρων τουτωνε[ί τι] προσεκκα[θ]αροῦμεν.

In what follows [or 'in the following books'?] we will continue with some further sorting out[72] of these celestial phenomena.

Now the topic of eclipses is one example of these promised further explanations, and, regardless of how we translate the beginning of the above sentence, Epicurus' promise strongly suggests that this continuation was to be found (at least) in the opening part of book XII. This has the further advantage of maintaining the parallel with the order of topics in the *Letter to Pythocles* which, skipping item (xxx), the stability of the earth, passes directly from item (xxix), the attack on astronomical devices, to a whole range of

(xxxi) further astronomical phenomena (phases etc. of moon; eclipses; day length).

---

[69] = 27.1 Arr.²   [70] See n. 13, p. 100 above.   [71] = 27.2 Arr.².

[72] On the problem of καθαίρειν and its derivatives in such Epicurean contexts, cf. Mansfeld (1994a), pp. 34–5.

At this point we seem to rejoin the *Letter to Herodotus*, at 73, where we left
it. Its sequence at 73–6 is: other worlds, origin of civilisation (exemplified
by the acquisition of language). Both of these topics are, as we have seen,
attested for book xii, although the only aspect of the history of civilisation explicitly recorded for it is the beginning of religion. After fully
describing the origin and general arrangement of our world in book xi
and at the beginning of book xii, Epicurus evidently went on to draw
some inferences about how far other worlds can be expected to resemble and differ from ours. He then resumed the history of our own world
by turning to the origins and development of mankind.[73] This enables
us to reconstruct book xii as follows:

BOOK XII

**(xxxi)   further astronomical phenomena (phases etc. of
moon; eclipses; day length);**

(xxxii)   other worlds;

(xxxiii) origins of civilisation.

Book xiii is harder to pin down. All that seems to be recorded for it is a
discussion of human relationships to god – affinity in some cases, non-
affinity in others – and possibly of other themes relating to piety.[74] It
would certainly be an appropriate point in his treatise for Epicurus to set
out some moral lessons about our relationship to the divine. Now that
he has completed his account of the rise of civilisation, including the
origins of religious belief, he is able to comment on what is true and what
false in popular religion in the light of the entire physical system, but
especially by invoking the mechanistic, non-theological explanations of
celestial phenomena in books xi–xii. And the extended final expository
section of the *Letter to Herodotus* (76–82), immediately following (xxxiii) the
origins of civilisation, dwells on just such a set of themes. We may therefore tentatively add to our chart

(xxxiv) *the correct attitude to divinity*.

This admittedly leaves one major question open. Where did Epicurus
cover the further range of meteorological phenomena – weather signs,
thunder, earthquakes etc., which I shall loosely call 'atmospheric and terrestrial phenomena' – dealt with in the later part of the *Letter to Pythocles*
(88–110) and in book vi of Lucretius? At least some of the final part of

---

[73] For the probable contents of the anthropological section, see Obbink (1996), pp. 306, 350–1.

[74] Philodemus, *Piet.* 1050–4 Obbink = fr. 88 Usener = 28 Arr.²: ἕν τε τῶι τρε[ισκαι]δεκάτωι περ[ὶ
τῆς] οἰκειότητος ἣ[ν πρός] τινας ὁ θεὸς ἔχ[ει καὶ] τῆς ἀλλοτρι[ότητος]. In addition, the admittedly corrupt fragment of P.Herc. 1111 in 19.5 Arr.² (see n. 13, p. 100 above) appears to attribute
to books xii and xiii of *On nature* some topic which also occurred in Epicurus' *On piety*.

the Letter may well be drawn from other source texts than *On nature*.[75] But we do not yet seem to have enough material to fill book XIII. Since weather signs, thunder, earthquakes and the like have an obvious importance to a section of the treatise in which Epicurus is debunking divine explanations of cosmic phenomena, we might well expect some treatment of them in this book. As we shall see next, in book XIV Epicurus will be making a completely new beginning, and unless the atmospheric phenomena are fitted into book XIII they likely to fall out altogether.[76] Tentatively therefore (hence the square brackets) I suggest the following completion for book XIII:

BOOK XIII
(xxxiv) the correct attitude to divinity;
[(xxxv) atmospheric and terrestrial phenomena.]

10. BOOKS XIV–XV

We have already seen in §3 that books XIV and XV constituted a pair. The closing stretch of XIV, of which substantial parts are decipherable in the papyrus, is undoubtedly polemical, and there is every reason to believe that the criticism of rival theories of the elements was the unifying theme of the two books. The scholion on *Letter to Herodotus* 40 tells us that item (vi), 'of bodies, some are compounds, others the constituents of those compounds', recurred in books XIV and XV, as indeed it would have done if Epicurus was here returning to the theme of the primary bodily elements in order to demonstrate the superiority of his own theory to the rival ones. This critique is not covered in either of our surviving epitomes – the *Letter to Herodotus* and the *Letter to Pythocles* – but we know from Diogenes Laertius (x 27) that there was a further epitome, now lost, the *Epitome of criticisms of the physicists* (Ἐπιτομὴ τῶν πρὸς τοὺς φυσικούς). It was presumably a summary of books XIV and XV.

Working backwards once again, the first thing to observe is that the wretchedly thin fragments of book XV strongly suggest that it contained

---

[75] The use of separate but occasionally overlapping texts would be an easy way to explain the oddity (cf. Arrighetti (1973), pp. 691ff.) that weather signs are treated twice in widely separated pasages (*Ep. Pyth.* 98–9, 115–16), as well as the surprising return to astronomy at 111–15 after a section (99–111) on atmospheric and terrestrial phenomena.

[76] We could, of course, try to squeeze the atmospheric phenomena in with (xxxi), the astronomical phenomena in book XII. But this would leave a surprising imbalance between the contents of books XII and XIII.

an extended critique of Anaxagoras.[77] Along with two critical references to 'those who have developed physical systems' (οἱ περὶ φύσεως πραγματευόμενοι or πεπραγματευμένοι),[78] forms or cognates of the word *homoiomereia* occur two or three times.[79] This latter was the term which thanks to the influence of Aristotle and Theophrastus came to be standardly attached to his theory of elements, although it was almost certainly not used by Anaxagoras himself. And we know that the Epicureans took up this usage.[80] Two further signs that Anaxagoras may be the target throughout are as follows.[81]

(a) The possible reference to atomic rearrangement (τὴν πα[ραλ]λαγὴ[ν] τῶν ἀ[τ]όμων) in fr. 14 of the book is, in such a context, reminiscent of Lucretius' argument against Anaxagoras at 1 897–914, that phenomena like combustion through friction are better explained by atomic rearrangement than by the Anaxagorean principle that there is a portion of everything in everything (see Ch. 7, §2).

(b) Anaxagoras' Principle of Predominance (B12 DK) ran as follows:

ἀλλ᾽ ὅτων πλεῖστα ἔνι, ταῦτα ἐνδηλότατα ἓν ἕκαστόν ἐστι καὶ ἦν.

But what each single thing most evidently was and is is whatever it has a majority of in it.

Each stuff, that is, despite containing portions of everything, has the phenomenal character of whatever ingredient in it exceeds the others. Or, as Lucretius puts it in his own corresponding critique, *sed illud | apparere unum cuius sint plurima mixta . . .*: 'But only that single thing is apparent which is present as a majority in the mixture . . .' (1 877–8). This same dictum of Anaxagoras is surely what underlies Epicurus' words in fr. 11 of book xv:[82]

---

[77] Millot (1977) properly notes some of the Anaxagorean allusions (pp. 28–9), although she does not draw any conclusions from them about the overall content of the book (p. 14).

[78] Forms of this expression clearly underlie frr. 24 and Q in Millot (1977).

[79] Frr. 7 and 25, and perhaps fr. 23 in Millot (1977).

[80] Cf. Diogenes of Oenoanda 6 II 4–7 Smith, quoted above p. 74; Lucretius I 830ff. (cf. above p. 48), with Rösler (1973).

[81] In addition, fr. 34 is about misconceiving the divine nature. It is not impossible (I can put it no stronger) that there is some allusion here to the charge of impiety that was brought against Anaxagoras at Athens for implicitly denying the divinity of the sun.

[82] The basis of what I am suggesting is already to be found in Millot (1977), pp. 17 and 29. What I have added, apart from trivial changes of punctuation, is (a) a suggested change of the final word from ὁμοιομε[ρῶν to ὁμοιομε[ρειῶν, in conformity to what seems to be the normal Epicurean representation of the Anaxagorean theory (cf. the references in n. 79 above); (b) a translation. I assume the subject and main verb carried over from the preceding sentence to be e.g. ἑκάστη οὐσία . . . νομίζεται.

καθ᾽ ὃ γὰρ [πρ]οϲαγορεύεται, ὅτι δῆ[λον, εἶ]ναι κατ᾽ ἐκε[ῖ]νο ἐκ τῶν [π]λείϲτων τῶν[δ]ὲ τινων [πε]ποιη[μ]ένη, ἐξ ὁμοιομε[ρειῶν . . .

For [it is claimed that] the respect in which it is spoken of – because it is evident – is the respect according to which it is made out of a majority of such and such things, namely the homoiomeries . . .

I conclude that book xv probably contained an extended critique of Anaxagoras.

The final columns (XXXIX–XLIII) of book XIV seem to have been devoted to an obscure critique of certain forms of eclecticism in physics. The critique may have been sparked by Plato's combination of Empedoclean and Pythagorean principles in his theory of elements, because prior to this last section Epicurus has been criticising in some detail the theory of elements in Plato's *Timaeus* (columns XXXIV–XXXIX). It is much less clear what preceded this in book XIV. Giuliana Leone, the modern editor of the book, notes an allusion to an argument for monism in col. XXXIII, and proposes that the critique switches from monism to pluralism immediately after that.[83] This is of course possible, but it would threaten to limit the critical content to a small fraction of the entire book. This is the book, remember, which we actually know to have been a massive 22,000 words long (see §4). Our assumption of thematic unity for books XIV–XV suggests that the surviving sections formed part of a more extended critique, filling most of the book (albeit, no doubt, after some methodological preliminaries).

Where does this leave us regarding the overall structure of XIV–XV? The relatively clear fact that the series of critiques dealt with Anaxagoras last is important, because it suggests that Epicurus is already organising physical theories along the lines set down by Aristotle (cf. *Phys.* 1 2, 184b15ff.) and Theophrastus:[84] first monism (Thales and co.), then finite pluralism (Empedocles and co.), and finally infinite pluralism (notably Anaxagoras) – the same sequence later adopted by Lucretius (1 635–920) and Diogenes of Oenoanda.[85] I shall be arguing later (Chs. 5 and 6) that Theophrastus' *Physical opinions* was a major source for Epicurus in *On nature*. It is also worth repeating that the Epicurean reading of Anaxagoras as the proponent of *homoiomereia*, which can now be traced back to *On nature* xv, is itself likely to reflect a considerable degree of

---

[83] Leone (1984), p. 34.   [84] See Mansfeld (1989), pp. 138–48.
[85] 6 1 10–11 9 Smith (1992), quoted p. 74 above.

dependence on Theophrastean doxography, rather than on Anaxagoras' unmediated text.[86]

Accepting provisionally that such an ordering controlled the sequence of topics in XIV–XV, the obvious guess to make is that XIV covered the monists and finite pluralists, ending with Plato (who, significantly, seems to have been the latest philosopher covered by Theophrastus' doxography), while XV was devoted to Anaxagoras. If this seems to allot too much space to Anaxagoras, we can remind ourselves that at the end of XIV Epicurus is locked into a methodological critique concerned with physical eclecticism: it may be that the early part of XV continued to investigate related methodological issues, before turning to Anaxagoras. Or, if Plato is there being accused of mixing Empedoclean elements with Pythagorean first principles, another possibility is that the first part of XV dealt with Pythagorean physics, which seems itself to have been classed, like Anaxagoras' theory, as a species of infinite pluralism.[87] I mention these possibilities merely in order to show that there is no obstacle in principle to our filling at least the bulk of books XIV and XV with the following sequence:

BOOK XIV
(xxxvi)   critique of monism;
(xxxvii)   critique of finite pluralism.
BOOK XV
(xxxviii) critique of Anaxagoras.

II. BOOKS XVI–XXXVII

From the later part of the treatise, we have substantial papyrus fragments of books XXV and XXVIII, and three skimpy citations – one of book XXXII, one of book XXXIV, and a third of a book somewhere in the thirties.[88]

Book XXV,[89] which survives in three parallel copies, is about psycho-

---

[86] See Schofield (1975).

[87] SE *PH* III 32. The alternative possibility that Democritus was the infinite pluralist criticised in the early part of *Nat.* XV is scarcely worth considering. Epicurus saw his own physics as a corrected Democriteanism (cf. Plut. *Col.* 1108E–F), and his view is undoubtedly reflected in Diogenes of Oenoanda's critique of the physicists, where Democritus is separated from the regular Theophrastean list of predecessors and reserved for criticism in the course of the exposition of Epicurean atomism (6 II 9 – III 1 Smith).

[88] A possible reference to book XVI in P.Herc. 558, 11.4–5, noted by Obbink (1996), p. 305, is better ignored for present purposes. The reconstruction of Crönert (1975), p. 149, ἐν δὲ τῶι ἑ]κκα[ι]δε[κάτωι is highly conjectural, and since the context seems to be a history of Socrates and/or Plato the reference would in any case probably not be to *On nature*.

[89] The number of the book was first recovered by Laursen (1987); it was previously *liber incertus*. There has been no complete edition of it since the one in Diano (1946), whose textual informa-

logical development, with a good deal of emphasis on the causal efficacy of the self and our capacity to choose what we become. It includes – miraculously preserved almost intact – a brilliant argument against determinism.[90] At the end of the book, Epicurus' résumé informs us that he has now given his exposition in two modes, the first in terms of feelings (the παθολογικὸς τρόπος), the second in terms of causes (the αἰτιολογικὸς τρόπος).

Now there is an old puzzle about when, where and how Epicurus arrived at his doctrine of the atomic swerve – the third principle of motion alongside impacts and weight, introduced to rescue us from the tyranny of physical determinism. Since this doctrine does not show up in the *Letter to Herodotus*, which we have now seen to cover only books I–XIII of *On nature*, there is a strong possibility that it was first developed in a later book of the treatise, where Epicurus had turned his attention to the problem of determinism. If so, we may guess that this was in book XXV or a neighbouring book. There is no reference to the swerve in the fragments of book XXV, but because these only represent the later part of it, perhaps the last third, and are anyway far from complete, we must be extremely cautious of any argument from silence. Since the swerve does occur in Lucretius' exposition, we will need to bear this book, or group of books, in mind in the next chapter, when considering his sources.

Book XXVIII is about language and other areas of epistemology – re-examining, as we have seen (§5), the former views of both Epicurus himself and Metrodorus. Book XXXII is cited in an unassigned Herculaneum fragment[91] as containing a brief definition of 'soul', summing up Epicurus' previous theorising about it. Book XXXIV is cited

---

tion was seriously inadequate, but who did at least print all three papyri alongside each other. Arrighetti (1973) prints as fr. 34 a combined text which proceeds by alternating between the three papyri as reported by Diano; it should be used with caution, since frequently letters which he prints in square brackets are in fact attested in one or both of the other papyri. For the earliest preserved part of the book we now have the excellent edition of Laursen (1995). Of the remainder, while we await Laursen's full edition, some parts must be read in Sedley (1983) and Long/Sedley (1987), §20 (with corrections in Laursen (1988)), others in Laursen (1992). It is to Laursen, and also to Puglia (1987), that we owe the identification of additional sections of papyrus as belonging to the same three rolls (P.Herc. 697, 1056, 1191) that provide the three parallel texts: the numbers of these additional papyri are included in the list I give on p. 98 above.

[90] For this passage, see above Ch. 3, §8. That the book is about psychological development is broadly agreed by Sedley (1983), p. 17, and Laursen (1995), p. 42, who there seems no longer to be pressing his suggestion in Laursen (1992), p. 153, that its theme was, more specifically, whether virtue can be taught.

[91] [32 Arr.²]; but see Sedley (1974), p. 89 n. 9 for a correction of the text: the word καί should be added before the book citation, ἐν τῶι β′ καὶ λ′.

for something said there about giving a criterion for things non-evident.[92] Finally, there is an indication in a barely decipherable passage of Philodemus, *De pietate* that in book thirty-something – probably xxxv[93] – Epicurus clarified some unspecified kind of 'benefiting' (ὠφέλεια) – apparently meaning some way in which the right attitude to the gods is beneficial to mankind.

This is far too little evidence to permit any conjecture regarding the overall structure of books XVI–XXXVII. The paucity of citations suggests that this later part of the treatise dealt largely with peripheral questions, and was not so widely studied. The one clear exception is book XXV, whose survival in triplicate implies, as we saw in §3, that it was highly valued in the Epicurean community. This impression is further confirmed by the fact that one of its arguments, the self-refutation argument against determinism, was picked out for summary in the collection of Epicurean sayings which have come down to us as the *Gnomologium Vaticanum*.[94]

12. CHRONOLOGY

A work as long as *On nature* cannot be written overnight. But when, and over how long a period, was it written? We are very fortunate that the papyri of three books from it carry at the end, below their titles, the Athenian archon-year in which they were composed. Thus we have the following firm dates:[95]

[92] Text in Polyaenus fr. 27 Tepedino Guerra (1991), p. 91.
[93] [33 Arr.²] = Philodemus, *Piet.* 1055 9 Obbink; see Obbink (1996), p. 474 in defence of the reading ἐν δὲ τῶι πέ[μπτωι καὶ] τριακ[οσ]τῶ[ι.
[94] *SV* 40, which seems to be a non-technical summary of the self-refutation argument in *Nat.* XXV (= Long/Sedley (1987), 20c 5): see further, p. 88 above.
[95] I say this despite the important proposal of Obbink (1996), pp. 351 2, that these *subscriptiones* give the dates of Epicurus' later redaction of the books in question, not that of original composition. He argues that the *subscriptio* to book XXVIII,

Ἐπ[ικ]ούρου
Περὶ φύσεως
κη′
ἐκ] τῶν ἀρχαίων [

ἐγ[ρ]άφη ἐπὶ Νικίου τοῦ μ[ετ]ὰ Ἀν[τι]φάτην
means, not that book XXVIII was *composed* in that archonship for which, he suggests, we should have expected συνεγράφη but that this was when it was copied into its present edited form, 'from the old exemplars', implying that a text had already existed for some time. I have several grounds for disagreement. (a) The dates of books XIV, XV and XXVIII (see immediately below) are ordered and spaced out in a way which fits the relatively laborious composition of a work much better than that of its editing. (b) Epicurus' own usual word for 'composing' a work *is* γράφειν (*Ep. Pyth.* 84, 85) or ἀναγράφειν (above pp. 100 1), but not συγγράφειν. (c) Even if we were to

book xiv: archonship of Clearchus = 301/300 BC;[96]
book xv: archonship of Hegemachus = 300/299 BC;[97]
book xxviii: archonship of Nicias 'the successor of Antiphates' = 296/295 B C.[98]

It is tempting to calculate as follows. Epicurus' production rate in the period 301–295 was two-and-a-half books a year. By projecting this onto the remainder of the work, we find that he started it in 306/305, soon after his move to Athens, and reached book xxxvii in 293 or 292.

But the temptation deserves to be resisted. During those fourteen or fifteen years Epicurus must have been composing many other works, towards his lifetime total of 300 volumes.[99] There is no possible reason to imagine that during this time the individual books of *On nature* were spaced out at regular intervals, like issues of a quarterly journal.

As a matter of fact, there is quite good reason to see the treatise as having been composed in two or more widely separated phases. I believe that the first phase, books i–xiii, belongs to his period spent teaching at Mytilene and Lampsacus, from 311/310 until 307/306, the year in which he moved to Athens and founded the Garden.[100] I offer three considerations in support of this.

The first piece of evidence for such a dating is negative. While three of the books datable after Epicurus' move to Athens carry, as we have seen, an Athenian archon-year, no archon-year has yet been found on

agree with Obbink (who does not quote evidence) that the parallel of other ancient *subscriptiones* confirms that those in *Nat.* should be expected to 'record information regarding copying, redaction, and correction, and thus date the work of a scribe or διορθωτής (possibly the publication of a particular version)', that would still give us no reason to infer that our texts are a hypothetical *second* version, rather than the original lecture version (which itself had quite possibly been preceded by a working draft). (d) This *subscriptio* probably also featured as a *superscriptio* at the beginning of the book, and the assumption that the date given is that of the original composition and delivery of the lecture thus finds some confirmation in the formula ἐδιδάχθη ἐπί (plus archon name) in the prefaces to Aristophanes' plays. (e) Even if the fourth line is to be construed as '[from] the old exemplars' (and I have proposed an alternative, which Obbink acknowledges, see n. 33, p. 105 above), it is certainly not to be construed grammatically with ἐγράφη, there being a substantial space between them (see Cavallo (1983), p. 59). (f) The Epicureans were scrupulous about recording the archon-dates of individual letters by Epicurus and his colleagues (see below), and these unambiguously refer to the original date of composition, not to that of some later edition of the letters. (Obbink, pp. 430–1, 450–1, is unlikely to be right that these dates were imposed on the letters only by later Epicureans: where would they have got the information from, unless the dates were already recorded on or with the letters? The fact that private letters from Egypt are usually undated is irrelevant to what was clearly an institutionalised Epicurean school practice.)

[96] This date was first deciphered by Leone (1984), see esp. pp. 37–8.
[97] Millot (1977), p. 26.   [98] Sedley (1973), p. 56.   [99] DL x 26.
[100] That some books of *Nat.* predate the move to Athens was already proposed by Bignone (1936), i 664 n. 130, ii 419 n. 16.

any of the four papyri from books II and XI. We may reasonably assume that the practice of dating his books by their Athenian archon-year began only when Epicurus moved to Athens. Although many such Epicurean datings survive in the writings of Philodemus and elsewhere, with individual letters written by the school's first generation regularly assigned an Athenian archon-year, *no* such dating has yet proved to be earlier than 307/306, when the Athens school was founded. Indeed, the first recorded archon-year in Epicurean history is that of Epicurus' foundation of the Athens school.[101]

The second piece of evidence for the dating is positive in character.[102] In §5 we met a passage of book XI in which Epicurus challenges mathematical astronomy: 'Why, after all, should you make the measurement from here, or the measurement from here, or the one from here, or this one, a more reliable measurement of risings or settings?' The evidence which he has adduced in the immediately preceding lines is as follows:

. . .] ἀνατέλλων, ἀνατείνοντες εἰς τὸ μέρος τῆς πάσης γῆς, οὗ μετέβημεν ἐκ τούτου ἡμῖν δυόμενος φαίνεται, οὐδὲ πολλὴν ἐνίοτε πάνυ γῆν με[ταβ]εβηκόσιν.

[The sun, if we walk towards the place from which it appeared to us] to rise, directing ourselves up into the mainland zone, appears to us to set where we previously passed by, sometimes even when we have not passed all that much ground.

Evidently he is describing the experience of walking eastwards at the time of sunset. You look back westwards at the sun, and it appears to be setting at a place where you were standing shortly earlier. (Virtually the identical phenomenon is described at Lucretius IV 404–13.) It follows, in Epicurus' view, that our terrestrial vantage points are useless for the objective tracking and measuring of a celestial orbit.

But there is something very odd about his description of walking eastwards: εἰς τὸ μέρος τῆς πάσης γῆς, which I have translated as 'into the mainland zone', means literally 'into the zone of total land'. If Epicurus were writing at Athens, that would be a highly misleading description of the narrow Attic peninsula to the east. It would be equally inappropriate to the island of Mytilene, where Epicurus taught briefly in 311/310.

[101] DL x 2. For the full set of Epicurean archon dates, see Dorandi (1990); also Dorandi (1991), pp. 62–3.

[102] I summarise here the argument which I presented briefly in Sedley (1976a), pp. 139–43, and fully in Sedley (1976b), pp. 31–6

But it does perfectly fit Lampsacus, on the Asian mainland, where Epicurus spent four years of his teaching career before the move to Athens. In an Asian context the prefix ἀνα- (as in Xenophon's *Anabasis*) standardly means 'in the direction of central Asia', and the unusual compound ἀνατείνοντες may well carry that sense. As for 'into the zone of total land', I know no exact parallels, but it does seem a highly appropriate expression for the Asian mainland, because in Thucydides VIII 46.3 the mainland of Asia is contrasted with 'the zone of the sea' (τὸ μέρος τῆς θαλάσσης), meaning the whole Aegean zone to the west.[103]

It looks, then, as if when book XI was being written Epicurus and his audience were living on the mainland of Asia,[104] in fact in the Epicurean school at Lampsacus. Given that books XI–XIII seem to form a closely linked group, we can be fairly confident that the entire series I–XIII was complete by the time Epicurus moved to Athens in 307/306. By then he had completed the exposition of his own cosmology, and it is not particularly surprising that he should have called a halt there, deciding only after an interval of six or more years to extend the work with a systematic refutation of rival theories of the elements in books XIV and XV. Before that resumption, which started in 301/300 BC, he may well have been fully occupied with other matters, such as the task of setting up the Athenian school.

A third, subsidiary argument for this chronology can now be added. The *Letter to Herodotus*, although purporting to epitomise *On nature*, in fact covers only books I–XIII, suggesting that at the time of its composition these books may have been the sum total of it. That already suggests a date before 301/300, when book XIV was written. But we can go further. The *Letter to Herodotus* can be argued on independent grounds to have 304 BC as its *terminus ante quem*: this is because it must predate the *Letter to Pythocles*, which refers to it (85), and Pythocles' biography makes it hard to date the letter to him later than 304.[105] If that is correct, books I–XIII were completed at least three years before the composition of book XIV.

---

[103] As I report in Sedley (1976b), p. 36, a detailed contour map of Lapseki (the modern site of Lampsacus) confirms that there is a path leading due east from the town, along which the western horizon would often be very close, sometimes less than 500 metres from the observer. So we can be confident that the phenomenon which Epicurus describes would be observable there.

[104] The present tense does not sit comfortably with the alternative possibility, suggested by Erler (1994), p. 97, that Epicurus might be *recalling* an observation taken at Lampsacus earlier in his career.

[105] For a defence of this chronology, along with a biography of Pythocles, see Sedley (1976b), esp. pp. 45–6.

This does not yet quite force them back into the Lampsacus period, but it is a strong further pointer in that same direction, since it confirms the existence of a substantial chronological break between books XIII and XIV.

13. CONCLUSIONS

On nature was a published lecture course in thirty-seven instalments. Books I–XIII were written in the period 311/310–307/306 BC, while Epicurus was teaching at Lampsacus, and the remainder was written at Athens. Books XIV and XV were written in 301/300 and 300/299 BC respectively. Book XXVIII was written in 296/295 BC. The dates of the remaining books are a matter of pure conjecture.

As a series of lectures delivered within the school, *On nature* was characterised by an expansiveness and an informality which gave it a very special place in the affections of Epicurus' followers. Certain books were especially highly prized, studied and quoted. These included I–II, XI–XV, and XXV.

The probable sequence of contents of books I–XV can be given in outline as shown in Chart I (the references in brackets are to the corresponding passages from Epicurus' epitomes (*Letter to Herodotus, Letter to Pythocles*, and the lost *Epitome of criticisms of the physicists*; page and line numbers refer to the Teubner text by P. von der Muehll).

Chart 1

Nat.			Epitomes
I	(i)	methodological preliminaries	*Hdt.* 37–8 (4.9–5.2)
	(ii)	nothing comes into being out of nothing	*Hdt.* 38 (5.2–3)
	(iii)	nothing perishes into nothing	*Hdt.* 39 (5.4–5)
	(iv)	the all never changes	*Hdt.* 39 (5.5–9)
	(v)	the all consists of bodies and void	*Hdt.* 39–40 (5.10–17)
	(vi)	some bodies are compounds, others constituents	
II	(vii)	nothing exists independently except bodies and void	*Hdt.* 40 (5.17–6.2)
	(viii)	bodies' constituents (distinguished in (vi)) are atomic	*Hdt.* 40–1 (6.3–10)
	(ix)	the all is infinite	*Hdt.* 41–2 (6.11–20)
	(x)	unimaginably, not infinitely, many atomic shapes	*Hdt.* 42–3 (6.21–7.8)
	(xi)	atoms are in perpetual motion	*Hdt.* 43–4 (7.9–8.2)
	(xii)	there are infinitely many worlds	*Hdt.* 45 (8.10–16)
	(xiii)	existence and mobility of images	*Hdt.* 46–8 (8.17–10.8)
III–IV	(xiv)	vision, visualisation, truth and falsity	*Hdt.* 49–52 (10.9–11.20)
	(xv)	the other senses	*Hdt.* 52–3 (12.1–20)
	(xvi)	thought	
V	(xvii)	atoms lack secondary qualities	*Hdt.* 54–5 (12.21–13.14)
	(xviii)	atomic dimensions	*Hdt.* 55–9 (13.15–15.16)
	(xix)	up and down	*Hdt.* 60 (15.17–16.5)
	(xx)	equal speed of atoms	*Hdt.* 61–2 (16.6–17.4)
VI–	(xxi)	nature of the soul	*Hdt.* 63–5 (17.5–18.10)
VIII	(xxii)	mortality of the soul	*Hdt.* 65–6 (18.10–16)
IX	(xxiii)	soul is not incorporeal	*Hdt.* 66–7 (18.16–19.12)
X	(xxiv)	metaphysics of properties and time	*Hdt.* 68–73 (19.16–21.21)
XI	(xxv)	origin of our world	*Pyth.* 88–90 (29.7–30.7)
	(xxvi)	origin of heavenly bodies	*Pyth.* 90 (30.8–14)
	(xxvii)	size of heavenly bodies	*Pyth.* 91 (30.14–31.6)
	(xxviii)	motions of heavenly bodies	*Pyth.* 92–3 (31.6–32.2)
	(xxix)	attack on astronomical devices	*Pyth.* 93 (32.2–7)
	(xxx)	stability of the earth	
XII	(xxxi)	further astronomical phenomena	*Pyth.* 94–8 (32.8–34.12)
	(xxxii)	other worlds	*Hdt.* 73–4 (21.24–22.18)
	(xxxiii)	origins of civilisation	*Hdt.* 75–6 (23.1–17)
XIII	(xxxiv)	the correct attitude to divinity	*Hdt.* 76–82 (23.18–26.18)
	[(xxxv)	atmospheric and terrestrial phenomena]	*Pyth.* 98–110 (34.13–40.15)
XIV	(xxxvi)	critique of monism	⎫ *Epitome of*
	(xxxvii)	critique of finite pluralism	⎬ *criticisms of the*
XV	(xxxviii)	critique of Anaxagoras	⎭ *physicists*

CHAPTER 5

Lucretius' plan and its execution

I. THE THESIS

In Chapter 3, I built my case for regarding Lucretius as an Epicurean
fundamentalist, feeding directly on the writings of his school's founder,
and uninterested in pursuing the history of philosophy beyond the
zenith which Epicurus himself represented. In Chapter 4, I have put
together a dossier on Epicurus' major physical treatise, *On nature*, seeking
to understand why it was at once the most demanding and the most
valued of all Epicurus' texts. Drawing on these findings, the present
chapter will defend the following account of Lucretius' procedure when
composing the *De rerum natura*.

Lucretius' sole Epicurean source, I shall argue, was Epicurus' *On
nature*, and, of that, mainly the first fifteen of its thirty-seven books.
Initially he followed its sequence of topics very closely, indeed almost
mechanically. But to some extent as he proceeded, and to a greater
extent during a phase of rewriting, he developed a radically revised
structure for the whole. At his death, the reorganisation of *DRN* I–III was
(so far as I can judge) complete. For books IV–VI, however, he had plans
which can still to some extent be discerned from his proems, but which
he did not live to put into operation.

The Lucretian material of which I am speaking is the physical exposition in the main body of all six books. I am assuming the remainder to
be his own original compositions – I mean in particular the proems, the
poetic manifesto at I 921–50 (and IV 1–25), at least the bulk of the *magna
mater* passage (II 600–60), the ethical diatribes which close books III and
IV, and the concluding account of the Athenian plague, of which I shall
have something to say at the end of this chapter.

Even in the central physical exposition, on which I shall be concentrating, it is no part of my intention to minimise Lucretius' original
contribution. Quite apart from his numerous distinctively poetic

134

achievements, no one need doubt for a moment that he has done much to develop, illustrate, expand and sharpen the arguments as he found them. My contention concerns the bare bones of the exposition. I shall maintain that these were lifted, more or less in their entirety, from *On nature* books I–XV.

Recovering this process of composition requires a good deal of effort and patience. But Lucretius' creative achievement in structuring his poem as we know it can only be appreciated when we see what material he started with, how he set about the task of reshaping it, and what further plans may have remained unfulfilled at his death.

2. LUCRETIUS' SOURCE

It used to be widely debated whether Lucretius' source text was Epicurus' *On nature*, his *Letter to Herodotus*, his *Great epitome*, or some combination of these, or, alternatively, whether he relied on more recent Epicurean writings.[1] Lately these questions about sources have fallen into the background, no doubt to the relief of many. There are even those, like Diskin Clay, who maintain that Lucretius worked directly from no source at all:[2]

There is suggestive, if not probative, evidence that Lucretius finally depended on no written text or texts for the philosophy he expounded in *De rerum natura*. He made Epicurus' philosophy his own and his preservitude to this thought seems to have made him free of any slavish attachment to a handbook survey of Epicurus' physiology. Epicureanism involved both a period of service to the true philosophy and an ultimate freedom.

As a picture of Epicurean education this portrayal has its attractions. But I do not see how it can be correct in Lucretius' own case. One half of my reply to it lies in Chapter 3, where I argued that Lucretius is demonstrably dependent on Epicurus' own writings, unmediated either by more recent philosophical developments or by training in an Epicurean school. The other half lies in the comparison, on which this chapter will be focused, between the structure of Lucretius' poem and that of *On nature*. The data which I shall present seem to me intelligible only if Lucretius is taken to be working directly from a text of Epicurus.

---

[1] For surveys of these views, see Schmidt (1990), pp. 12–23, and, more selective, Erler (1994), pp. 414–16. Schmidt in particular defends the view that more recent Epicurean writings play a large part – a thesis originating largely from Lück (1932).

[2] Clay (1983), p. 31. For Clay's arguments against *On nature* as source, see *ib.* pp. 18–19.

Chart 2

Nat.			DRN
I	(i)	methodological preliminaries	
	(ii)	nothing comes into being out of nothing	I 149–214
	(iii)	nothing perishes into nothing	I 215–264
	(iv)	the all never changes	
		(L1) *the existence of the invisible*	I 265–328
		(L2) *the existence of void*	I 329–417
	(v)	the all consists of bodies and void	I 418–29
	(vi)	some bodies are compounds, others constituents	—
II	(vii)	nothing exists independently except bodies and void	I 430–82
	(viii)	bodies' constituents (distinguished in (vi)) are atomic	I 483–634
			I 635–920
	(ix)	the all is infinite	I 951–1051
		(L3) *critique of geocentric cosmology*	I 1052–1113
	(x)	unimaginably, not infinitely, many atomic shapes	(II 333–580)
	(xi)	atoms are in perpetual motion	II 62–215
		(L4) *the swerve of atoms*	II 216–93
		(L5) *more on motion*	II 294–332
			II 333–580
		(L6) *compounds*	II 581–729
			II 730–990
	(xii)	there are infinitely many worlds.	II 1023–1174
	(xiii)	existence and mobility of images	(IV 26–238)
III–IV	(xiv)	vision, truth and falsity	(IV 239–468)
		(L7) *refutation of scepticism*	(IV 469–521)
	(xv)	the other senses	(IV 522–721)
	(xvi)	thought	(IV 722–822)
		(L8) *critique of biological teleology*	(IV 823–57)
		(L9) *nutrition, motion, sleep, dreams, sex*	(IV 858–1287)
V	(xvii)	atoms lack secondary qualities	(II 730–990)
	(xviii)	atomic dimensions	—
	(xix)	up and down	—
	(xx)	equal speed of atoms	—
VI–	(xxi)	nature of the soul	III 94–416
VIII	(xxii)	mortality of the soul	III 417–1094
IX	(xxiii)	soul is not incorporeal	—
			IV 26–1287
X	(xxiv)	metaphysics of properties and time	
XI		(L10) *mortality of our world*	V 55–415
	(xxv)	origin of our world	V 416–508
	(xxvi)	origin of heavenly bodies	—
	(xxvii)	size of heavenly bodies	(V 564–613)
	(xxviii)	motions of heavenly bodies	V 509–33
	(xxix)	attack on astronomical devices	—
	(xxx)	stability of the earth	V 534–63
			V 564–613
XII	(xxxi)	further astronomical phenomena	V 614–770
	(xxxii)	other worlds	—
	(xxxiii)	origins of civilisation	V 771–1457
XIII	(xxxiv)	the correct attitude to divinity	VI 50–91
	[(xxxv)	atmospheric and terrestrial phenomena]	VI 96–1286
XIV	(xxxvi)	critique of monism	(I 635–711)
	(xxxvii)	critique of finite pluralism	(I 712–829)
XV	(xxxviii)	critique of Anaxagoras	(I 830–920)

But which text? While it is quite understandable that Lucretian scholars should have got bored with Quellenforschung, it is surprising that no Lucretian scholar has set out to reopen the question of Lucretius' source materials in the light of our constantly improving range of evidence on Epicurus' *On nature*. Even while I was completing this book, valuable new data on the contents of *On nature* were continuing to appear in print.[3] As the fruits of Chapter 4, we now have before us a reconstructed table of contents for *On nature* books I–xv (Chart 1, p. 133 above). Our next move must be to place this table of contents alongside that of the *De rerum natura*. I shall be referring to Chart 2 (p. 136) repeatedly in the remainder of this chapter: please insert a bookmark.

The analysis of *On nature* I–xv combines the data gathered in Chapter 4. On the right, I show how the sequence of topics in the *DRN* matches up with it. Wherever Lucretius includes a topic which we have not so far located in *On nature*, I have added this in the second column, marked '(L1)', '(L2)' etc. There are ten such additions.[4] Where Lucretius includes a topic which we have located in *On nature*, but in a different position in the sequence, I have signalled this with an arrow.

Despite these disparities, it leaps to the eye that there is an extensive and non-accidental correspondence between the sequence of topics in *On nature* and that in the *DRN*. Lucretius includes some topics not found in the *Letter to Herodotus*, and the Letter includes some topics not found in Lucretius, but that need reflect no more than two partly different policies used in excerpting material derived (directly or indirectly) from *On nature*.

Moreover – and this is of the utmost importance – one of the disparities of sequence can be shown to depend on a transposition which Lucretius himself made during the writing of the poem, after having initially followed the exact order found in *On nature*. As we saw in Chapter 2, §4, the proem to book IV preserves, side by side, two alternative programmatic passages. The later of the two (26–44) was written when the book was expected to follow what we now call book III, on the soul and its mortality. The earlier version (45–53), accidentally left in during the process of editing, preserves an earlier plan in which the book followed directly after book II.[5] Thus originally Lucretius took items (xii) and (xiii)

---

[3] In Dirk Obbink's magisterial new edition of Philodemus, *On piety* (Obbink (1996)).

[4] I have excluded non-expository passages, such as the proem and the poetic manifesto at I 921–50.

[5] This was long ago shown by Mewaldt (1908), and has been widely accepted. Of later discussions critical of Mewaldt, see esp. Pizzani (1959), pp. 157–67, and Gale (1994b), pp. 4–5. But their strongest objection, that book IV assumes some knowledge of book III, is not decisive. It may simply

in their original sequence from *On nature* II, so that *DRN* IV's topic — images, perception and other soul and body functions — followed directly after that of the multiplicity (and impermanence) of worlds at the end of book II. It was only after he had begun drafting that sequence that Lucretius decided to postpone perception and related topics until after what is now called book III, on the soul and its mortality. Given, then, that one of the arrowed transpositions is demonstrably Lucretius' own, there is a serious possibility that the others were also made by him during the process of writing.

In the case we have just examined, Lucretius' original sequence — (xii), (xiii) — was identical to that in *On nature* II, and also, consequently, to that in *Letter to Herodotus* 45–6. In principle, then, he could be following either of these texts,[6] or indeed some third, unknown text which took over the same sequence. The favourite candidate for this unknown text has long been the *Great epitome* (Μεγάλη ἐπιτομή),[7] a work of which we know only because it is cited three times in the scholia on the *Letter to Herodotus*. Before proceeding further, it will be best for me explain why I believe that *On nature* is itself the unmediated source.

The hypothesis that the *Letter to Herodotus* may have been Lucretius' primary source offers few attractions. It is certainly not enough to pick out the occasional phrase from it which Lucretius can be said to have directly translated, since there need be little doubt that any such phrase occurred in *On nature* too.[8] The hypothesis must of course assume that Lucretius supplemented the Letter with a great deal of other Epicurean material. But it is not easy for its proponents to explain why Lucretius should have so closely matched the sequence of *On nature* even at points where the Letter offered no guidance. For example, a look at Chart 2 will

show that Lucretius became aware during the course of writing book IV that he would eventually need to transpose it — see p. 150 below. And the findings of Ch. 2, §4, where we saw how the first version contained a translation of technical terminology alien to Lucretius' eventual method, lend new confirmation to Mewaldt's conclusion that this represents an early draft of the poem. In defence of Mewaldt against the alternative proposal of Drexler (1935) that Lucretius' change of mind was the other way round — to move book IV *to* a position after book II — see Ferrari (1937).

[6] Those who have supported *On nature* as primary source include Mewaldt (1908), von der Muehll (1922), pp. III–IV, Boyancé (1963), pp. 53–6, and Arrighetti (1973). The case for the *Letter to Herodotus* as primary source, whose groundwork was laid by Woltjer (1877) and Brieger (1882), has most recently been urged by Fowler (1996). Cf. also Asmis (1983), on which see n. 5, p. 193 below.

[7] That the *Great epitome* is Lucretius' main source was the proposal of Giussani (1896–8), 11–11.

[8] E.g. Bailey (1947), 1 25: 'as will be seen from time to time in the commentary, his relation to it [the *Letter to Herodotus*] is so close that it is almost impossible to resist the conclusion that he was translating it' (although Bailey does not make it Lucretius' *primary* source). For an effective reply to this inference, see Boyancé (1963), p. 55 n. 1.

show that he largely preserves the order of topics in *On nature* XI–XII, despite the fact that neither the *Letter to Herodotus* nor, for that matter, the *Letter to Pythocles* could have offered sufficient reason to do so. Neither letter includes item (xxx), yet Lucretius has preserved its original place in the sequence, as the final columns of *On nature* XI confirm.

Stronger evidence against the *Letter to Herodotus* as source is forthcoming from the end of *On nature* II. This includes perhaps the one point in the surviving portions of the treatise which it is possible to correlate precisely with the corresponding lines of Lucretius. Discussing images, Epicurus marks his transition from the preceding topic of their speed of generation to that of their speed of travel as follows:[9]

περ[ὶ] δὲ τῆς κατὰ τὴν φορὰν ὑπαρχούσης ταχυτῆτ[ος] νῦν λέγειν ἐπιχ[ειρ]ήσομεν. πρῶτον μ[ὲ]ν γ[ὰρ] ἡ λεπτότης μακρὰν τῆς ἀπὸ τῶν αἰσθήσεων λεπτότητος ἀ[πέχου]σα, ταχυτῆτα τῶν εἰδώλων κατὰ τ[ὴν φορὰ]ν ἀνυπέρβ[λητον ἐ]νδείκνυται [. . . (*lacuna c. 35 words*) . . . ὑπερβαλλόν]τως κοῦφα· εἰ δ' [ὑ]περβαλλόντω[ς κοῦ]φα, δῆλον ὡς καὶ ὑπερβαλλόντως ταχεῖα κατὰ τὴν [φ]ορὰν.

Now we will try to speak about the speed which belongs to them in respect of their motion.

First, their fineness, which far exceeds the fineness revealed by the senses, indicates the images' unsurpassed speed of motion [. . . (*lacuna c. 35 words*) That fineness[10] makes them] exceedingly light, and if they are exceedingly light it is clear that they are exceedingly fast in respect of their motion.

The identical transition from the images' speed of generation to their speed of motion is made by Lucretius at IV 176ff., in lines which perfectly illustrate his talent for putting flesh on the bare bones supplied by Epicurus:

> nunc age, quam celeri motu simulacra ferantur
> et quae mobilitas ollis tranantibus auras
> reddita sit, longo spatio ut brevis hora teratur,
> in quem quaeque locum diverso numine tendunt,
> suavidicis potius quam multis versibus edam; 180

[9] 24.36 7 Arr.² = Vogliano (1953), p. 81, fr. E cols. IV v. Arrighetti indicates, p. 579, that his readings of this part of P.Herc. 1149 are drawn from previous editions, not from an autopsy. Yet, strangely, he reports a number of letters as missing or uncertain which in Vogliano's text appear certain — even some which show up clearly in the early nineteenth-century facsimiles. I have therefore, despite some puzzlement, reverted to Vogliano's report of the papyrus, which, fortunately, does not differ in its actual reconstruction of the text. This is one of the Herculaneum papyri of which we still await a truly modern edition, and it remains quite likely that the eventual text will prove to differ in some respect.

[10] Since the full proof of the images' fineness can hardly have been contained in the short lacuna, Epicurus must be relying on an earlier such proof, for whose location in the sequence see Ch. 4, §7.

> parvus ut est cycni melior canor, ille gruum quam
> clamor in aetheriis dispersus nubibus austri.
> principio persaepe levis res atque minutis
> corporibus factas celeris licet esse videre.
> in quo iam genere est solis lux et vapor eius . . . ·   185
>
> Come now, how fast is the motion with which the images travel,
> and what mobility they possess in swimming through the air, so
> that it takes them but a short time to go a long way, whatever
> direction they may be tending in with their varying inclination,
> I shall explain in sweet-speaking rather than numerous verses,
> just as the short song of the swan is better than that honking of
> cranes which spreads through the airy southern clouds.
>   First, you can often see that things made out of light and tiny
> particles are swift-moving. Among such things are the light and
> heat of the sun . . .

When these two passages are placed side by side, it looks entirely credible that we have before us the actual text from which Lucretius was
working. They both announce their *demonstrandum*, and proceed to their
first argument (πρῶτον μέν = *principio*)[11] in an almost identical manner.
Lucretius adds the swan comparison, declaring his determination to
brighten up the argument. And his diction – both when sketching the
demonstrandum itself and when elaborating the arguments to which he
now proceeds – may be judged to fulfil that promise. In the proem to III
Epicurus was, philosophically speaking, the swan, Lucretius a mere
swallow (see Ch. 2, §12). This time however, when it is the literary prizes
that are being handed out, Lucretius casts himself as the swan. Who, by
contrast, are the cranes, whose interminably raucous honking is so subtly
captured by the cacophonous enjambment at 181–2? Lucretius may have
in mind the earlier Roman prose writers on Epicureanism – such as
Catius, whose own writing on visual images provoked such derision (see
Ch. 2, §4) – and perhaps even Epicurus himself.[12] Lucretius thus displays
little modesty about his own literary superiority within the Epicurean

---

[11] One prominent feature of Lucretius' method is the clear labelling of successive arguments, *principio, deinde, praeterea* etc. Epicurus can be seen at 24.42 Arr.² to make his own transition between
separate arguments for the speed of images with the words 'Again, then, it becomes evident that
the images have unsurpassed speed in their motion. But also in the following kind of way it will
be possible to produce a proof about the speed of images. For since . . .' This clear division is
evidently what underlies Lucretius' organisation of his own arguments. Epicurus' greater
expansiveness is a feature of the lecturing style.

[12] There is no need to insist that the isolated Greek-derived word *cycnus* is this time a conscious
Graecism. If, on the other hand, we suppose that the Greek–Roman contrast of the proem to
book III (described in Ch. 2, §12) *is* being revived here, then Lucretius is claiming for himself a
Greek literary mantle (see Ch. 1) which has bypassed Epicurus himself.

tradition. The philosophical hard core of the passage is itself neverthe-less visibly being supplied by Epicurus.[13]

More important still, in both texts the argument in question belongs at the end of exactly the same sequence. As we noted in Chapter 4, §7, Epicurus' sequence in the final part of *On nature* II is:

(a) existence of images,
(a)* their fineness,
(b) their speed of generation,
(c) their velocity.

This is identical to the sequence which we find in Lucretius IV 54–216.[14] But we also saw there that in this particular case the *Letter to Herodotus* (46–8) has a slightly changed order

(a) the existence of images,
(c) their velocity – including (a)*, their fineness, merely as a premise,
(b) their speed of generation.

Here then there can surely be no possible doubt that Lucretius' debt to *On nature* has not been mediated by use of the *Letter to Herodotus*.[15]

Thus in a passage where, for once, we can administer a direct test, the *Letter to Herodotus* is ruled out as Lucretius' source. This strengthens the impression of its irrelevance to our task, and drives us back to a choice between *On nature* itself and the *Great epitome*. If the mysterious *Great epitome* is assumed to have been sufficiently great, in principle almost any-thing found in *On nature* could have recurred in it. But it seems an awfully implausible candidate for Lucretius' source text. This title (a) does not feature among those which Diogenes Laertius catalogues as Epicurus' leading works (X 27–8) or as the sources for his physics (*ib.* 30, where he lists not only *On nature* but also, implicitly, the *Letter to Herodotus* and *Letter to Pythocles*);[16] nor (b) is it cited by any ancient source apart from the

---

[13] Contrast Clay (1983), pp. 18–19. His objection there to taking *Nat.* as Lucretius' source – includ-ing for this passage – is 'There is no hint of translation or paraphrase.' But why should we have expected there to be?

[14] Cf. Barigazzi (1958), p. 254. The denial of this fact by Lackenbacher (1910) p. 232 is based on a simple mistake. He thinks that Lucretius' first argument for (c) is founded on the images' 'light-ness', while Epicurus' first argument for (c) is founded on their 'fineness' (λεπτότης). But these are both the same property! Lucretius' first argument refers (IV 183–4) to *levis res atque minutis cor-poribus factas*, and that this latter expression is equivalent to 'fineness' for him is made plain at 110–15.

[15] Also, as Mieke Koenen has kindly pointed out to me, at *Nat.* II, 24.12.1 Arr.², [ἀν]ακλάσεις is evi-dence that in *Nat.* Epicurus has cited the phenomenon of reflection earlier on in his arguments for εἴδωλα. There are corresponding discussions of reflection in Lucretius at IV 98–109, 150–67. He could have got these from *Nat.*, then, but not from *Ep. Hdt.* 46–8.   [16] Quoted p. 110 above.

scholiast on the *Letter to Herodotus*; nor (c) has any text that could plausibly be identified with it turned up in the library of Philodemus.

By contrast, as we learnt in Chapter 4, *On nature* (a) was the most prominent of all Epicurus' works, (b) is by far his most widely cited work on physics, and (c) can be seen from the Herculaneum library to have been collected and valued by Epicureans in Lucretius' own day. In view of all this, the common impression that it was virtually unreadable, generated by the woeful state of the papyri, cannot be correct (see Ch. 4, §5). Moreover, even allowing – as I prefer to insist (see Ch. 3) that Lucretius is unlikely to have been a member or active associate of Philodemus' school, we at least have incontrovertible evidence that copies of *On nature* were obtainable in Italy. Lucretius had to get his own texts of Epicurus from somewhere, and the papyri of *On nature* which survived at Herculaneum may well include some of the exemplars from which his own copy was made. There was surely no better archetype of Epicurus available in Italy than Philodemus' ancient copies of *On nature*, imported from the Garden in Athens.

These arguments are circumstantial. But I think it is possible to go further. One thing that would not easily have survived into an epitome, however large, is the quirks of personality which Epicurus displayed in the lectures *On nature*. In Chapter 4, §5, where I said a little about personal touches in *On nature*, one example was Epicurus' measured way of dealing with his illustrious and not so illustrious predecessors. In *On nature* xxv, he says of the early atomists' failure to see the consequences of determinism[17]

οἱ δ' αἰτιολογήσαντες ἐξ ἀρχῆς ἱκανῶς, καὶ οὐ μ[όν]ον [τ]ῶν πρὸ αὐτῶν πολὺ διενέγκαντες ἀλλὰ καὶ τῶν ὕστερον πολλαπλ[α]σί[ως], ἔλαθ[ο]ν ἑαυτούς, καίπερ ἐν πολλοῖς μεγάλα κουφίσαντες, ε[ἰ]ς τὸ τ[ὴ]ν ἀνάγκην καὶ ταὐτόματ[ο]ν πάντα α[ἰτ]ιᾶσθαι.

The first men to give an adequate account of causes – men greatly excelling not only their predecessors but also, many times over, their successors – although in many matters they alleviated great problems, turned a blind eye to themselves in order to blame everything on necessity and accident.

It would be hard not to notice how closely this stylised mixture of praise and criticism is echoed at Lucretius 1 734ff., where Empedocles and his 'lesser' followers are likewise gently rebuked:

[17] The passage is most conveniently cited as Long/Sedley (1987), 20c 13. The interpretation of μεγάλα κουφίσαντες is due to Arrighetti (1979). The reading ε[ἰ]ς is uncertain, but discussion of it is unnecessary here.

hic tamen et supra quos diximus inferiores
partibus egregie multis multoque minores,   735
quamquam multa bene ac divinitus invenientes
ex adyto tamquam cordis responsa dedere
sanctius et multo certa ratione magis quam
Pythia quae tripodi a Phoebi lauroque profatur,
principiis tamen in rerum fecere ruinas   740
et graviter magni magno cecidere ibi casu..

But this man and the greatly inferior and far lesser ones whom
I mentioned above, although in making their many excellent
and godlike discoveries they gave responses, as from the shrine
of the mind, in a holier and much more certain way than the
Pythia who makes her pronouncements from Apollo's tripod
and laurel, nevertheless came crashing down when they dealt
with the elementary principles of things. Great as they were,
their fall here was a great and heavy one.

Leucippus and Democritus were 'many times over' (πολλαπλ[α]σί[ως])
superior to their successors; Empedocles' successors were inferior to
him, literally, 'by outstandingly many degrees' (*partibus egregie multis*, 735).
Leucippus and Democritus solved great problems; Empedocles and his
successors made many excellent discoveries. Yet both parties made cat-
astrophic judgements concerning the issue in hand.

There is at least one clear trace of a similar comparative critique in an
earlier book of *On nature*.[18] It seems to be a style of judgement characteristic of this lecture course. Lucretius' comment on Empedocles and his
followers thus has Epicurus' unmistakable fingerprint: in all probability
he is directly echoing Epicurus' criticisms of Empedocles from book XIV,
characteristically qualified by praise in the form of a historical ranking.

Another such echo is suggested by the same passage from *On nature*
xxv. There Epicurus goes on to single out Democritus, not by name, but
just as τὸν ἄνδρα, 'the great man'. This term of respect is reflected in
the later Epicureans' use of οἱ ἄνδρες, 'the Great Men', to designate the
four authoritative founders of their school (pp. 67–8 above). Once again,
Epicurus' own usage is mimicked by Lucretius, who on both occasions
on which he cites a doctrine of Democritus refers to it as *Democriti quod
sancta viri sententia ponit*.[19]

---

[18] *Nat.* XI, K IV + |M| II Vogliano (1940) p. 49=26.44 Arr.²: those who have explained the earth's
stability by reference to air 'we should consider no better than these men' (i.e. those who appeal
to symmetry alone, e.g. the Platonists) 'in many matters' (ἐν πολλοῖς again) – 'but in many
matters utterly, comprehensively, vastly better' (ἐν πολλοῖς [δὲ κ]αὶ μάλιστα τῶι ὅλωι τρόπωι
πολλῶι βελτίους).   [19] III 371, V 622.

It is hard to believe that these personal touches in the comparative evaluation of predecessors, highly visible in Epicurus' expansive lecture course, had so clearly shown through in a condensed handbook such as the *Great epitome* must have been.

Of course Lucretius is selective. He has omitted many topics and arguments altogether, and has cut down considerably on the large amount of polemical content that shows through in the fragments of *On nature*. His doing so is fully accounted for by (a) the need to fit the main argument of fifteen books of *On nature* into six books of Latin hexameters, and (b) the lower levels of philosophical expertise, and perhaps even tolerance, to be expected of his Roman readers. Nevertheless, even in what remains the imprint of *On nature* shows through clearly not only in the philosophical content of Lucretius' poem but also in its style.

I conclude that to posit *On nature* itself, rather than some derivative of it, as Lucretius' source is not only the most economical hypothesis, but also the one which can best explain our data. I do not, of course, deny that for his Epicurean ethics – which he knew and understood extremely well – he had read more widely. Nor is it capable of demonstration that he never supplemented *On nature* with other works of Epicurean physics. But I know no feature of his poem which is better explained by that hypothesis, and I shall argue below (§7) that at least one feature of it, namely Lucretius' actual method of composition, is on the contrary better explained by the supposition that he relied exclusively on the full-length treatise.

3. THE STRUCTURE OF *DE RERUM NATURA*

As we have already noted, it was only during the process of writing that Lucretius adopted the transposition which put books III and IV into their present order. This decision to depart from Epicurus' own order was a crucial factor in producing what now stands out as the carefully balanced six-book structure (Chart 3).

The structural features of this arrangement are very well recognised, and do not need elaborate rehearsal here. Notable aspects include the sequence of three pairs of books, expanding from (A) the microscopic level, through (B) the human level, to (C) the cosmic level. Within each pair, the first book sets out the nature and lifespan of the items in question – (I) atoms, (III) human soul, (V) world – and the second goes on to account for a range of phenomena related to those same items. The poem also falls into two pairs of three books, each ending on the theme

Chart 3

(A) Atoms
{
  I (a) Proem: praise of Venus as life force, and of Epicurus for discovering the nature of the infinite universe
     (b) The basic elements
     (c) The infinity of the universe

  II (a) Proem: the Epicurean good life
     (b) Microscopic and macroscopic properties
     (c) The multiplicity of worlds
}

(B) Man
{
  III (a) Proem: praise of Epicurus for freeing us from fear of god and of death
     (b) The soul and its mortality
     (c) Diatribe against the fear of death

  IV (a) Proem: Lucretius' poetic mission
     (b) Perception and other soul/body functions
     (c) Diatribe against sexual passion
}

(C) World
{
  V (a) Proem: Epicurus as the greatest god
     (b) The world and its mortality (including astronomy)
     (c) The origin of life, civilisation and religion

  VI (a) Proem: praise of Athens for its greatest gift to civilisation, Epicurus
     (b) Cosmic phenomena
     (c) The Athenian plague
}

of death (IIIc, VIc), to counterbalance the opening celebration of birth and life in Ia. All this, and much more, hung on Lucretius' decision during the course of writing to move book IV to its present position.

The remaining transpositions cannot so decisively be shown to be Lucretius' own, rather than already imposed by the author of some hypothetical intermediary source on which Lucretius might be imagined to rely. But now that we have acknowledged the principle that he did transpose material during the process of composition, it becomes more plausible (as well as economical) to suppose that these are his too.

4. BOOKS I–III

A good example is the shifting of (xxxvi)–(xxxviii), the refutation of rival theories of matter, from its late position in books XIV–XV of *On nature* to the place it now holds in book I of Lucretius (635–920). The apparent match in the structure of the two passages (monism, finite pluralism, Anaxagorean *homoiomereia*) is encouraging evidence that *On nature* XIV–XV was Lucretius' source. As we have seen (pp. 125–6 above), this whole structure, including the *homoiomereia* interpretation of Anaxagoras, originally reflected Epicurus' use of Theophrastean doxography. That the Lucretius passage is shaped by the same doxographical approach is well recognised.[20] For example, at 1 647ff. Lucretius hypothetically attributes to Heraclitus a theory of rarefaction and condensation of fire which appears to have entered the tradition only with Theophrastus.[21]

Epicurus had held over his critique of rival theories of the elements until he had completed his own physical and cosmological exposition in books I–XIII of *On nature*. The decision to bring the critique forward to occupy a much earlier place, immediately after the initial demonstration of atomism in the first part of book I, is almost certainly Lucretius' own. From a methodological point of view the critique now comes surprisingly early. I shall be examining this aspect fully in Chapter 7. For present purposes I shall concentrate on just one of the main advantages achieved by the transposition.

The transfer of the critique to this early position helps Lucretius to engineer a major structural feature of the first pair of books (see Chart 3 above). It enables him to postpone until the end of book I the theme (IC) of the universe's infinity and the absurdity of the alternative, inward-looking cosmology which constructs our world around an absolute centre.[22] This horizon-expanding motif is then mirrored at the end of the second book (IIC), where Lucretius argues for the existence of other worlds and (an aspect of the argument not brought out at (xii) in the *Letter to Herodotus* condensation) the transient nature of our own. The emphasis achieved by this pair of matching closures delivers what he has effectively promised since the proem (1 62–79): a liberating intellectual journey with Epicurus in which we will push on through the constricting barriers of our own world and into the infinite universe beyond.

[20] Rösler (1973), Mansfeld (1990), pp. 3153–4.
[21] Theophrastus, *Phys. op.* fr. 1 Diels (1879), p. 475.14–18, = fr. 225 FHS&G (= Fortenbaugh et al. (1992)), p. 406.15–19.
[22] Barigazzi (1950), in a very valuable study of (xxx), the argument about the earth's stability at the end of *Nat.* XI, points to links between it and the critique of geocentrism in (L3). However, he does not explicitly suggest that Lucretius has brought this material forward from (xxx) to (L3), and thinks it likely, as I do too, that (L3) was already in place in *Nat.* I, adjacent to (ix), the infinity of the all. The main thrust of (L3) is that space cannot have a centre or any other structural or causal properties (see Ch. 3, §6); and that is already justified by the arguments which precede it (v), which includes the total non-resistance of void at 1 430–44, and (ix). The target in (xxx) may conceivably include the same people (see however Panchenko (1994), pp. 47–55), but there the issue is the stability of the earth, not the structure of space as such.

There are other signs of Lucretius' intervention in the sequence of topics in book II. One relates to items (xii), the multiplicity of worlds, and (xvii), that atoms lack secondary qualities. These became consecutive topics as soon as the intervening material on perception etc. had been transferred to book IV (see the second descending arrow in Chart 2).[23] Lucretius then decided to reverse their order. This was his way of postponing the topic of the plurality and transience of worlds until the end of book II, producing what we have just seen to be the appropriate match between its closure and that of book I.

Another case is the atomic 'swerve'. This theory is not yet present in the *Letter to Herodotus* account of the causes of atomic motion (43–4), and therefore was very probably introduced only in a later book of *On nature*. I suggested in Chapter 4, §11 that this was either in book xxv, where the issue of determinism was visibly in focus, or in a book flanking it. Book xxv, we have also seen (Ch. 4, §§3 and 11), was apparently one of those especially prized by Epicureans. Hence it should be no great surprise in such a case that Lucretius for once drew on material from the later part of Epicurus' treatise. For that is what he seems to have done. He has brought the swerve thesis forward to an early position in book II (L4 = II 216–93), where it quite properly takes its place as a third cause of atomic motion alongside impacts and weight. Furthermore, this has in turn required Lucretius to anticipate at the same early point item (xx), the topic of the equal speed of atoms, needed as a premise in the argument for the swerve (II 225–39).[24]

I do not in this context want to discuss the theoretical merits or demerits of these transpositions, from the point of view of Epicurean physical methodology. What they illustrate for my present purposes is how books I–II are the product of delicate restructuring by Lucretius of Epicurus' original material: I shall be discussing the nature of this transformation in Chapter 7. I see no sign anywhere in books I–III that the restructuring

---

[23] The original proem to IV (45–53), which represents a very early stage in the composition of the poem and precedes Lucretius' decision to move the book's material to its present position (see n. 5, pp. 137–8 above, and §5 below), does not make it explicit that item (xvii) was already at the time of writing located in book II. But I assume that at any rate once the transposition had been decided on – quite early on in the composition of the book, see p. 150 below – it became clear to Lucretius that any further material on atoms in (xvii)-(xx) must either be incorporated into book II or simply omitted. In fact he chose to omit most of it.

[24] This is not arrowed in Chart 2 as a transposition, because the topic is not covered in its own right at II 225–39. He only refers there to the equal speed of atoms moving vertically downwards in inter-cosmic space. The main topic of (xx), that of the equal speed of atoms at all times, even within compounds, is simply omitted by Lucretius.

was not fully carried out (although in the case of book III there is no clear
evidence that Lucretius actually had to make any structural change,
apart from his omission of (xxiii) on the metaphysical issue of
incorporeality).[25] So far as I can tell, apart from corruptions acquired
during later transmission, the first three books may well be exactly as
Lucretius would have intended them to be.[26]

5. BOOK IV

When we turn to the last three books, the picture is very different. The
state of book IV is the prime item of evidence. I have already mentioned
the transitional state of its proem, where the original programmatic lines
have accidentally remained in the text. The later version of these lines
differs from the earlier one in some very revealing ways. By comparing
the two versions we saw, in Chapter 2, §4, how Lucretius overhauled his
announced range of vocabulary for *eidōla*. Here, however, I want to concentrate on just one aspect: his preview of the book's contents. Unlike
the original version, the revised version tells us emphatically that the
book's main purpose is to dispel the fear of ghosts (IV 26–41):

> atque animi quoniam docui natura quid esset
> et quibus e rebus cum corpore compta vigeret
> quove modo distracta rediret in ordia prima,
> nunc agere incipiam tibi, quod vementer ad has res
> attinet, esse ea quae rerum simulacra vocamus;   30
> quae quasi membranae summo de corpore rerum
> dereptae volitant ultroque citroque per auras,
> atque eadem nobis vigilantibus obvia mentes
> terrificant atque in somnis, cum saepe figuras
> contuimur miras simulacraque luce carentum,   35
> quae nos horrifice languentis saepe sopore
> excierunt; ne forte animas Acherunte reamur
> effugere aut umbras inter vivos volitare
> neve aliquid nostri post mortem posse relinqui,
> cum corpus simul atque animi natura perempta   40
> in sua discessum dederint primordia quaeque.

---

[25] If Lucretius' argument in III is thought to acquire its structure largely from doxography — as
argued by Mansfeld (1990), pp. 3143–52, although I do not myself find the grounds he offers particularly compelling — the doxographical influence would be likely to have come through
Epicurus from Theophrastus' *Physical opinions* (cf. §8 and Ch. 6 below). That would suggest that
Lucretius has in the main retained Epicurus' own sequence.

[26] If there are any residual signs of lack of a final revision in these books, they concern no more
than local fine tuning (e.g. perhaps III 620–1, 806–18; see Kenney (1971), *ad loc.*), not the overall
arrangement of material.

And now that I have taught you what is the nature of the mind, from what things it gets its power when combined with the body, and how when torn apart it returns to its elements, I shall now begin to deal with what is closely relevant to this: how there are what we call images of things, which, like membranes snatched from the outermost part of things' bodies, fly hither and thither through the air; and how these same things strike us both awake and asleep and terrify our minds, when, as often, we see strange shapes, and images of those who have passed on – which have often woken us in terror as we lay slumbering; lest we should think, perhaps, that souls are escaping from Acheron, or that shades flit around among the living, or that something of us can survive after death, when both the body and the nature of the mind have been destroyed and dissolved, each into its own elements.

The main function of book IV within the middle pair of books is thus laid bare. Book III has shown that the soul is mortal and death not to be feared. Book IV's account of psychic functions will complement this by showing that encounters with 'ghosts' are not evidence that something of us does after all survive death. That this was to be the central message of book IV is confirmed by the proems to books I and V (I 132–5, V 59–63), both of which emphasise precisely the same role for book IV. Yet what we actually find on the topic of ghosts in book IV is a mere 11 lines (757–67). None of the important questions is addressed. Are the images of the dead which invade our dreams ones which emanated from those same people before they died, even centuries ago? Or are they images which our minds pick out merely because they bear some resemblance to those people? And how are waking visions of ghosts – referred to explicitly in the proem – to be explained? These are important questions for an Epicurean to be able to answer. As far as I know, the only explicit evidence – albeit from the virulently hostile Plutarch[27] – attributes to the Epicureans the belief that images can stay in circulation even long after the death of the people from whom they emanated. But this at the very least needed saying, explaining and justifying. Above all, Lucretius owes his readers a well-reasoned assurance (which was certainly forthcoming from other Epicureans, and almost certainly from Epicurus himself)[28]

[27] Epicurus fr. 394 Usener = Plut. *De def. or.* 420B C.
[28] Diogenes of Oenoanda 10 v 2–6 Smith. Since the point is argued there as a disagreement with Democritus, it probably stems ultimately from Epicurus himself. Moreover, there is excellent reason to suppose that this disagreement was already to be found in Lucretius' source text, since it is likely to be what motivates the criticism of Democritus reproduced by Lucretius at III 370–95, for making soul-atoms and body-atoms alternate throughout the living organism: only on such an account could atom-thin films from the body be thought themselves to have soul.

that such images could not actually be alive. Extraordinarily, Lucretius
devotes more lines in his proems to announcing that book IV will explain
ghosts than he devotes in book IV to actually explaining them. It seems
self-evident that book IV is not in the final state which Lucretius envisaged for it at the time when he wrote its revised programme of contents.

There is good reason to suspect that before he had advanced very far
with the writing of what is now book IV Lucretius came to realise that he
would eventually be moving it to come after the account of soul. As early
as IV 121 there is an explicit reference to *anima* and *animus*, presupposing
readers' familiarity with the technical distinction between these developed in book III.[29] But it seems equally clear to me that he had not, at
this stage, worked out the pivotal role that ghosts would eventually have
to play in the book: that intention is acknowledged only in the proems,
which can therefore be assumed to represent a very late stage in
Lucretius' planning.

As for the actual contents of book IV as we have it, there is reason to guess
that they still closely reflect Epicurus' original sequence of material,
without the benefits of Lucretius' planned reworking. The list, excerpted
from Chart 2, is:

Chart 2a

(xiii)	existence and mobility of images	IV 26–238
(xiv)	vision, truth and falsity	IV 239–468
	(L7) *refutation of scepticism*	IV 469–521
(xv)	the other senses	IV 522–721
(xvi)	thought	IV 722–822
	(L8) *critique of teleology*	IV 823–57
	(L9) *nutrition, motion, sleep, dreams, sex*	IV 858–1287

Although the position of book IV, following book III on the soul, and likewise its primary content, encourage the impression that it is concentrating on mental phenomena, the addition of (L8) and (L9) appears to
introduce an amorphous mixture of soul and body functions. Neither
the critique of biological teleology – where we are urged not to believe
those who say that legs were made for walking with, etc. – nor the
ensuing account of nutrition, has anything directly to do with the
Epicurean soul. Puzzlingly, as F. Solmsen noticed,[30] what links the items
listed is, if anything, that they are all functions of the *Aristotelian* soul.
Even here, however, the critique of teleology fits such an account loosely

[29] Much later, at IV 877–906, the distinction is even more clearly presupposed and exploited.
[30] Solmsen (1961a).

at best. Attempts have been made to find an equally good rationale for their grouping based on principles purely internal to Epicureanism, but with only limited success.[31] I hope that the following conjecture is an improvement.[32]

The cardinal rule in the second half of the poem is this: if you want to make sense of a puzzling sequence of topics adopted by Lucretius, since he demonstrably has not completed his own reorganisation of the material, ask why *Epicurus* should have ordered it in this way. To answer such a question with regard to book IV, we must consider the above list in its full context on Chart 2 (p. 136 above). It is actually quite easy to see why, having explained perception and thought in *On nature* III–IV, Epicurus should have continued with the remaining vital functions in (L9). Significantly, the very next topic was to be

(xvii) *Atoms lack secondary qualities,*

and this, in Lucretius' version (much fuller than *Letter to Herodotus* 54–5), includes some proofs that atoms lack vital properties (II 865–990). Clearly the full discussion in *On nature* set out to show systematically that atoms lack not only all secondary sensible properties (colour, taste etc.) but also all vital properties. Hence Epicurus felt the necessity to analyse the full range of both sensible and vital properties before turning to (xvii), showing in particular how vital properties always depend on complex structures and processes which single atoms cannot possess. As for (L8), the critique of biological teleology, while its tenuous relevance to psychological properties and functions makes it look curiously out of place in Lucretius IV, it would have been entirely at home in its original Epicurean context. Any full explanation of vital functions was, for Epicurus, likely to include a vehement rejection of Plato's elaborate account of these in the *Timaeus*, where the organs in which they are located had been described as providentially produced for those very functions by divine creators.[33]

Epicurus' plan, it seems, was not to turn to the analysis of soul itself – item (xxi) on his agenda – until the nature of atoms had been fully

---

[31] Cf. Furley (1967), p. 213 for criticisms of Giussani and Bailey's explanations, although Furley's own proposal — 'The whole passage from 722 to 961 might be entitled: "No need for any explanation other than *simulacra*"' — does not fit IV 858–76 or 907–61 very comfortably (cf. Schrijvers (1976), p. 232).

[32] One simple explanation for this unexpectedly Aristotelian thematic link would be the hypothesis that Epicurus was himself working from Theophrastus' *Phys. op.*, which as an Aristotelian doxographical work naturally grouped its topics on Aristotelian principles. I have made this suggestion in Sedley (1997a). It is compatible with the proposal which I offer here, but is not required by it.

[33] For teleology in the *Timaeus* as Epicurus' (and derivatively Lucretius') target, cf. Ch. 3, §5.

sorted out, in order that it should be incontrovertible that the vital properties of soul depend on its complex structures and processes, not on its
components. It is significant here that in the great majority of the
Presocratic theories to which Epicurus was reacting vital properties were
already irreducibly present in the basic stuff or stuffs of the world. The
concern to combat this supposition, in favour of his atomistic bottom-
up model, was clearly an overriding factor in Epicurus' organisation of
his physical exposition.

Lucretius' eventual decision, in the interests of his poem's overall
architectonic, was to analyse soul in book III *before* turning to the individual vital properties in IV. It is this reversal of Epicurus' expository
order that accounts for the otherwise puzzling heterogeneity of the
issues covered in the later part of book IV. We may recall that, on the
clear evidence of the proems, Lucretius had plans for re-focusing the
content of book IV. We need not doubt that these would have included
an enhancement or clarification of its thematic unity.

6. BOOK V

Given what we have learnt about Lucretius' intentions in book IV, it is
worth asking whether the proems reveal any other unfulfilled plans on
his part. Remarkably, it will turn out that they do. But let me approach
the point indirectly.

The sequence of topics in book V is curious. Lines 509–770, on astronomy, constitute a surprising interruption between two phases of the
history of the world, coming as they do after the development of the
cosmos itself but before the emergence of life and civilisation. Once
again there is good reason to attribute the sequence not to any concern
of Lucretius' own, but to one which may well have motivated Epicurus,
namely the need to respond to the account of creation in the teleologists'
bible, Plato's *Timaeus*. For there the motions of the heavens and earth
occupy a closely analogous position, between the origin of the world
(28b-34a) and the origin of mankind (41a ff.), being integral to the intervening construction of the world soul. One can imagine that Epicurus,
in developing his own account of the world's origin in *On nature* XI–XII,
felt the need to respond point by point to the *Timaeus*.

This anti-Timaean motive is in fact borne out by a closer look at item
(L10) on Chart 2 (p. 136 above), the mortality of the world. (There is no
reason to doubt that this topic occurred at just the same position in *On
nature*, even if we happen to have found no independent attestation of

the fact.) Lucretius' series of arguments against the divinity of the world
– that the world cannot be alive (126–55), that the gods cannot have
created it, for lack of either a motive or a model to give them the idea
(156–94), and that it is not good enough to be divine handiwork
(195–234), look like a co-ordinated response to *Timaeus* 29e–30c, where
the world is the good product of a benevolent creator, and is animate,
being modelled on the ideal Living Being. In Chapter 3, §5 we found evidence that the literal creationist reading of the *Timaeus* which is presupposed by Lucretius' response was the one favoured in the Academy
of Epicurus' own day, under the headship of Polemo. This too helps to
confirm that Lucretius is following Epicurus closely in book v.[34]

The fact that Lucretius' order of exposition in book v derives from
Epicurus should in any case be plain simply from a glance at items
(xxv)–(xxxiii) on Chart 2. In the entire sequence there is just one demonstrable transposition.[35]

If, as by now seems overwhelmingly likely, the astronomy in Lucretius
v owes its present position to Epicurus' polemical concerns, one might
have expected Lucretius eventually to transpose it. Outside that polemical context it belonged much more naturally with the discussion of
other cosmic phenomena which I have conjecturally assigned to *On
nature* XIII, and which are picked up by Lucretius book VI.[36] Did
Lucretius intend to reorder his topics in this way? When we turn to the
proems, we find that indeed he did. The programmatic proem to book
v, 64–90, places the astronomy at the end, *after* the history of civilisation: he announces that he is going to expound (a) the world's mortality
and its origin; (b) then (*tum*, 69) the origins of life and civilisation
(exemplified here, as in the *Letter to Herodotus*, by language, but also by
the origin of religious terror); and (c) in addition (*praeterea*, 76) the celestial motions. I see no reason to doubt that this programme was, as

[34] See also Ch. 6 for evidence that the next part of (L10), Lucretius' arguments in favour of the
world's destructibility at v 235ff., represents Epicurus' response to Theophrastus.
[35] Assuming that it was Lucretius himself who moved (xxvii), the smallness of the heavenly bodies,
to a less prominent position, his motive can only be a matter of conjecture. Epicurus had wished
to stress its damaging implications for the accuracy of astronomical observations (cf. Sedley
(1976b)), and Lucretius (cf. his omission of the attack on astronomical devices, Ch. 3, §7) was not
interested in pursuing that kind of critique. My guess therefore is that Lucretius initially omitted
it, like many other topics, but that when he got to the beginning of book XII he found an argument that he really wanted to include – resulting in v 592–613, his finely crafted passage on how
the sun, though small, can illuminate the entire world – but which required that he should first
belatedly insert the argument to prove that the sun *is* small.
[36] Epicurus' selection of topics for the *Letter to Pythocles* is itself an acknowledgement of this fact: see
Chart 1 p. 133 above.

elsewhere in his proems, meant to correspond to the actual order of exposition.[37]

The transposition of the astronomical passage to the end of book v, had he lived to effect it, would admittedly have sacrificed one advantage, namely the thematic link between the history of civilisation at the end of v and the proem to vi, where Epicurus is ranked prominently among the gifts of Athenian civilisation. But, compensatingly, the transposition would have eliminated the unwelcome interruption in book v's history of the world, and led to a smooth continuity between the end of v, on astronomy, and the primary content of vi, the remaining cosmic phenomena. In fact, the proem to vi also appears to allude to that same planned continuity between the two books (vi 43–6):

> Et quoniam docui mundi mortalia templa
> esse ⟨et⟩ nativo consistere corpore caelum,
> et quaecumque in eo fiunt fierique necessest,
> pleraque dissolui, quae restant percipe porro.

> And since I have taught that the world's regions are mortal, and that the heaven is made of a body which had birth, and I have accounted for the majority of the things which go on and must go on in it, now hear the remainder of them . . .

It is also worth noting that the programmatic lines in the proem to book v promise (76–90) a heavily theological message for the astronomical section, namely that failure to understand the true working of the heavens leads to a morally ruinous misconception of the divine nature. This is a message which the actual astronomical passage as we have it (v 509–770) fails to deliver. Just as the middle pair of books was to have the joint function of dispelling the fear of death, so the final pair was destined to have (even more prominently than in our version) the function of dispelling the fear of god. I imagine that in the planned rewriting there was to be a strongly theological motif in the astronomical close of book v – perhaps even including the famously missing account of the gods promised at v 155 (*quae tibi posterius largo sermone probabo*).

---

[37] Townend (1979) offers a similar argument for a different account of Lucretius' original plan, arguing that I 127–35 reflects a stage at which he intended the sequence v, vi, iii, iv. I disagree. These lines are not in any normal sense programmatic. Lucretius' reasoning is: there are dangers attached *both* to false views about the gods (80–101), *and* to false beliefs about the soul (102–26); therefore it is necessary to learn *both* (*cum*, 127) about the real explanation of celestial phenomena (127–30), *and* (*tum*) about the real nature of the soul (130–5). The sequence is dictated, not by the subsequent contents of the poem, but by the order of the two warnings in 80–126.

7. LUCRETIUS' METHOD

I have offered reasons for supposing book IV to be still very much in the organisational state in which Epicurus himself had bequeathed the material. As for book V, no such surmise is needed, because a glance at Chart 2 is enough to confirm that, with possibly only one exception (item (xxvii)), Lucretius has indeed conserved Epicurus' order. In §§5–6 I have argued that for both books he was visibly planning a radical overhaul, but did not live to carry it out. We can speculate what the final product might have looked like, but there is little doubt that he would have decided on further changes as he proceeded with the rewriting. The most that it is safe to say is that the rewriting might well in the end have been as subtle and complex as the reorganisation that can actually be discerned in books I and II (see §4 above, and Ch. 7).

Before proceeding to consider book VI, it is worth putting together some interim conclusions on Lucretius' method of composition and its motivation. According to the reconstruction which I have proposed, he initially downloaded (if I may be forgiven the computing metaphor) large quantities of material into Latin hexameters, following the sequence of his sole Epicurean source closely, indeed almost mechanically. He had already at this stage radically recast at least the diction of the arguments into his own evolving poetic mode – we saw evidence of this reshaping process in book IV (Ch. 2, §4) – but had not significantly departed from the overall sequence as he found it. It was largely in a second phase that he set about reorganising it into the familiar structure by which we know it today, although even then he did not live to fulfil all of his plans for books IV–VI. Three points may now be made explicit about the earlier draft. (a) It was probably longer than the final draft: since each of books IV–VI is longer than any of books I–III,[38] we can infer that the uncompleted second phase involved some trimming. (b) It was already in verse. (c) It was already divided into books. The original programme of book IV, which we examined earlier, unambiguously testifies to both (b) and (c).

These three facts in turn virtually rule out the hypothesis of a further stage, an initial draft in Latin prose. If Lucretius had started out with a prose draft, as Virgil is said to have done when writing the *Aeneid*,[39] we

---

[38] Book I, 1117 lines; II, 1174 lines; III, 1094 lines; IV, 1287 lines; V, 1457 lines; VI, 1286 lines.

[39] Donatus, *Vita Verg.* 23: Virgil made a detailed prose draft of the *Aeneid*, already divided into 12 books, so that when versifying it he could move from passage to passage *ad lib.* The question whether Lucretius started the same way is properly raised by Smith (1966), p. 82 n. 3.

might surely expect him to have proceeded to plan the reorganisation of his material *before* he turned it into verse. In fact, though, the opening of book IV is evidence of major reorganisation taking place at a time when (a) the material was already in Latin hexameters and divided into books, yet (b) it was still in an early enough draft to retain the order of material bequeathed by Epicurus. The hypothesis of a prose draft prior to this stage looks explanatorily redundant.

Even without a prose draft, Lucretius was adopting a circuitous route to his final goal, since much of his first verse draft undoubtedly required radical rewriting in the final version. Why should he have gone about the task in this apparently time-wasting way? One part of the answer surely lies in the size and character of the *On nature*. In Chapter 4 we saw that the entire treatise would have filled nine or ten volumes of Oxford Classical Text, and that books I–XV alone would have filled four such volumes. That was a very considerable quantity of material for Lucretius to work through when making his selection of arguments. It would have been extremely hard for him to move back and forth between widely separated passages in different rolls of Epicurus' work, while trying at the same time to keep control over the internal structure of the emerging poem. Without the aid of tables of contents, indexes, chapter and page references, etc., this would have been a daunting task, and perhaps ultimately an unmanageable one.

Once the hypothesis of a prose draft is excluded, then, Lucretius' initial decision to versify the *aurea dicta* largely if not entirely in their own transmitted sequence turns out to have been, from a practical point of view, the natural one to take. Nor was it a foolish decision. Epicurus had himself been scrupulous about maintaining what he considered a philosophically correct sequence for his own argument in *On nature*, and indeed the *magnum opus* had advertised itself (as we saw in the closing sentence of book XXVIII – see Ch. 4, §5 – but no doubt the same claim was made in earlier books too) as being delivered in a philosophically proper sequence. If Lucretius initially hoped to preserve most of that same order in his poem, he had Epicurus' active encouragement to do so.

It was only during the actual process of versification, as the philosophical epic took shape, that Lucretius came to see the merits of a radical restructuring. If the reorganisation meant sacrificing some of Epicurus' methodological rigour, any loss would be vastly outweighed by gains in architectonic unity and rhetorical power. The first half of the poem is eloquent testimony to the wisdom of his decision. So far as concerns the planned restructuring of the second half, however, only a few clues survive in the proems to afford us a glimpse of the new organic whole into which, at the time of Lucretius' death, the *De rerum natura* was still undergoing its final transformation.

8. BOOK VI

So far I have deliberately left book VI almost entirely out of account. My hope is that what we have learnt about books I–V will be able to throw light on a long-standing puzzle about the final book.

After an opening disquisition on the proper attitude to divinity, the great bulk of book VI is devoted to a series of atmospheric and terrestrial phenomena. I have suggested tentatively that the corresponding part of *On nature*, book XIII, covered this same pair of topics ((xxxiv) and (xxxv)). Moreover, since we have learnt that at the time of Lucretius' death books IV and V had not yet had the same overhaul that he had given to the first half of the poem, it is only to be expected that book VI in its present state should also follow Epicurus' original order of exposition closely.

Our only clue to the internal order in which Epicurus' section on these phenomena proceeded is the corresponding part of the *Letter to Pythocles* (98–116). This does not match Lucretius VI at all closely. But it is a part where the *Letter* seems to be combining two or more different sources (see Ch. 4, §9), and we cannot be confident how far the internal structure of *On nature* XIII can be recovered from it. In proposing a match between *On nature* XIII and *DRN* VI, I start with an appeal to probability, based on what we have learnt about the composition of the two preceding books, where very strong reasons emerged for deriving Lucretius' order from the corresponding books of *On nature*.

A closer look at Lucretius' sequence of topics in book VI proves, at the very least, consistent with this supposition. It shows a strong likelihood that the sequence derives ultimately from Theophrastus. And we have already found some reason to regard Theophrastus' *Physical opinions* as one major influence on Epicurus' own exposition, and, through him, on Lucretius'. (Chapter 6 will amply confirm that picture.)

We can see this by placing Lucretius' order alongside that found in Aetius (Chart 4, p. 158 below).[40] That Aetius' own order stems from Theophrastus' foundational doxographical work – as one would in any case have predicted[41] – receives some confirmation if we place on the

---

[40] Cf. the table in Runia (1997).
[41] For continuing general acceptance of the thesis of Diels (1879), who traced the origins of the 'Aetius' doxography ultimately to Theophrastus, see e.g. Mansfeld (1990).

Chart 4

Lucr. VI		Aetius III 1–IV 7	Thphr. *Metars.*
		milky way	
		comets	
96–159	thunder	thunder	thunder
160–218	lightning	lightning	lightning
219–422	thunderbolts	thunderbolts	thunderbolts
423–50	prēstēr	prēstēr	
		typhoons	
451–94	cloud	cloud, mist	cloud
495–523	rain	rain	rain
524–34	[rainbows, snow, wind, hail, frost]	dew, snow, frost, hail, rainbows	snow, hail, dew, frost
		wind	wind
		winter and summer	
		the earth (number,	
		size, shape,	*halo of moon*
		position, stability)	
535–607	earthquakes	earthquakes	earthquakes
608–38	sea	sea	
639–711	Etna		
		tides	
		halo of moon	
712–37	Nile	Nile	
738–839	Avernian Lake		
840–905	springs and wells		
906–1089	magnets		
1090–1137	disease		

right-hand side the sequence of headings found, not in the *Physical opinions* itself (which is lost), but in what is now thought to be Theophrastus' *Metarsiologica*, which survives, abridged, in Syriac and Arabic[12] (I use italics to highlight an isolated discrepancy).

Lucretius' sequence, although selective, conforms very closely to that in Aetius. The one minor departure is at 524–34, but it is clear what has happened there. Following his explanations of cloud and rain, he deals with the next group – the remaining aspects of weather – *en bloc*, by offering a few words in explanation of one of them, rainbows, and instructing his readers thereafter to work out their own explanations for the remainder. Allowing for this deliberate abridgement, the parallelism holds even there.

The material in Theophrastus is incomplete, but its degree of coincidence with the Aetius order is sufficient to guarantee that, as expected,

---

[12] On this text, see Ch. 6, §6 below.

that order drew its origins from Theophrastus' work. Moreover, Theophrastus' exposition anticipates so much of the detail of Lucretius' that it is indisputably, even if at one or more removes, a major influence on it: I shall say more in illustration of this in Chapter 6, §6.

In combination, these facts strongly encourage the further inference that the Lucretian material, which matches the same order almost perfectly, reflects Epicurus' use of Theophrastus.[43]

The way in which the Theophrastean expository sequence functions is best seen by following the complete set of topics, assembled from all three sources. It works its way steadily downwards from the upper levels of the atmosphere to the earth and its contents. (The one exception, for which I have no explanation to offer, is the halo of the moon, differently – but equally anomalously – placed by Aetius and Theophrastus.)[44] Thus the waterspout, *prēstēr*, no doubt preceded cloud and rain in the list because it was usually taken to descend from above, being fiery in nature, whereas cloud was regarded as produced from the air itself or by exhalations from below. It is particularly significant here that Lucretius does not fully endorse this standard difference. Like Epicurus (*Letter to Pythocles* 104–5), he discounts the fiery nature usually attributed to the *prēstēr*, and derives it purely from cloud.[45] One might therefore have expected him, had he been creating the order himself, to have located it after cloud in the sequence, especially as he allows as one source of cloud formation the arrival of matter from *above*, even from outside the cosmos (481–94). The fact that he does not merely confirms that his material came to him in an order already conferred on it by Theophrastus' doxographical method.

This does not in itself prove that Lucretius' material came to him from a book of Epicurus shaped by its reliance on Theophrastus, rather than from his own independent use of doxographical sources.[46] But if I have

---

[13] Cf. Mansfeld (1992a), p. 326: 'But what we find in Theophrastus can be paralleled point by point from Lucretius. We therefore must assume that Lucretius, at least for his sections dealing with thunderbolts, did not use the *Letter* [sc. *to Pythocles*], and may surmise that a much longer *epitome* of Epicurus' views on cosmology and meteorology was available to him (assuming he did not consult the difficult *Physics* [meaning *On nature*]). It follows that in the books of his *Physics* on which this *epitome* was based Epicurus followed Theophrastus very closely: at any rate this can be proved for the argument about thunderbolts.' (For this comparative material on thunderbolts, see Ch. 6 §6.)

[14] As evidence that *some* kind of displacement has taken place, it is worth noting that in Theophrastus this chapter includes the theological excursus which Daiber (1992), p. 280, and Mansfeld (1994a), p. 316, agree to be itself misplaced.

[15] This in itself may well be influenced by Theophrastus' own view on *prēstēr*; see p. 182 below.

[16] The latter option is favoured by Runia (1997).

been right to explain the programmes of books IV and V by the hypothesis that their sequence was derived from Epicurus' in *On nature*, the same explanation inevitably commends itself for book VI as well.

There is, on the other hand, one item in book VI which can hardly reflect *On nature*. As is well known, the book's final part (1138–1286) is a long and gruelling description of the great plague at Athens during the Peloponnesian War, borrowed directly from Thucydides. Just as the entire poem opened with a celebration of life drawn from a fifth-century Sicilian, so it closes with a grim tableau of death drawn from a fifth-century Athenian.[47]

There is much unresolved dispute about this passage. While it is widely agreed that the horror story of mass death somehow serves to counterbalance the poem's opening focus on birth and life and the denunciation of the fear of death which provides the climax for the first half of the poem, it is not so widely accepted that the close as we have it can be as Lucretius meant it finally to be. In confirmation of this doubt, it is worth observing that the passage has what we have now seen to be the hallmark of a Lucretian first draft: that is, despite occasional omissions or additions, it retains the exact order of material found in its Greek source, Thucydides II 47–54.[48] This time there is no way of blaming his procedure on the sheer size of the source text, but we may still surmise that, even when working from a relatively short Greek passage, what had by now become his habitual method suggested itself once again, as the best way to ensure as full *coverage* of the Thucydidean material as he evidently wanted, prior to reworking it to fit the poem's still developing architectonic.

Those who believe, as I do, that Lucretius must have intended to rework the plague passage and to make its moral explicit,[49] can draw comfort from the general picture I have painted. If my story is right, Lucretius' plans for organising his individual books around an overarching moral framework had not, at the time of his death, been fully put into effect for the second half of the poem. If book VI does not yet

[47] Among the many excellent studies of the plague passage, I have found those of Commager (1957), Bright (1971), and Clay (1983) especially helpful.
[48] For demonstration of this, see Bright (1971), p. 608. The one apparent exception is 1247–8, but I am persuaded by Bright's argument in defence of Bockemüller's transposition of 1247–51 to a concluding position after 1286, which restores the correspondence.
[49] Although Bockemüller's transposition (see previous note) may, as urged by Fowler (1996), p. 889, give the final lines some appropriate closural features, such minor repairs do not in my view come near to supplying a morally credible closure to the poem as a whole.

have a fully finalised closure, in the light of the current state of books IV and V that is exactly what we should expect. We are therefore at liberty to ask how he might have meant to close book VI, without shackling ourselves to a doctrinaire insistence on the integrity of the existing text as a finished product. Given that the book as we have it is already exceptionally long,[50] there is also a strong possibility that the description of the plague itself was destined to be significantly reduced in the final draft, before the concluding moral was grafted on to it.

Much the most promising guess to have emerged from discussions of this problem is that Lucretius meant here to show how the other achievements of civilisation are dwarfed by Epicurus' contribution to it. Athens, the proem to book VI points out, was the cradle of civilisation for 'ailing mortals' (*mortalibus aegris*, VI 1), giving them both corn and laws: Athens, that is, helped foster both our bodily and our moral needs. But, the proem continues, Athens also gave us Epicurus, whose godlike discoveries have outlived him to spread 'life's joyful solaces'. It was he who truly satisfied our physical and moral needs, by teaching us the limits of pleasure and by dispelling our fears.

The return to Athens at the end of the book must have been meant to take this message forward. Lucretius surely wanted us to learn that when the Athenians faced the worst that fortune could hurl against them,[51] the other benefits of their civilisation were powerless: only Epicurus' wisdom, had it yet come to birth, could have dealt with the horrors of the plague, both physical and moral. He is the one who has taught us to tolerate bereavement and bodily pain with genuine optimism, and not to cling desperately to life as if death were an evil. In other words, the plague must carry a message for *us*, and this is supported both by my earlier finding (Ch. 2, §11) that here Lucretius is not, as often elsewhere, seeking to emphasise any gulf between Greece and his readers' own world, and by the way in which he omits the circumstantial details of the Athenian plague in order, it seems, to maximise the generality of its lessons.[52]

Now it seems idle to pretend that the intended message is in fact conveyed by the closing section of the poem.[53] Some would interpret the

---

[50] See n. 38, p. 155 above.
[51] Cf. VI 29–32 for anticipation of this theme in the book's proem.
[52] This aspect is well brought out by Bright (1971). Cf. also Segal (1990), p. 231: 'Athens is remote enough from Lucretius' Roman audience to be exemplary, but real enough to be terrifying.'
[53] Cf. Long (1992a), p. 498: 'If Lucretius were concerned to disclose and cure anxieties about dying painfully, the plague would be about as effective as a horror movie for inducing pleasant dreams.'

plague passage as a final test: have Lucretius' readers really learnt their Epicureanism? But even that interpretation must presuppose that we have at least been taught the relevant principles, so that we are now ready to apply them for ourselves.[54] I wonder how many readers of this passage have ever been left feeling that, thanks to the poem's lessons, if they had been there they would have been less helpless than the wretched Athenians were in the face of such grisly suffering. The expected Epicurean teachings about the right responses to painful death are not yet fully in place. We have learnt much from book III about why we should not fear *being* dead, and those lessons will certainly prove to bear on the conduct of the plague victims. But where have we been taught how to remain happy through severe and even terminal physical suffering?

On this matter Epicurus' teachings were well known, and his own death the great model. He had maintained that even excruciating pain need not mar our happiness, both because we can be confident that it will be short-lived,[55] usually to be followed by the totally painless state of death, and because even while it is going on it can be outweighed by the joyful recollection of past pleasures. Cicero, for one, showed how well he understood the pivotal importance of these tenets in his eloquent expansion of the Epicurean *tetrapharmakos* (*De finibus* I 40–1):

That pleasure is the ultimate good can be most easily seen from the following picture. Let us imagine someone who enjoys great, numerous and continuous pleasures of both mind and body, unobstructed by any pain or by the prospect of it. What state could we call more excellent or choiceworthy than this one? For someone in such a condition must possess the strength of a mind which fears neither death nor pain, on the ground that death is painless, and that long-term pain is usually bearable, serious pain short-lived, so that intense pain is compensated by brevity, long-term pain by lightness. Once we have added to this the provision that he is not in awe of divine power, and that he does not allow past pleasures to evaporate but enjoys constantly recalling them, what further improvement could be possible?

These teachings on neither fearing, nor being made wretched by, even the most intense physical suffering are absolutely central to Epicurus' ethics, and their relevance to the plague victims is obvious. Yet nothing has yet been said about them in the poem. As it stands, Lucretius' exam sets us at least one large question to which he has nowhere hinted at the answer.

---

[54] See Clay (1983), pp. 225, 257–66, who cites I 402–3, V 1281–2, VI 68–79, 527–34 in support of the do-it-yourself interpretation. In all these cases, it seems to me, we have been supplied with the necessary materials or explanatory model.   [55] *KD* 4, *SV* 3–4.

The *tetrapharmakos* or 'fourfold remedy', which summarised the cardinal first four tenets of the Epicurean *Kyriai doxai*, ran as follows:[56]

God presents no fears, death no worries. And while what is good is readily attainable, what is terrible is readily endurable.

Up to this point in the poem the first three have all been magnificently preached. The first tenet, that god is not to be feared, is a central theme of the entire poem, emphasised in the proems to books I and III, and consolidated at VI 48–79; indeed, I have argued (§6 above) that Lucretius meant to give it even greater emphasis in the final version of books V–VI. The second, that death is nothing to us, is of course the prime lesson of book III, and, as we have seen, was intended to be that of book IV as well. The third tenet, that good can be readily attained (by imposing a natural limit on our desires), is the theme of the proem to book II, and the proem to book VI glorifies it as the chief benefaction bequeathed to us by Epicurus, as if Lucretius, in embarking on the final lap, were consciously reminding us that this lesson too is in place. But the last of the four cardinal tenets, that pain is readily endured, is totally missing. The plague passage is the best possible evidence that Lucretius meant to add it.[57]

The genetic account of the poem which I have defended in this chapter offers a satisfying explanation of the omission. Lucretius, we have seen, first took over the raw material he needed from his Greek sources *en bloc*, and only in a second phase reworked it to blend with the poem's emerging master-plan. In the case of the plague, as of much else in the second half of the poem, the reworking simply had not yet taken place when he himself died.

What Lucretius still owed his readers was Epicurus' explanation of how tolerance of physical pain depends on our mental attitude to it. To confirm such an account of the poet's intentions, the most that we can hope for in his paraphrase of Thucydides is the occasional clue to his eventual aims. Fortunately, some excellent work has been done on Lucretius' use of Thucydides, and it does indeed confirm that he was heading in some such direction. A series of valuable analyses have

---

[56] For the text, see Long/Sedley (1987), 25J, or Angeli (1988), p. 173. Although both the *tetrapharmakos* and the present arrangement of *KD* may postdate Epicurus, *Ep. Men.* 133 fully confirms that Lucretius would have known the four canonical tenets from Epicurus' own writings.

[57] There is, admittedly, a disparity between the first and the second pair of ethical tenets. The former are themselves founded on the lessons of physics, to which the poem is formally dedicated, while the latter are not. Nevertheless, the third tenet receives enough emphasis in the poem (albeit without formal argument) to encourage the expectation that Lucretius intended no less for the fourth as well.

brought out a number of points where Lucretius departs from the letter of Thucydides' text. His strategic omissions of Thucydidean material and inclusion of additional medical details serve, *inter alia*, to magnify the horror and hopelessness of the situation. Along with this comes a marked tendency to psychologise.[58]

Sometimes the psychologising adjustments emphasise people's horror of death as such. For example, where Thucydides' plague victims on occasion survive thanks to the loss of diseased bodily parts (II 49.7), Lucretius' interpretation is that the fear of death actually drove them to sever their own limbs and organs (1208–12):

> et graviter partim metuentes limina leti
> vivebant ferro privati parte virili,
> et manibus sine nonnulli pedibusque manebant   1210
> in vita tamen, et perdebant lumina partim:
> usque adeo mortis metus his incesserat acer.

> And some of them, through the burden of fear at the onset of death, stayed alive by cutting off their genitals with a knife; others stayed on without hands and feet, but alive; others lost their eyes. So far had the grim fear of death entered them.

Elsewhere Lucretius elaborates on the mental distress brought about by their current plight itself. For instance, where Thucydides (II 49.3) describes the physical symptoms as being μετὰ ταλαιπωρίας μεγάλης, 'with much (physical) distress', Lucretius not only takes this as describing their mental state (which in itself would be an understandable error), but expands it as follows (1158–9):

> intolerabilibusque malis erat anxius angor
> adsidue comes et gemitu commixta querella.

> Their unbearable sufferings were at all times accompanied by a torment of troubledness,[59] and by groaning mixed with lamentation.

Symptoms, not in Thucydides, that the disease is in its terminal stages include (1183–4)

> perturbata animi mens in maerore metuque
> triste supercilium, furiosus voltus et acer . . .

---

[58] Especially Commager (1957), Bright (1971). It is possible to accept Commager's findings without endorsing his conclusion, that Lucretius is presenting the plague itself as moral illness.

[59] That *anxius angor* does not specifically signify 'anxiety' is shown by III 993, where the same phrase describes the torment of one in love (cf. Commager (1957), p. 106). Hence there is no reason to read this passage as focusing especially on the fear of death.

a mind distraught in its grief and fear, a gloomy brow, a frenzied
and grim expression . . .

One further discrepancy is that where Thucydides describes the
crowding of country-dwellers into the city, Lucretius (VI 1252–5) instead
gives the impression that the plague spread death into the countryside. I
imagine that this deliberate shift prepares the ground for a warning
about universality: such sufferings are not a hazard exclusive to civic life,
but one which every human being must be prepared to confront and
deal with. Epicurus, we should recall, had established his Epicurean
community outside the city walls of Athens, thereby reminding us of his
already memorable dictum that 'when it comes to death, we human
beings all live in an unwalled city'.[60]

These and similar clues as to how Lucretius was beginning to shape
his source material lend strong support to the hypothesis that the eventual moral message was to be a quintessentially Epicurean one about
facing terminal suffering with *the right frame of mind* – a frame of mind
which will enable us to eliminate fear and to tolerate pain cheerfully if it
should come our way. Whoever we are and wherever we live, if we have
not learnt this lesson we cannot face the future with truly Epicurean
equanimity.

Like Lucretius', so too Epicurus' last written words had been a
description of terrible physical suffering – his own. Yet his happiness, he
wrote, was unmarred:[61]

I wrote this to you on that blessed day of my life which was also the last.
Strangury and dysentery had set in, with all the extreme intensity of which they
are capable. But the joy in my soul at the memory of our past discussions was
enough to counterbalance all this.

This triumph of philosophical serenity over the most intense physical
pain was surely what Lucretius was preparing to bring into focus at the
close of his poem. The panic, terror and misery of the pre-Epicurean
Athenians, in the face of bodily suffering hardly worse than Epicurus'
own terminal illness, are a brilliantly graphic backdrop to this final lesson
in the Epicurean ethical canon.

[60] *SV* 31. [61] DL X 22.

CHAPTER 6

The imprint of Theophrastus

I. THEOPHRASTUS AND THE WORLD'S DESTRUCTIBILITY

The aim of this chapter is to consolidate a picture, which has been growing in the preceding two chapters, of the vital role of Theophrastus in Lucretius' poem.

I shall start with a close look at one particular text, Theophrastus, fr. 184 FHS&G,[1] which I shall argue lies directly behind a series of arguments in Lucretius book v.

Philo (ll. 1–4, *De aeternitate mundi* 117) reports as follows:

Theophrastus, however, says that those who assert that the world[2] is subject to coming-to-be and passing away were led astray by four principal considerations: (1) the unevenness of the land, (2) the withdrawal of the sea, (3) the dissolution of each of the parts of the whole, (4) the perishing of whole kinds of land animals.

The text then goes on to amplify these four arguments (ll. 4–89, *Aet.* 118–31). Finally comes a refutation of each of the four in turn.

The four arguments attacked by Theophrastus were identified by Zeller[3] as belonging to Zeno of Citium. As a result, the first part of the same text became Zeno fr. 56 in Pearson's collection,[4] and Zeno fr. 106 in vol. I of von Arnim's *Stoicorum Veterum Fragmenta*.[5] They are still often regarded as Zenonian,[6] despite the reservations that have been voiced

---

[1] = Fortenbaugh/Huby/Sharples/Gutas (1992), to which all my Theophrastus fragment numbers refer. The fragments I shall be discussing are in fact edited by R. W. Sharples. In the main I reproduce his translation, with a few modifications, noting any changes which could be thought to be of substance. Fr. 184 will be cited by line number in FHS&G, followed by chapter reference to *De aeternitate mundi*. Since I drafted a large part of the content of this chapter (now published as Sedley (1998a)), the discussion of this fragment in Kidd (1996) has appeared. I am glad to find myself in complete agreement with his conclusions.

[2] Here and elsewhere I shall translate κόσμος 'world' ('universe' Sharples).   [3] Zeller (1876).

[4] Pearson (1891).   [5] Arnim (1903–5).

[6] See e.g. the long appendix in Graeser (1975), pp. 187–206, 'Zenons Argumente gegen Aristoteles' These von der Ewigkeit der Welt'; Long/Sedley (1987), II 275.

from time to time about the passage's credentials.[7] Zeller's proposal is chronologically hard to sustain,[8] and I shall be maintaining that a better explanation of the arguments' origin is available. But let me now briefly discuss one of the items cited by Zeller in his support, since it may indicate something about the passage's character.

In developing the third argument, from the perishability of the world's parts to the perishability of the whole, the text includes the following (ll. 45–8, *Aet.* 125):

Do not the strongest (κραταιότατοι) stones moulder and decay, and because of the weakness of their constitution (ἕξεως) – that is the tension of their *pneuma* (πνευματικὸς τόνος), a bond (δεσμός) which is not unbreakable but only difficult to undo – do they not crumble and dissolve . . .?

The language is unmistakably Stoic, as Zeller was quick to point out. True, but does that show that Theophrastus (died 288–286 BC) in his old age must have been defending Aristotelian cosmology against the new upstarts in the Stoa? Far from it. This formal extension of *pneuma*, in varying states of tension, beyond living beings to become a universal causal agent, is hard to date earlier than Chrysippus, a full generation after Zeno.[9] And we can go further than this. The language used, speaking as it does of the πνευματικὸς τόνος which binds even stones together, is unmistakably the Stoic-influenced language characteristic of Philo himself.[10] Indeed, it seems clear that the language of the entire passage is primarily Philo's own.[11] This must put us on our guard against any assumptions about how much of the content goes back to Theophrastus. But we will nevertheless see reason to regard its principal arguments as authentic, and in what follows I shall permit myself to go on calling the passage's author Theophrastus.

---

[7] Especially Diels (1879), pp. 106–8; Arnim (1893), who, despite inveighing against the attribution of the arguments to Zeno, proceeded to print them as a fragment of Zeno in Arnim (1903–5); Wiersma (1940); McDiarmid (1940).

[8] In §7 below I argue that the Theophrastus text was early enough to draw a response from Epicurus in *On nature* XI XIII, datable (see Ch. 4 §12) before 307/6. Yet Zeno was still a student till *c.* 300.

[9] See e.g. Solmsen (1961b); Lapidge (1978).

[10] Cf. Philo, *Deus* 35–6, λίθων καὶ ξύλων δεσμὸν κραταιότατον ἕξιν εἰργάζετο [*sc.* God], ἡ δ' ἐστὶ πνεῦμα ἀναστρέφον ἐφ' ἑαυτό. ἄρχεται μὲν γὰρ ἀπὸ τῶν μέσων ἐπὶ τὸ πέρατα τείνεσθαι. Cf. *Bel.* 80; *Heres.* 242, τῶν πνευματικῶν τόνων, οἳ συμφυέστατος δεσμὸς ἦσαν.

[11] See further Wiersma (1940). In addition to his evidence, note e.g. l. 56 (*Aet.* 127) τί χρὴ μακρηγορεῖν περὶ . . ., l. 93 (*Aet.* 132) ὦ γενναῖοι , and l. 132 (*Aet.* 138) τριπόθητον, all typically Philonian flourishes. Kidd (1996), pp. 137–8, notes the very Philonian λεωφόρος l. 13 (*Aet.* 119), and Diskin Clay has pointed out to me the citation of Euripides fr. 839 Nauck/Kannicht at ll. 169–71 (*Aet.* 144), a fragment also quoted by Philo at *Aet.* 5 and 30.

2. THE FOURTH ARGUMENT

I want to take the four arguments in their reverse order, since it is the last which most clearly demonstrates Theophrastus' influence on Lucretius.[12] This fourth argument we have already seen labelled as 'the perishing of whole kinds of land animals'. The details, when they come, match this description crudely at best (ll. 80–3, *Aet.* 130):

The fourth and remaining argument is to be stated precisely in the following way, they say. If the world were eternal, living creatures too would be eternal, and especially the human race, in so far as it is superior to the others. But that the human race's origin is recent is clear to those who wish to inquire into natural matters.

After a brief argument for the recentness of mankind's arrival, interrupted by a lacuna, the passage concludes (ll. 87–9, *Aet.* 131):

But if mankind is not eternal, neither is any other living creature; so neither are the places in which these live, earth and water and air. And from this it is clear that the world is perishable.

Clearly a more complex argument has been condensed.[13] Roughly, it seems to run:

(a) Mankind is of recent origin.
(b) What has a temporal origin has a temporal end [a standard assumption].
(c) Therefore mankind will one day perish.
(d) Other species are less favoured than mankind, so will perish too.
(e) Since the species inhabiting earth, water and air will perish, those elements will themselves perish [no reason given].
(f) Since three of the four cosmic masses will perish, the world itself will perish.

---

[12] After writing the first draft of this chapter, I unearthed many of the same points of comparison between the Theophrastus fragment and Lucretius v in the long chapter 9 of Bignone (1936). His thesis is that Zeno, Theophrastus and Epicurus were all engaged in a debate sparked by Aristotle's *De philosophia*: Zeno produced the four arguments against Aristotle, Theophrastus replied to them, and then Epicurus rehabilitated them. Although I shall argue that this cannot be entirely the right story, Bignone's discussion does contain many acute observations on the links between the Theophrastus and Lucretius texts (following the lead of Norden (1893)). Typically of Bignone, they are hidden in a jungle of confused speculation which makes them hard to pick out (especially for those already repelled by the author's incessant self-congratulation). For instance, although his conclusion is that the Epicureans were responding to the Theophrastus text, he frequently talks as if it were the other way round (ii 450, 456–8, 472–3). All this has had the effect of making his real discoveries pass virtually unnoticed. Even Boyancé (1963), pp. 214–21, while endorsing Bignone's general thesis about the polemical motivation of Lucretius v, totally fails to pick up the crucial role of Theophrastus fr. 184. On this topic, cf. also Solmsen (1951).   [13] This point is well made by Runia (1986), p. 83.

It is not yet clear why in Theophrastus' introductory summary of this argument – 'the perishing of whole kinds of land animals' – the species covered by (d) and (e) should have been narrowed down to land animals, but we can safely postpone the answer to this puzzle for a while. More urgently, we might ask whether Philo's paraphrase distorts the original balance of the argument, by concentrating almost exclusively on step (a), the recent origin of mankind. But it will become clear that this was, at least, the step on which Theophrastus chose to concentrate his criticism, and on which he therefore probably concentrated his summary too. Significantly, it is also the part of the argument singled out for defence by the Epicureans.

The details of step (a) are given as follows (ll. 82–7, *Aet.* 130–1):

But that the human race's origin is recent is clear to those who wish to inquire into natural matters; for it is reasonable, indeed necessary, that the crafts should exist alongside mankind and be of the same age, not only because what is systematic is proper to what is rational by nature, but also because it is not possible to live without these. So let us consider the date of each craft, disregarding the stories told about the gods by the tragic poets [lacuna].

Unfortunately the promised survey of the crafts has vanished into the lacuna at the end. But we can infer something of its contents from the argument at Lucretius v 324–34:[14]

praeterea si nulla fuit genitalis origo
terrarum et caeli semperque aeterna fuere,   325
cur supera bellum Thebanum et funera Troiae
non alias alii quoque res cecinere poetae?
quo tot facta virum totiens cecidere neque usquam
aeternis famae monumentis insita florent?
verum, ut opinor, habet novitatem summa recensque   330
naturast mundi neque pridem exordia cepit.
quare etiam quaedam nunc artes expoliuntur,
nunc etiam augescunt; nunc addita navigiis sunt
multa, modo organici melicos peperere sonores.

Besides, if earth and heaven had no origin of birth, and always existed, being eternal, why is it that other poets have not also sung of other things before the Theban War and the sack of Troy? Into what place have all those deeds of men again and again fallen, and nowhere been planted to flourish in the eternal monuments of fame? But actually, I believe, the world is new

---

[14] Lucretius concludes this passage, at 335–7, with a comment on the newness of his own philosophical task; this is presumably his own personal touch, and can be ignored for present purposes.

and of recent birth,[15] and did not begin long ago. That is why even now some crafts are being perfected, even now developing. Only now have certain improvements been made to ships, just recently did musicians create their melodious sounds.

Now the mere correspondence of Lucretius' argument with the truncated one recorded by Theophrastus does not yet demonstrate that the Epicureans learnt it from Theophrastus. The hypothesis of a common source would do as well. But the supposition of direct Theophrastean influence will become unavoidable as soon as we see that the Epicureans have adjusted their version of the argument to take account of Theophrastus' criticisms.

Theophrastus' first criticism is as follows (ll. 172–6, *Aet.* 145):

Certainly, to continue, it is complete foolishness for the human race to be dated by the crafts. For if anyone follows this absurd argument they will show that the world is quite new, having been put together hardly a thousand years ago, since those who we are told were the discoverers of the crafts do not go back more than that number of years.[16]

It is not clear why Theophrastus infers that the world will be *no* older than mankind. He may be assuming, either on his own account or by inference from step (e), that the principal cosmic masses have only the same lifespan as the species which inhabit them. But whatever his reasons, it seems clear that his inference was accepted and accommodated by the Epicureans.[17] Lucretius, as we have just seen, builds it into his version of the argument that both the crafts, and the world itself, are indeed of very recent origin – barely older than the Theban and Trojan wars. It is evident that this must be an Epicurean concession rendered expedient in order to meet the Theophrastean objection, rather than a standard tenet. For in an argument at the end of book II, undoubtedly echoing an original passage of Epicurus,[18] Lucretius has already argued for the world's perishability on the premise that, far from being young, it has already passed its peak and entered its terminal decline.

---

[15] For this translation of *recensque naturast mundi*, see Clay (1983), pp. 86–7.

[16] The figure 1,000 years confirms that we have here Theophrastus' own formulation, not Philo's. Plato, in Theophrastus' own lifetime, could speak of the arts as 1,000 or 2,000 years old (*Laws* 677d), but no one in Philo's day, four centuries later, could plausibly still have put the figure as low as 1,000 (especially someone living in Egypt, whose civilisation was by common consent much older than that of Greece).

[17] This fact seems to preclude the possibility that the inference used a teleological premise, namely that the cosmic masses exist purely for the sake of their respective inhabitants.

[18] II 1118–74. It relies on the analogy of the world's growth and decline to those of a living being, 1118–43, an analogy already invoked for the same purpose by Epicurus, see fr. 305 Usener.

Theophrastus' objection to the argument continues as follows (ll. 176–204, *Aet.* 146–9):

If then we are to say that the crafts are as old as mankind, we must do so not carelessly and lazily, but with the help of research concerning nature. What research? Destructions of things on land,[19] not of all of them together but of most of them, are attributed to two principal causes, indescribable onslaughts of fire and water; they say that each of these descends in turn, after very long cycles of years. So, when a conflagration occurs, a stream of fire from heaven is poured out from above and scattered far and wide, spreading over great regions of the inhabited earth; when there is an inundation, all the substance of water rushes down in the form of rain;[20] rivers fed by their own springs, and winter torrents, not only flow in spate but exceed the usual level to which they rise and either break down their banks or leap over them, rising to the greatest height. Then they overflow and pour out over the adjacent plain. This is first of all divided into great lakes, as the water always settles into the hollow parts, but as the water continues to flow in and submerges the intervening strips of dry land by which the lakes are separated, in the end it becomes a great expanse of sea as the many lakes are joined together.

And by these conflicting forces those who dwell in opposite places are destroyed in turn. The fire destroys those who dwell on the mountains and hills and in places where water is scarce, since they do not have abundant water, which is the natural defence against fire. And conversely the water destroys those who dwell by rivers or lakes or the sea; for evils are accustomed to fasten on those close at hand, at first or even solely.

When the greater part of mankind perishes in the ways stated, apart from countless other minor ways, of necessity the crafts fail too; for it is not possible to see knowledge on its own, apart from its practitioner. When the common diseases[21] abate, and the race begins to grow and flourish from those who were not previously overcome by the troubles that pressed upon them, then the crafts too begin to arise again; they have not come into being for the first time then, but had become rare[22] because of the reduction in the number of their possessors.

Theophrastus' point is of course that the data to which the fourth argument appeals – the newness of the crafts – could equally well be accounted for by periodic cataclysms in an eternal world. Two aspects are worth noting in passing.

First, we can now see that it must be Theophrastus himself who chose, at the beginning of the fragment, to characterise the fourth argument as

[19] τῶν κατὰ γῆν ('things on the earth', Sharples). Or perhaps 'land species'.
[20] 'Every sort of water rushes down', Sharples. But I think ἅπασαν τήν is more likely to mean 'all' than 'every'. I also prefer not to delete κατομβρίαν, with Diels, but to emend it to κατ' ὄμβρον, 'in the form of rain'.
[21] I translate νόσοι 'diseases', not 'ills' with Sharples, in order to bring out a link with Lucretius – see below. [22] ὑποσπανισθείσας: '(previously) neglected', Sharples.

based on 'the perishing of whole kinds of land animals'. For near the beginning of his reply to it, just quoted, he notes that it is primarily the virtual destruction of *land* species that could equally well be accounted for by periodic conflagrations and floods. Water dwellers would clearly be largely immune to both, nor would one expect birds to be badly affected by either, given the availability of water as a refuge from fire, and high ground from flood (ll. 192 7, *Aet.* 148). Revealingly, then, he turns out to be labelling the argument from the outset, not in the terms in which its proponents would present it, but with an eye to the nature of the refutation he is already planning. His project is not to catalogue others' arguments in the manner of a neutral observer, but to engineer a dialectical confrontation. We will be able to make use of this observation later.

Second, as David Runia has expertly brought out,[23] the description of conflagration and flood draws heavily on *Timaeus* 22 – not actually with any verbatim quotation, but with an extended interpretative paraphrase. Runia argues, reasonably enough, that this 'slavish dependence on an authoritative text' is more likely to betray Philo's hand than Theophrastus'. He points out that, while Theophrastus as an Aristotelian can be expected to subscribe in general terms to the theory of periodic cataclysms,[24] Aristotle seems to have concentrated on floods (especially *Meteor.* 1 14), to the exclusion of conflagrations.

Runia's conclusion is certainly appealing. On the other hand, the passage does not really read like anybody's appeal to authority. On the contrary, that the debt is specifically to Plato is, if anything, disguised by the paraphrastic style and the inexplicit attribution, 'they say' (φασίν, l. 181, *Aet.* 146 fin.). I strongly suspect that the Timaean material was already included by Theophrastus, motivated not by reverence for Plato but by a dialectical strategy. But to this too we will return later.

What can be asserted with some confidence is that, with or without the Timaean details, the reference to conflagration as well as flood was already in the Theophrastean reply as Philo found it. That is because Lucretius, immediately following his own appeal to the newness of the crafts, can be seen making a direct countermove to the Theophrastean

---

[23] Runia (1986), pp. 83 4.
[24] Aristotle (*De philosophia* fr. 8 Ross; *Met.* Λ 8, 1074b10 13) taught that the crafts and other forms of learning were all but wiped out by periodic cataclysms, but regenerated from the remnants much the same theory as is applied to the crafts in the Theophrastus text. For Theophrastus himself there appears to be no independent evidence, but fr. 584A shows that he subscribed to *some* sort of genetic theory of human civilisation, and it is hard to think what that can be if not the cataclysm theory.

reply, and doing so with explicit reference to fire as well as flood (v 338–50):

quod si forte fuisse antehac eadem omnia credis,
sed periisse hominum torrenti saecla vapore,
aut cecidisse urbis magno vexamine mundi,   340
aut ex imbribus assiduis exisse rapaces
per terras amnis atque oppida coperuisse,
tanto quique magis victus fateare necessest
exitium quoque terrarum caelique futurum.
nam cum res tantis morbis tantisque periclis   345
temptarentur, ibi si tristior incubuisset
causa, darent late cladem magnasque ruinas.
nec ratione alia mortales esse videmur,
inter nos nisi quod morbis aegrescimus isdem
atque illi quos a vita natura removit.   350

If however you happen to believe that all the same things existed previously, but that the generations of humans perished through scorching heat, or that cities fell because of a great cosmic upheaval, or that as a result of incessant rain the rivers overflowed to sweep over the land and engulfed the towns, you are all the more defeated, and must admit that earth and heaven will also be destroyed. For when the world was beset by such terrible diseases and dangers, if at that time a more ruinous cause had settled on it, it would have faced destruction across its breadth and massive catastrophe. The reason why we are seen by each other to be mortal is precisely that we fall ill with the same diseases as those people whom nature has removed from life.

Unmistakably, the Epicureans have taken account of the Theophrastean reply and tried to turn it to their own advantage, arguing that to cite cataclysmic events like conflagrations and floods as explaining the newness of the crafts is to allow that the world might perish in those events.[25] Lucretius' description even echoes Theophrastus in certain details.[26] In particular, where Theophrastus, echoing a simile at *Tim.* 23a7, had spoken of the cataclysms as 'diseases' (νόσοι, l. 200, *Aet.* 149) which eventually

---

[25] But for the interruption at 351–79, it might seem natural to read 380–415 as continuing this same argument. But note that while 338–50 has a highly hypothetical character, provoked by the need to answer Theophrastus, 380–415 changes tone and argues from mythical evidence that there actually have been a conflagration and a flood. While this may indirectly echo *Tim.* 22c, it does not seem to be part of the reply to Theophrastus.

[26] Cf. Bignone (1936) II 475. The attribution of the flood to heavy rain making rivers overflow is a further shared feature of the two passages, but no doubt too commonplace to carry any weight here.

abate, Lucretius too calls them diseases (*morbis*, 345), but adds pointedly – drawing on the lessons of book III (especially 472–3) – that in our own experience there is an intimate link between disease and mortality.

It emerges, then, that the palpable dialectical interplay between Lucretius V 324–50 and Theophrastus' presentation and refutation of the fourth argument for the world's impermanence is so tight that it can only be explained on the assumption that the Epicureans were responding directly to Theophrastus.

3. THE THIRD ARGUMENT

Moving backwards now to the third argument, we will be able to detect a similar pattern. This is the argument from 'the dissolution of each of the parts of the whole'. The expansion of this at 41–79 (*Aet.* 124–9) contains some strange intrusions – not just what we have seen to be Philo's own inserted remarks about the 'pneumatic tension' of stones, but also a long and grotesque comparison of fire to suicidal Indian snakes squashed under the fallen bodies of the elephants they have just killed. (Whether you blame this latter oddity on Theophrastus or on Philo seems arbitrary – it simply depends on which one you are prepared to have the worse opinion of.) It can be outlined as follows. Each of the four cosmic masses – earth, water, air and fire – consists of parts which eventually perish: stones crumble, water becomes putrid, air becomes sickly, fire burns itself out. Therefore the universe, consisting of these mortal parts, is perishable too.

Lucretius at exactly the corresponding point – V 235–323, immediately preceding his version of the fourth argument – similarly argues that the world has a temporal beginning and end on the ground that each of the four cosmic elements is unstable. Significantly he even, twice over, takes the four elements in the same order as Theophrastus. This sequence – earth, water, air, fire – follows the cosmic strata outwards from earth to the heavens, and is not used elsewhere by Lucretius except in a passage where, unlike here, he is specifically describing the layered structure of the world (V 449–59, 495–8; contrast the different orders of the elements adopted at I 567, 715, 744, V 142–3, 248–9). This correspondence helps confirm the impression that he is taking his lead from the Theophrastean text.

Theophrastus' own reply to the version of the argument which he reports is that ordered cyclical change of the elements into each other points if anything towards the everlastingness of the world (cf. Aristotle, *GC* 337a1 ff.): destructibility would follow only if all the parts perished simultaneously. This time the Lucretian version less obviously contains any direct response. But he does take up the point about cyclical change, and develops it in a different direction. He describes each of the four cosmic masses neither as perishing *tout court*, as in the argument reported by Theophrastus, nor as perishing into the neighbouring element, as in Theophrastus' reply, but as undergoing an internal cyclical change in the form of dispersal and accumulation. Earth is eroded, but replenished with decaying organic matter. Sea and rivers evaporate but are refilled. The air is constantly both absorbing and depositing particles shed by other things. And the sun, moon and stars are constantly both shedding light and renewing their supply of it.

How is this meant to prove their overall destructibility? There seems good reason to believe that Lucretius is reproducing, if imperfectly, Epicurus' own revision of the argument reported by Theophrastus. For where that argument had inferred the perishability of the world from the *perishing* of its parts, we are told that Epicurus, like Lucretius in our passage, inferred it from the *change* which the world's parts undergo.[27] Adding the clues supplied by Lucretius, we can perhaps reconstruct the full Epicurean argument as follows. Theophrastus has argued that, provided the perishing of the elements is their cyclical destruction into one another, there need be no implication of eventual overall destruction. But on the contrary, such radical change would itself amount to instant annihilation (see Lucretius 1 782ff.), leaving the natural cycle with no enduring substrate to account for its evident regularity – the regularity invoked by the main Epicurean arguments for atomism. In reality a process like, say, evaporation, which Theophrastus calls the destruction of water into air, is the dispersal of water's unchanging atomic particles into the atmosphere. So too quite generally, the destruction Theophrastus speaks of takes the form of the *dispersal and accumulation* of each cosmic mass. This does, unlike Theophrastus' theory, account for cosmic regularities. But if it is possible for a thing to be dispersed in part, it is at least possible for it to be dispersed in its entirety.[28] And given infinite time, every possibility is sooner or later realised.[29] Therefore each cosmic mass will eventually disperse in its entirety.

Read this way, the Epicurean argument looks like a considered reply

---

[27] Scholion on *Ep. Hdt.* 74: φθαρτούς φησι τοὺς κόσμους, μεταβαλλόντων τῶν μερῶν.

[28] For a version of Theophrastus' argument which tries to refute this inference, see Alexander, *Quaest.* 1 23 (transl. with notes by Sharples (1992)), which could conceivably be responding to the Epicureans.

[29] For Epicurean use of the principle of plenitude, see fr. 266 Usener, and cf. Lucr. 1 232–3, III 855 61. The same principle underlies the argument of Melissus which started this entire debate (B7.2): 'If it were to become changed by a single hair in 10,000 years, it would all perish in the whole of time.'

to the debate constructed by Theophrastus, accepting his criticism that
the original argument failed to allow for the cyclical character of elemental change, but re-analysing that cycle in atomist terms which justify
the expectation that the cosmic order must eventually disintegrate.

4. THE FIRST AND SECOND ARGUMENTS

I hope by now to have made a sufficiently persuasive case for reading the
entire sequence of arguments at Lucretius v 235–350 as a systematic
Epicurean defence against Theophrastus of the third and fourth arguments for the world's impermanence, as reported and criticised by him.

The first argument, from 'the unevenness of the land', is that, if the
world had existed from infinite time past, erosion would by now have
completely flattened the mountains (ll. 4–17, *Aet.* 118–19). Theophrastus'
reply (ll. 91–128, *Aet.* 132–7) is that, mountains being volcanically caused,
their erosion is counterbalanced by new growth. It is worth noticing that
Lucretius does in passing, at the end of his version of argument 3, echo
this same argument. After working his way through the four elemental
masses, as we saw, he adds to his list of unstable items the two things with
the strongest claim to indissolubility: solid rock (v 306–17) and the vault
of heaven (318–22). The fragility of solid rock is illustrated not only with
the decay of buildings but also with mountain erosion (v 313–17):

Do we not see rocks roll down, torn from high mountains, unable to endure the
mighty force of a finite timespan? For they would not suddenly be torn away
and fall if they had from infinite time past suffered without damage all the harsh
treatment of the ages.

This pointedly recalls the Theophrastean erosion argument (between
them, in fact, they seem to be the *only* recorded arguments inferring the
world's impermanence from the timescale of mountain erosion). But the
tactic has changed. The original argument had relied on the incomplete-
ness of mountain erosion to show that it had started only a finite number
of years ago. Lucretius' version instead uses the actual phenomenon of
mountain erosion to show that even the most solid objects, like lumps of
rock, are subject to dissolution within a finite timespan — hence the same
should be true of the world as a whole. Crucially, this reworked version
is not directly vulnerable to Theophrastus' objection. We may put it
down as yet another Epicurean rehabilitation of the arguments pilloried
by Theophrastus.[30]

---

[30] Arnim (1893) notices the connexion between the Theophrastean and Lucretian arguments, but
is clearly unjustified in inferring that Theophrastus was himself reproducing an Epicurean argu-

Finally, the second argument is the one from 'the withdrawal of the sea' (ll. 18–40, *Aet.* 120–3). It may be summarised as follows. The sea has steadily diminished in size, as is shown (a) by islands which have within recorded history appeared out of the sea, (b) by the pebbles and seashells found in inland areas. We may infer that earth and air are likewise diminishing, and that all three elements will end up as fire.

Theophrastus objects (ll. 129–58, *Aet.* 138–42) that there is just as much evidence that elsewhere the sea has spread in historical times, so that an equilibrium between land and sea is being maintained. Once again, his reply is directly drawn from Aristotle (see *Meteor.* I 14; cf. Theophrastus, *Metaphysics* 10a28–9), but the actual evidence he cites is more widely gathered, including the Atlantis myth cited from the *Timaeus*.

Unlike the other three, Lucretius altogether omits this argument. To have adopted the premise that the sea is diminishing would clearly have militated against the claims he makes at v 235–323 when rehabilitating the third argument, namely that each cosmic mass, including the sea, undergoes cyclical change in the form of dispersal and counteracting replenishment.[31] For once, the Epicureans may have thought Theophrastus' rebuttal well founded.[32]

5. THE PROVENANCE OF THEOPHRASTUS FR. 184

We can now turn to the character of the work in which Theophrastus presented and criticised the four arguments. I have already noted two features. One is that right from the outset he presents the arguments not in their own right but as materials for a dialectical confrontation. The other is that although the rebuttals clearly accord in general terms with his own Aristotelian views, they incorporate a good deal of material drawn from non-Aristotelian sources, such as the *Timaeus* with its thesis of periodic conflagrations and its Atlantis myth. It is as if the dialectical confrontation which he is engineering is meant not to be overtly one between Aristotelians and non-Aristotelians.

I can now add to these observations one about the heterogeneous provenance of the four arguments themselves. It is clearly a mistake to treat them as a unified body of argument, traceable to a single philosopher or school. Nothing is known of the origins of the first and fourth arguments, but something can be said about the other two. The second,

---

ment. Quite apart from the chronological problem, this overlooks the important difference between the two versions.

[31] Cf. Lucretius VI 608–38 on the equilibrium between the sea's depletion and replenishment.
[32] Cf. Bignone (1936) II 492–3.

from the sea's withdrawal, and also Theophrastus' own refutation of it, are both drawn directly from Aristotle, *Meteorologica* I 14 (especially 352a17 ff.). Aristotle in fact later (II 3, 356b6 ff.) names Democritus as its author. However, we may doubt whether Theophrastus wanted to attach it exclusively to Democritus. For one thing, we know that he spoke of Anaximander and Diogenes as proponents of the thesis that the sea will eventually dry up.[33] For another, he also incorporates into the argument a reference to seashells on dry land as testimony to the sea's withdrawal, an observation known to stem from Xenophanes.[34] Finally the further idea, also incorporated into the argument, that all the elements will eventually turn to fire could hardly be represented as Democritean, but may on the other hand reflect Theophrastus' reading of Heraclitus — that the world as a whole originates from fire and eventually returns into it.[35] It seems, in short, that Theophrastus was trying to associate the argument with a wide range of earlier philosophers, and not to record the views of any one person.

There is certainly no necessity to see in the second argument a specific allusion to the Stoic 'conflagration' (*ekpyrōsis*) theory — even though the Stoics did in due course take up the Theophrastean interpretation of Heraclitus, as well, incidentally, as adopting a version of the second argument itself.[36] Nor need the third argument — the one from the perishability of the world's parts to that of the whole — presuppose Stoicism, as many have thought, despite the fact that a Stoic version of it is recorded.[37] Zeller reasoned that, since it was Aristotle who made the world's eternity an issue for the first time, the objections recorded by Theophrastus must be post-Aristotelian, and that Zeno is the first suitable proponent to assign them to. But here it may be objected that the debate had multiple sources — witness for instance Democritus' contribution — and that it stemmed in large measure from Plato's *Timaeus* and the controversy, which was to run thoughout the remainder of antiquity, as to whether its description of the world as γενητός refers to a literal genetic origin.

Speusippus and Xenocrates took creation in the *Timaeus* as a purely

[33] Theophrastus fr. 221.   [34] Hippolytus, *Ref.* I 14.5.

[35] Fr. 225. See e.g. Kirk (1954), pp. 318ff., 327ff., Kerschensteiner (1955), for the generally accepted view that Theophrastus (i) interpreted Heraclitus this way and (ii) influenced the later Stoicising presentation of him. (Long (1975–6) disputes (ii) but accepts (i).) The evidence is not unambiguous, but his attribution (fr. 225, 18–21) to Heraclitus of a fated time-limit on cosmic change is probably a development of Aristotle's view (*De caelo* I 10, 279b14) that Heraclitus agrees with Empedocles in making the world everlastingly move between alternate generation and destruction.   [36] DL VII 141 *fin.*   [37] DL VII 141.

expository device, but it can hardly be doubted that at least some early Platonists, like their ex-colleague Aristotle[38] in their own day and their fellow-Platonists Plutarch and Atticus in the second century AD, defended the genetic reading. It is easy to imagine that the third argument's inference, from the perishability of the world's parts to that of the whole, originated in the interpretation of its mirror image at *Tim.* 28b: the argument that the world is something 'which becomes' (γιγνόμενον) and that it therefore, as a whole, 'has become'.

We are told (frr. 241A–B) that Theophrastus in his work *On physical opinions* (Περὶ τῶν φυσικῶν δοξῶν), while acknowledging the Speusippean interpretation of the *Timaeus* as a possible one, based his own criticisms of Plato on the genetic reading. It is more than likely that this was the context from which fr. 184 is drawn. Jaap Mansfeld has convincingly argued that this massive work – probably in eighteen books, and variously called *Physical opinions* or *On physical opinions* – was not a history of physics, but a collection of materials for use in dialectical debate about physical issues, and included Theophrastus' own counter-arguments to the positions supported by others.[39] The dialectical structure that has emerged in fr. 184 fits this description to perfection.[40]

6. METEOROLOGY

In Chapter 5, §8, we encountered Theophrastus' meteorological text, conjecturally identified as the *Metarsiologica*, an abridged form of which is extant in Syriac and Arabic.[41] Since the first partial discovery and publication of this text in 1918, and the subsequent work of Reitzenstein,[42] it has been recognised that it bears a direct causal relation to Epicurean meteorology, especially as we meet this in book VI of Lucretius. Theophrastus does not just anticipate the Epicurean method of multiple explanations. Many of the specific explanations which he

---

[38] Aristotle (*De caelo* 279b32) attributes the non-genetic reading to 'some people', which is not most obviously interpreted as signalling the unanimous view of the Academy. On Aristotle's reading, see also Baltes (1976), pp. 5–22.

[39] Mansfeld (1992b). I also accept his persuasive defence of the title as (*On*) *physical opinions*, not (*On*) *the opinions of the physicists*. The significance of this, as he shows, is that the work concentrated on the opinions themselves, not on their authors.

[40] This is the work to which Diels (1879), pp. 106, 486–91, following Usener, assigned the fragment, numbering it *Phys. op.* fr. 12.

[41] The full text of this was published for the first time by Daiber (1992). That it is an abridgement of the *Metarsiologica* (a two-book work), and not as Daiber thought the whole of it, is argued convincingly by Mansfeld (1992a).   [42] Bergsträsser (1918), Reitzenstein (1924).

catalogues are effectively identical to those in Lucretius. Moreover, the recognition of direct influence has become even more inescapable since 1992, when Hans Daiber gave us the first full edition and translation of the Theophrastus text. In addition to the many specific aetiologies, and the methodological principle of multiple explanation, it turns out to contain a theological excursus which is astonishingly close in content to an equivalent passage in Lucretius vi. Since these links have already been very effectively set out and explored by Jaap Mansfeld,[43] I can be brief in illustrating them.

In *Metars.* 6.67–81, Theophrastus offers naturalistic explanations for two alleged facts: (1) that thunderbolts are more frequent in spring, and (2) that they are more frequent in high places. Both points are later cited in the theological excursus, where Theophrastus argues that thunderbolts, along with the other meteorological phenomena, are not the work of god (14.18–25):

> If thunderbolts originate in god, why do they mostly occur during spring or in high places, but not during winter or summer or in low places? In addition, why do thunderbolts fall on uninhabited mountains, on seas, on trees and on irrational living beings? God is not angry with those! Further, more astonishing would be the fact that thunderbolts can strike the best people and those who fear god, but not those who act unjustly and propagate evil.

Lucretius, after giving an answer to question (1) – why thunderbolts are more frequent in spring –[44] which simply expands on the content of Theophrastus' own, turns to the same question of divine retribution (vi 379–422). His comments include the following (387–99, 404, 421–2):

> But if it is Jupiter and the other gods who shake the gleaming precincts of heaven with spine-chilling noise, and who hurl fire wherever it pleases each of them, why do they not ensure that those who have recklessly committed abominable crimes are struck and breathe out flames of lightning from their pierced breast, as a grim warning to mortals? Why instead does someone with nothing shameful on his conscience, for all his innocence, get engulfed in flames and swallowed up and swept away by whirlwind and fire descending from heaven? Why, too, do they waste their efforts aiming at deserted places? Is it that when they do that they are excercising their arms and hardening up their muscles? Why do they allow their father's bolt to be blunted in the ground? And why does he himself let them, instead of saving it for his enemies? . . . How does he come

---

[43] Mansfeld (1992a).

[44] vi 357–78. As Mansfeld (1992a), p. 326 notes, Lucretius adds autumn. This may just be his, or Epicurus', addition to the explanandum, since it is in fact an awkwardness for Theophrastus that his explanation of thunderbolts' frequency in spring should imply that they are equally common in autumn (which may be why he avoids mentioning autumn at all in his explanation).

to hurl it into the sea? . . . Why does he usually aim for high places, and why do we see most traces of his fire on the tops of mountains?

Taken severally these questions might sound like stock jokes, and indeed one or two of the same digs at traditional religion are made elsewhere in Lucretius' poem.[45] But the asking of these very same questions by our two authors in the very same context, one in which both are to a large extent invoking the same multiplicity of naturalistic explanations for the same set of meteorological phenomena, rules out coincidence. There really is a shared body of argument here, and we are dealing with one of those rare topics on which Epicureans and Aristotelians could see eye to eye – the exclusion of direct divine causation from the sublunary world.

Before the full publication of the Theophrastus fragments, it was usually thought that this text was a doxographical one, probably part of the *Physical opinions*, cataloguing the meteorological explanations of earlier philosophers. It is now at least clear, as Daiber himself has shown, that the text is arguing Theophrastus' own case. However, it would be risky to press for too sharp a contrast here. The views catalogued by Theophrastus in it are, as a matter of fact, largely collected from his predecessors (as Daiber's commentary brings out), and even in this abridgement[46] their defence is in places put in a form which implies a dialectical confrontation. Besides, we must remember that it is equally true of the long fr. 184 on the world's destructibility, which is certainly doxographical and probably from the *Physical opinions*, that (a) Theophrastus is arguing for his own view most of the time, and (b) the views of earlier philosophers are gathered and synthesised into a single whole, without any apparent emphasis on their attribution to individuals. The meteorological text differs from fr. 184 at least to the extent that Theophrastus is arguing for, not against, the position synthesised out of the work of earlier thinkers, but we have no reason to suppose that that too did not happen sometimes in the *Physical opinions*.

However, it is not my aim to close altogether the gap between the *Metarsiologica* and the *Physical opinions*. What I want to point out is how easily the very same material as we read in the former might have been redeployed in the latter, for different but closely related purposes.

---

[45] II 1101–4.

[46] Mansfeld (1992a), who is responsible for the proposal that it is an abridgement, points out that it is far too short to be the whole of the *Metarsiologica*, which ran to at least two books. However, I am much less confident than he is that the abridgement involves only the omission of some whole sections, with no condensation within the surviving sections (cf. Mansfeld's n. 8, p. 316).

There is in fact very good reason to suspect that the Epicurean arguments in Lucretius VI are based, not on a direct reading of the *Metarsiologica*, but on the equivalent section of the *Physical opinions*. Although the actual material is largely the same in Lucretius VI and the *Metarsiologica*, its organisation differs just enough to suggest that the latter is not the direct source. For one thing, there is relatively little detailed correspondence between the order of explanations adopted for each phenomenon.[17] More significant, however, is the position of *prēstēr* in the exposition. I remarked in Chapter 5 (see p. 159 above, and Chart 4 on p. 158) that Lucretius, like the doxographers, places this phenomenon in an early position (VI 423–50), before cloud and rain, thus respecting the majority ancient view that it is fiery in nature, descending from the heavens. I observed that this does not reflect Lucretius' own Epicurean view of it, which derives it purely from cloud, and that the order followed can therefore be seen to be determined by a doxographical source, not by considerations internal to Epicureanism. Now in the *Metarsiologica* Theophrastus shows himself more or less to share the Epicurean view of *prēstēr*, which he may well have influenced. And since this is not a doxographical work, he for once departs from the doxographical order and instead subsumes *prēstēr* under the heading of winds (*Metars.* 13.43–54). This discrepancy between Lucretius and the *Metarsiologica* confirms the impression that Lucretius' material, even here, is likely to be most directly derived not from the *Metarsiologica* but from Theophrastus' doxographical presentation of the same material in the *Physical opinions*.

7. THEOPHRASTUS, EPICURUS AND LUCRETIUS

We have now examined two major parts of Lucretius' exposition in books V and VI which incorporate or respond to Theophrastus' work, very probably in his *Physical opinions*. Given our earlier findings in Chapter 5, §§6 and 8, it hardly needs arguing here that Lucretius drew this material, not directly from Theophrastus, but from Theophrastus' younger contemporary Epicurus, whose *On nature* XI–XIII he proves to have been following so closely throughout these two books.

It is now time to recall that a similar role for Theophrastus looked likely in a previous context. Both Epicurus and Lucretius, we saw (Ch.

---

[17] E.g. for the explanations of thunder, see Reitzenstein (1924), p. 26, or the Lucretian parallels cited by Daiber (1992), pp. 272–3. Even for the theological excursus examined above, Mansfeld (1992a), pp. 326–7, points out that the same arguments are used but in different orders.

4, §10, Ch. 5, §4), classify previous physical theories on the Aristotelian principle which Theophrastus made the standard doxographical one: monism, finite pluralism, infinite pluralism. They also seem reliant on that same doxographical tradition in their actual presentation of these doctrines – especially in using the rubric of 'homoiomereia' for Anaxagoras' theory.[48] It is worth recalling that *On nature* xiv seems to end the critique of the finite pluralists with Plato: this may reflect the apparent fact that Theophrastus took his doxography down only as far as Plato, and omitted his contemporaries, including Aristotle himself.[49]

Another possible case of Theophrastean influence is the following. The better-preserved parts of *On nature* xiv include criticisms of Plato which, as Wolfgang Schmid pointed out, can be thought to reflect Aristotle's in *De caelo* iii 7–8.[50] In view of what we have already seen of Theophrastus' methods, it will be both plausible and economical to guess that the Aristotelian criticisms had been redeployed by him in his report and critique of Plato's element theory, and were in turn taken up by Epicurus.

This leads me on to a further consideration. Epicurus in general shows little, if any, positive influence from Aristotle's own theories and concepts. At least, attempts to locate such influence in his thought, for instance in his theory of free will, have in every case proved at the very least controversial. And we should indeed be wary of expecting him to have looked, for positive ideas, to a philosophical tradition so alien to his own.[51] But he does much more recognisably show a negative Aristotelian influence. In particular, his theory of minima involves a detailed attempt to circumvent Aristotle's criticisms of comparable theories in *Physics* vi,[52] and his treatment of void probably responds similarly to the arguments against void in *Physics* iv.[53] I long assumed that the *Physics* was one Aristotelian text which, because of the threat it posed to atomism, Epicurus did take the trouble to study.[54] But in view of the pattern we have seen, it seems much more likely that those Aristotelian criticisms reappeared in Theophrastus alongside his doxographical reports of

[48] Pp. 125–6, 146 above; cf. Schofield (1975).
[49] This is certainly true of the *De sensibus*, and, as far as I know, is confirmed by silence about later philosophers in his fragments. [50] Schmid (1936). [51] Cf. Sedley (1989b), pp. 117–18.
[52] This was shown above all by Furley (1967). For further development of the same theme, cf. Long/Sedley (1987), §§9 and 11. [53] See Inwood (1981).
[54] Not much can be made of Philodemus, P.Herc. 1005, fr. 111 (Angeli (1988), pp. 166–7), in which a letter by a first-generation Epicurean, not necessarily Epicurus himself, is quoted as mentioning Aristotle's *Analytics* and Περὶ φύσεως. Even if one assumes that this latter is the *Physics*, there is no indication whether he has read it, or, if he has, at what date (the immediately following letter is dated 280/279, which would be too late to play a part in our story).

atomism, and once again that may well be the route by which they found
their way to Epicurus.

Aristotle's school treatises appear to have been relatively neglected in
the Hellenistic period.[55] (It would be a curious irony if this proved to be
largely due to the Hellenistic philosophers' reliance on Theophrastus'
doxography, which excluded Aristotle from its scope!) Such a conclusion
is not universally shared, but when the denial of it appeals, as it sometimes does, to likelihood – how *could* they have ignored Aristotle? – that
is uncomfortably reminiscent of the widespread, but equally unfounded,
refusal to believe that Lucretius could have ignored Stoicism (see Ch. 3).

Although numerous attempts have been made to discern Aristotle's
direct influence on Epicurean texts, including the poem of Lucretius, the
strongest objection seems to me to lie in the contrast with Theophrastus.
At least some of the cases where Theophrastus has influenced an argument in Lucretius are quite simply unmistakable, in spite of the fact that
only a tiny fraction of Theophrastus' work has survived. I hope that the
argument over the world's destructibility, which has taken up the bulk of
this chapter, will commend itself as one such case. But at any rate what
we have seen to be the (for once positive) influence of Theophrastus'
meteorology on Lucretius book VI is so transparent that as far as I know
it has never been denied. Why are there no equally unmistakable
Aristotelian imprints? The difference makes it much more believable
that it was primarily through Theophrastus, and not through the direct
impact of Aristotle's treatises, that Aristotelianism helped shape the
Epicureanism which we can read in the poem of Lucretius.

It is noteworthy that Epicurus wrote a work *Against Theophrastus*, in at
least two books, the only surviving fragments of which concern
physics.[56] Since the *Physical opinions* was serving Epicurus as his source-
book for earlier views, not for Theophrastus' own, *On nature* itself cannot
always have offered him adequate opportunity for direct replies to the
less acceptable of Theophrastus' own physical opinions. That he should,
as an offshoot, feel the need to write a separate treatise against
Theophrastus becomes entirely understandable.

It is surely not an accident that no corresponding treatise 'Against
Aristotle' is attested. There is no need to suppose that what drew
Epicurus to Theophrastus was an interest in Aristotelianism as such. We
therefore have no warrant for expecting further Aristotelian influences

---

[55] I here declare a large measure of agreement with Sandbach (1985).
[56] Epicurus frr. 29–30 Usener, where the topic is whether colour exists in the dark.

to show through in our Epicurean texts, ones acquired through a reading of Peripatetic doctrinal writings. The Theophrastus who made his mark on Epicurus, and as a result can be detected again and again in the pages of Lucretius, was not – except incidentally – Theophrastus the Aristotelian. Rather, it was Theophrastus the collector, synthesiser and critical purveyor of doctrines from the earlier history of physics.

We have encountered a substantial quantity of Theophrastean material in Lucretius. That Lucretius has absorbed this through Epicurus, and not by his own direct reading of Theophrastus, seems overwhelmingly probable. The findings of Chapter 3 make it intrinsically unlikely that Lucretius would strike out on his own in such a way. For Epicurus, on the other hand, Theophrastus' *Physical opinions* was a recently published encyclopaedia of physical argument, the first work of its kind and an ideal source for someone who, in writing a global treatise on physics, sought a synoptic view of the state of play down to his own time. We in any case know enough about Epicurus' own debt to Theophrastus in meteorological methodology to be quite confident that here at least Theophrastus' influence on Lucretius was mediated by him. In this chapter I have tried to show why, in other areas too, the visible response to Theophrastus is most likely to reflect Epicurus' polemical concerns, rather than Lucretius' own.

CHAPTER 7

The transformation of book I

1. THE CONTENTS

I argued in Chapter 5 that Lucretius, for reasons perhaps connected with the enormous size of his Greek source text, initially drew large quantities of material from it *en bloc*, following its order of exposition fairly mechanically. In a second phase, he set about reorganising it into the carefully structured six-book poem that we know. But he did not live to complete the task. By the time of his death he had got as far as reversing books III and IV into their present numbered order; and he had, as far as I can tell, fully reworked the contents of books I–III. However, he had plans for the reorganisation of books IV–VI which can be recovered from his proems, but which he did not live to put into effect. In their present state, books IV–VI to a large extent simply reproduce the sequence of the corresponding books of *On nature*. It is likely that the same was true of the opening books in the first phase of composition.

In this chapter I want to give an idea of what the completed reorganisation of his material in books I–III may have involved. But I shall select for the purpose the contents of book I only. Even here I shall largely pass over the proem, which I have dealt with separately in Chapter 1.

Chart 5 (pp. 188–9 below) shows the overall layout of the book, with equivalences to Chart 2 (p. 136 above) added in italics.[1]

2. *DRN* I AND *ON NATURE* I–II

We have seen in Chapter 5 that the basic structure of this book reflects that of its source text, Epicurus, *On nature* I–II. This dependence can now be observed in one specific detail. If we bypass Epicurus' methodological preliminaries in book I, which are replaced in the *DRN* by Lucretius'

---

[1] There is nothing innovative about this table, apart perhaps from my inclusion of 705–11 in the final argument against the monists, rather than treating it as making a new beginning.

Chart 2b

Nat.			*DRN*
I	(i)	methodological preliminaries	—
	(ii)	nothing comes into being out of nothing	I 149–214
	(iii)	nothing perishes into nothing	I 215–264
	(iv)	the all never changes	—
	(L1)	*the existence of the invisible*	I 265–328
	(L2)	*the existence of void*	I 329–417
	(v)	the all consists of bodies and void	I 418–29
	(vi)	some bodies are compounds, others constituents	—
II	(vii)	nothing exists independently except bodies and void	I 430–82
	(viii)	bodies' constituents (distinguished in (vi)) are atomic	I 483–634
		Criticisms of rival theories of the elements	*I 635–920*
		Interlude: Lucretius' poetic mission	*I 921–50*
	(ix)	the all is infinite	I 951–1051
	(L3)	*critique of geocentric cosmology*	I 1052–1113
		Closing words	I 1114–17

own proem, the line at which Lucretius first hooks up to his Epicurean source is precisely identifiable. At 136–45 he declares his determination, despite the poverty of the Latin language, to illuminate Memmius' understanding of the world – to seek out the poetry 'by which you may be able to take a view deep into hidden things'. This line, *res quibus occultas penitus convisere possis* (145), which marks the transition to physical exposition (148, *naturae species ratioque* = Epicurean φυσιολογία: see above pp. 37–8) and specifically to the first argument, that nothing comes into being out of nothing, unmistakably echoes the words with which Epicurus marked his own transition to that same opening argument. These are, in the *Letter to Herodotus'* presumably condensed version, ταῦτα δὲ διαλαβόντας συνορᾶν [*sc.* δεῖ] ἤδη περὶ τῶν ἀδήλων (*Ep. Hdt.* 38): 'Having made these distinctions, it is now time for us to take a view of hidden things.' The rare compound *convisere* scrupulously echoes Epicurus' characteristic verb συνορᾶν.

Thereafter the parallelism between *On nature* I–II and Lucretius I is so close that coincidence can be ruled out. The above table of comparison (Chart 2b) borrows its contents from Chart 2 (p. 136).

From (ii) onwards, Epicurus' list contains just two items which do not occur at precisely the same point in Lucretius' sequence. Item (iv) is the only significant omission, and I shall consider shortly Lucretius' motive for omitting it. The other, (vi), does not occur in the *Letter to Herodotus* either at this point: in both Lucretius and the Letter it occurs only in its repetition at (viii), where it does its main work.

Of the items present in Lucretius but absent from Epicurus' epitome,

Chart 5

1–145 Proem

(1–43) Prayer to Venus

(44–9) The detached nature of divinity

(50–61) Topic of book 1: atoms

(62–79) Epicurus as liberator

(80–101) The evils of religion

(102–35) Wrong and right views on life after death

(136–45) Lucretius' poetic task

146–264 The principles of conservation

(146–8) The philosophical task

(149–214) Nothing comes into being out of nothing = *(ii)*

1 (159–73) regular place of growth

2 (174–83) regular season of growth

3 (184–191) regular duration of growth

4 (192–8) regular dependence on nutrition

5 (199–207) upper limits on size

6 (208–14) effects of ploughing

(215–64) Nothing is destroyed into nothing = *(iii)*

418–82 Only body and void have *per se* existence = *(vii)*

1 (418–29) The 'all' is bodies and void

2 (430–48) No third *per se* thing is conceivable

3 (449–58) Attributes (*coniuncta* and *eventa*) do not exist *per se*

4 (459–63) Nor does time

5 (464–82) Nor do facts about the past

483–634 Body exists in the form of atoms = *(viii)*

(483–502) This is surprising, but . . .

1 (503–10) there must exist pure body

2 (511–19) what contains void must itself be solid

3 (520–39) alternation of body and void

4 (540–50) conservation of matter

5 (551–64) imbalance of destruction and generation

6 (565–76) soft and hard

7 (577–83) durability of stuffs

8 (584–98) regularity of species

9 (599–614) impossibility of detachment of minimal parts

1 (742–5) omission of void

2 (746–52) admission of infinite divisibility

3 (753–8) softness of elements

4 (759–62) mutual hostility of elements

5 (763–9) if elements become other stuffs, why call them more basic?

6 (770–81) or, if not, they lack explanatory power

7 (782–802) if there is intertransformation of elements, they perish

8 (803–29) atomism does the same job better

(830–920) Anaxagoras = *(xxxviii)*

(830–46) Anaxagoras' theory explained

1 (847–58) his stuffs are perishable

2 (859–74) everything will consist of stuffs unlike itself

3 (875–96) 'there is everything in everything' can be refuted empirically

4 (897–914) tranformations are better explained by atomism

5 (915–20) *reductio ad absurdum* of 'the part resembles the whole'

1 (217–24) destruction would be instantaneous

2 (225–37) matter would have run out by now

3 (238–49) all destruction would be equally easy

4 (250–64) natural change is cyclical

265–328 The existence of the invisible = (L1)

1 (271–97) wind

2 (298–304) odour, temperature, sound

3 (305–10) evaporation

4 (311–21) erosion

5 (322–8) growth and shrinkage

329–417 The existence of void = (L2)

1 (335–45) motion

2 (346–57) permeation

3 (358–69) relative weight

4 (370–83) redistribution in a plenum impossible

5 (384–97) artificial creation of void

(398–417) There are many more such arguments.

10 (615–27) (... which must exist, to explain size differences)

11 (628–34) separated minimal parts would lack generative powers

635–920 Refutation of rival theories of matter

(635–711) Monists: Heraclitus = (xxxvi)

(635–44) Heraclitus is overrated

1 (645–54) fire could not explain diversity of stuffs

2 (655–64) indispensability of void

3 (665–89) if fire becomes something else, it perishes

4 (690–700) he turns the senses against themselves

5 (701–11) to choose fire, or any other single element, is arbitrary

(712–829) Pluralists: Empedocles = (xxxvii)

(712–15) Introduction of finite pluralism

(716–41) Empedocles' merits, and failures ...

921–50 Interlude: Lucretius' poetic task

951–1051 The infinity of the all = (ix)

Space cannot be bounded:

1 (958–67) there is something beyond any limit

2 (968–83) what if you throw a spear past the supposed boundary?

3 (984–97) in a finite universe, all body would accumulate at the bottom

4 (998–1001) the 'all' could have nothing external to bound it

Body, as well as space, must be infinite:

(1008–51) otherwise it would be infinitely dissipated

1052–1113 Critique of geocentric cosmology = (L3)

1114–17 Closing words

some can be briefly dealt with. The interlude at 921–50, containing Lucretius' poetic manifesto, is Lucretius' own contribution, and we need seek no Epicurean original. Likewise the closing words of the book. Item (L3), the criticism of geocentric cosmology, will almost certainly be drawn from an original critique present in Epicurus, *On nature* but naturally enough omitted from the epitome, which concentrates on Epicurus' positive findings. I have argued for its provenance from Epicurus in Chapter 3, §6.

As for the refutation of rival theories of matter, I have argued in Chapters 4 and 5 that Epicurus held over his critique of rival theories of the elements until he had completed his own physical and cosmological exposition in books I–XIII of *On nature*, and that in the *De rerum natura* the decision to bring the critique forward to occupy a much earlier place, immediately after the initial demonstration of atomism in the first part of book I, was Lucretius' own. From a dialectical point of view the critique now comes surprisingly early. The incapacity of the rival theories to explain phenomena, as atomism can explain them, is the main burden of the critique. Yet, although by this point Lucretius has isolated atoms and void as the only independently existing things, he has done none of his work on their power to account for the full range of phenomena: that is the task especially of book II, and to some extent of the entire remainder of the poem. Methodologically, Epicurus' order is sounder than Lucretius'. Lucretius nevertheless gains much by the transposition. Here I would list three main advantages achieved.

First – and this is well enough recognised[2] – the critique enables Lucretius to broach the theme of how philosophy might best be written. Paradoxically, it is the prose-writer Heraclitus who is pilloried for seeking to persuade by mere innuendo (638–44), while the poet Empedocles, Lucretius' proudly acknowledged literary forebear, is praised for his godlike lucidity of exposition.[3] This contrast insinuates onto the agenda the very theme – the defence of philosophical poetry – which will move to centre stage in the famous poetic manifesto (921–50) immediately following the critical section.

Second, one of atomism's greatest claims to fame is its explanatory *economy*. In the critical passage, Lucretius twice illustrates this with his favoured alphabetic analogy: you can account for any observed material

---

[2] Kollman (1971), Tatum (1984); cf. Milanese (1989), pp. 134–9.
[3] Cf. above pp. 13–14, where I argued that the comparison of Empedocles with the Delphic oracle at 1 738–9 is meant to contrast him favourably with the oracle's proverbial ambiguity, associated also with Heraclitus.

change as mere rearrangement within a modest stock of atomic types, just as shifts between one word and another can be achieved by redistributing a small set of alphabetic letters (817–29, 907–14). If friction in the branches of trees produces fire, atomism effortlessly explains how (907–14):

> iamne vides igitur, paulo quod diximus ante,
> permagni referre eadem primordia saepe
> cum quibus et quali positura contineantur
> et quos inter se dent motus accipiantque,   910
> atque eadem paulo inter se mutata creare
> ignes et lignum? quo pacto verba quoque ipsa
> inter se paulo mutatis sunt elementis,
> cum ligna atque ignes distincta voce notemus.

> So do you now see, as I have said before, that for the very same primary particles it often makes a huge difference with which others and in what arrangement they are held, and what motions they impart and receive in relation to each other; and that the same ones, with a little interchange, create fire (*ignes*) and wood (*lignum*)? Just as the words themselves have only undergone a small change in their elements (= 'letters') when we use different sounds to designate *ligna* and *ignes*.

In this alphabetic shift from *ligna* to *ignes*, which parallels the combustion of actual wood through friction, the point is not the rearrangement of an identical set of elements, since the two words are not anagrams, so much as the exposure, by a disruption of its outer parts, of what already lay hidden within a structure – fire in the case of the wood, and its analogue the letter-group *ign* in the case of *lignum*.

Such explanatory economy is a relative matter, and it is only in the context of a comparison of atomism with rival physical theories that the point could have been so effectively made: how much better to posit simple atomic rearrangement than to believe, with Anaxagoras, that wood contains fire, and indeed that everything contains everything. Hence, if this merit of atomism was to be adequately exploited, the critical section could not be postponed. The sense of urgency which this betrays is our first indication of an important guiding factor in Lucretius' transformation of his Greek material: the need to maximise the persuasive impact of his argument in its early stages. Epicurus had been addressing an already committed and presumably patient philosophical audience; Lucretius is only too well aware that his reader may put the poem down as soon its impact starts to wane (I 943–5: *haec ratio plerumque videtur | tristior esse quibus non est tractata, retroque | volgus abhorret ab hac*).

Third, the transfer of the critique to this early position helps Lucretius create a major structural feature for the first pair of books. By delaying the theme of infinity until the end of the book, it generates the matching closures of books I and II, expanding our horizons beyond the boundaries of our own world. I have dealt with this already in Chapter 5, §4.

To sum up, the transference of the critical passage to the early position which Lucretius assigns to it can be seen as part of an elaborately contrived restructuring, well explained by the nature of Lucretius' persuasive project and the poem's overall architectonic.

I now turn to Lucretius' own demonstrable omission: item (iii), Epicurus' argument for the immutability of the 'all', which in the *Letter to Herodotus* (39) is summarised as follows:

Moreover, the all was always such as it is now, and always will be. For (a) there is nothing into which it changes, and (b) beside the all there is nothing which could pass into it and produce the change.

This is a desperately obscure argument, and the reason for its obscurity was brilliantly explained by Jacques Brunschwig in a little-known article first published in 1977.[4] What Epicurus actually means – or rather, what his argument will with hindsight turn out to amount to – is that (a) there can be no *space* beyond the universe for it to lose anything into, and (b) there can be no *body* beyond it to enter it and add to its contents. But for very sound methodological reasons, Epicurus cannot say that here. That the all consists of body and space will be demonstrated only in the next stage of his argument; it therefore must not be presupposed here, on pain of circularity. And that is why Epicurus must content himself with the entirely unspecific assertion that there is simply 'nothing' outside the universe to permit subtraction or addition.

Playing his cards this close to his chest is entirely germane to Epicurus' philosophical project, but similar reticence would be ruinous if replicated so early in book I of Lucretius' poem. Hence Lucretius omits the argument here, even though he was quite happy in later books to invoke it as soon as the items in question could be unmasked as space and body (II 303–7, III 816–18 = V 361–3). Whether he omitted it in book I because he did not understand it, or because, although he understood it, he

<hr>

[1] Brunschwig (1977), esp. p. 18 of the 1994 translation. I have some residual disagreements with Brunschwig on points of detail, expressed in Long/Sedley (1987) vols. I and II, §4, but they do not affect the present issue.

found it damaging to the lucidity of his own argument, it is hard to be certain. But I tend to the former explanation since, as I shall now be arguing, preserving Epicurus' methodological rigour in the order of his exposition was in any case not a consideration to which Lucretius attached priority. Lucretius, that is, would not have thought it out of the question to name space and body prematurely, even where methodological rigour had prevented Epicurus himself from doing so.

3. SEEDS

The proof of this greater flexibility lies in Lucretius' readiness to smuggle in countless advance allusions to atoms, long before their existence has been demonstrated – a degree of licence which Epicurus would never have permitted himself, but which has obvious rhetorical advantages to a writer eager to advertise the explanatory merits of atomism with all speed.[5]

Epicurus (*Ep. Hdt.* 38) begins his physical argument by maintaining that

. . . nothing comes into being out of what is not. For in that case everything would come into being out of everything, with no need for seeds (σπέρματα).

'Seeds' here means just that – biological seeds.[6] These symbolise the unchanging regularities of natural processes, whereby a given organism can only grow from the appropriate seeds, and not emerge out of thin air, as might have been expected if things came into being out of nothing at all.

Lucretius, at the corresponding point (stage (ii)), may appear at first to echo this argument from 'seeds' accurately enough (159–62):

nam si de nilo fierent, ex omnibu' rebus
omne genus nasci posset, nil semine egeret.
e mare primum homines, e terra posset oriri
squamigerum genus . . .

---

[5] This theme of rhetorical anticipations in Lucretius is perceptively explored by Asmis (1983). My main difference from her analysis, so far as book 1 is concerned, is that I suppose both the *DRN* and the *Letter to Herodotus* to derive from Epicurus' *On nature*, with each making its own independent selection of arguments, whereas she treats any departure from the *Letter to Herodotus* on Lucretius' part as a conscious one, as if it were itself a primary source for him.

[6] In Greek Epicurean texts σπέρμα never demonstrably signifies 'atom'. There is no foundation for the view of Reiley (1909), p. 39, and Vlastos (1950), n. 13, that Epicurus uses the word in this sense. They cite *Ep. Hdt.* 38, 74 and *Ep. Pyth.* 89; but in 74 the 'seeds' are apparently biological, and in 89, although it is impossible to tell what kind of 'makings' of worlds or their parts the word represents, the conjoined metaphor of 'irrigation' makes it unlikely that we are dealing with discrete atoms.

For if they came into being from nothing, every species would
be able to be born out of everything, and nothing would need a
seed. To start with, human beings would be able to spring up out
of the sea, and the scaly tribe out of the land . . .

The imagined flouting of environmental constraints on birth provides
the materials of the wonderful *adynaton* that follows, and no reader is
compelled to doubt at this stage that the required 'seed' is a literal biological one. The singular *semine* certainly strengthens that impression – a
single organism needs no more than one originative seed, but many
constituent particles.[7] However, first impressions can mislead. Look
what follows just lines later (167–71):

quippe ubi non essent *genitalia corpora* cuique,
qui posset mater rebus consistere certa?
at nunc *seminibus* quia certis quaeque creantur,
inde enascitur atque oras in luminis exit   170
materies ubi inest cuiusque et *corpora prima.*

For in a situation where there were no *generative bodies* for each
kind, how could things have a fixed mother? But as it is, because
each kind is created from fixed *seeds*, it is born and emerges into
the realm of light from the place where each thing's *matter* and
primary bodies are to be found.

The 'seeds' here reappear in company which radically changes their
profile. The words which I have italicised are all Lucretian variant terms
for atoms. Precisely the same terms were conveniently announced as
such barely a hundred lines earlier, in the programmatic part of the
proem (58–61):

quae nos materiem et genitalia corpora rebus
reddunda in ratione vocare et semina rerum
appellare suemus et haec eadem usurpare
corpora prima, quod ex illis sunt omnia primis.

. . . which it is our practice, when giving an account, to call
things' 'matter', their 'generative bodies' and their 'seeds', as
well as using the regular term 'first bodies', because they are the
primary things from which all things come.

The echo of these lines is too sustained and accurate to be accidental.[8]
Hence even within his very first argument against generation *ex nihilo*

---

[7] In retrospect this consideration will prove not to have been decisive: the singular of *semen* at 185,
206 and 221 undoubtedly functions as an uncountable noun designating a group of constituent
particles.
[8] Lucretius' anticipation here therefore amounts to a great deal more than what Asmis (1983), p.

(161–73) Lucretius has appeared to shift ground: by the end of it, the focus has proved to be not on biological regularity at the level of seeds but on material regularity: natural species can only grow in environments which provide a stock of the right constituent particles for them. Strictly speaking nothing yet asserts the atomicity (indivisibility) of these material 'seeds', but no one need doubt that Lucretius is already here advertising the explanatory merits of the very particles with which, as we have been carefully forewarned, book i will be concerned.

That he is doing so is guaranteed by the entire run of the ensuing arguments against absolute generation and annihilation (174–216), which constantly invoke the constraints imposed by the availability of matter, and which do so by continuing to deploy Lucretius' pre-announced vocabulary for atoms.[9] In his fourth argument, in pointing to the dependence of plant growth on the ingestion of rain, he even manages to contrive a first airing for the alphabetic model of atomic rearrangement (196–8):

> ut potius multis communia corpora rebus
> multa putes esse, ut verbis elementa videmus,
> quam sine *principiis* ullam rem existere posse.

> Hence you can more readily believe that many things share many bodies in common, just as we see words share their elements [='letters'], than that anything should exist without primary particles.

Here *principiis* is a quite unequivocal allusion to atoms.

Yet all this is done without relinquishing the advantageous biological connotations offered by the atomic vocabulary. The second argument observes that things only come into being at times when the right *semina rerum* (176) have 'flowed together', a confluence immediately redescribed as the 'creative union' (*genitali | concilio*) of *primordia* (182–3). This last word, *primordia*, is another standard term for atoms, already announced as such back at i 55, and yet who can doubt that in such talk of the creative union in which seeds flow together the language of biological procreation is being exploited to the utmost? The regularities which Lucretius is invoking are ultimately material – as they must be if the need for an atomic substructure is to be insinuated – yet matter is being

59, suggests, his simple (and perhaps even uncontroversial) assumption that what things are dissolved into are 'bodies'.

[9] *semen/semina* 169, 176, 189, 206, 221; *materies/materia* 171, 191, 203, 245, 249; *corpora prima* 171 (cf. 196, 242, 246, 249); *primordia* (along with *principia*, standardly used by Lucretius as its proxy in the oblique cases, for metrical reasons) 182, 198, 210, 244; *genitalia corpora* 167.

treated as if its creative powers were themselves virtually sexual. The association is strongly encouraged by the very vocabulary of *genitalia corpora* and *materies* – the latter derived from *mater*, with which it is effectively identified at 167–8 (quoted on p. 194 above).

The same conflation is even more pronounced in the third argument, where Lucretius is appealing to the slowness of plant and animal growth, and has already insisted on the time required for the 'gathering of seed' (*seminis ad coitum*, 185) in the growth process. Although 'seed' here must designate atomic matter, the distinction between this and biological seed becomes even harder to maintain when, at 188–91, we read

> quorum nil fieri manifestum est, omnia quando
> paulatim crescunt, ut par est, *semine certo,*
> *crescentesque genus servant;* ut noscere possis
> quidque sua de materie grandescere alique.

> It is evident that no such thing [i.e. instant growth] happens, since all things grow gradually, as one would expect, *from a fixed seed, and in growing preserve their kind,* so that you can tell that each grows and is nourished from the matter proper to it.

The direct association of an organism's dependence on 'fixed seed' with its unalterable membership of a species can hardly fail to put the biological connotations of the word uppermost in the reader's mind.

In the sixth argument (208–14) the need for agriculture is attributed to the presence of *primordia rerum* in the soil which, by use of the plough, we *cimus ad ortus*. These are of course particles of nutrients. But when the plough is said to 'stimulate them to growth' they once again threaten to take on the profile of seeds, germinating when the plough brings them to the surface.

Finally, in the further set of arguments against literal annihilation, Lucretius even manages to convey to us the characteristically atomic structure of things, and of indestructible particles separated by void (221–4):[10]

> quod nunc, *aeterno* quia constant *semine* quaeque,
> donec vis obiit quae res diverberet ictu
> *aut intus penetret per inania dissoluatque,*
> nullius exitium patitur natura videri.

> But as it is, because individual things are composed of *everlasting seed,* until a force has impinged on them to smash them apart by

----

[10] For the same point, see Asmis (1983), p. 60.

its impact, *or to penetrate inside them through their voids and disintegrate them*, nature does not allow anything to be destroyed.

I have no wish to reprimand Lucretius for his methodological transgression. To start his arguments off by creating an image of nature in which the observed regularities of biological creation constitute a continuum extending all the way down to the level of primary particles is a brilliant rhetorical coup, promising the reader almost miraculous creative powers for the atoms. Epicurus, by contrast, had started from observed natural regularity and worked painstakingly downwards in the direction of atomic particles. To arrive there, he had first to establish that body and space (ordinary body and ordinary space, witnessed in our everyday experience of moving objects) are the only things with independent existence, and then to infer that at the lowest level there must be bodies altogether unpunctuated by empty space, and hence atomic.

In particular, Epicurus in *On nature* II, at step (viii) of his argument (see Chart 2b, p. 187), had moved to the introduction of atoms by re-invoking premise (vi), 'Moreover, of bodies themselves, some are compounds, others the constituents of those compounds' (*Letter to Herodotus* 41). He was thus able to start from the undeniable fact that there are compound bodies, and, via the equally undeniable fact that compounds must have constituents, to go on to demonstrate the atomicity of the ultimate constituents. Lucretius' equivalent move (1483–634) gets off to a less auspicious start at 1483–4:

> corpora sunt porro partim primordia rerum
> partim concilio quae constant principiorum.

> Moreover, some bodies are the primary particles of things,
> others are ones which are composed from the aggregation of
> primary particles.

The editors regularly comment that Lucretius has here followed Epicurus closely, or even translated him.[11] This misses the crucial difference in strategy. Instead of working dialectically from an uncontroversial notion to a controversial one, in accordance with Epicurus' methodology, Lucretius reverses the strategy and places the atoms themselves up front as his primary exhibit. But one can see why. Having jumped the gun by familiarising his readers from the start with the concept of these primary particles, he has forfeited the chance to replicate Epicurus' dialectical derivation of them. Instead, he must put his

---

[11] 'Followed closely': Bailey (1947) *ad loc.* 'Translated': Munro (1886), Ernout/Robin (1962) *ad loc.*

best foot forward, capitalising on the notion of primary particles which he has been working so hard to impress on his readers.

4. DIVINITY

The miraculous procreative powers of atoms also provide backing for an accompanying denial. Where Epicurus had stated his opening thesis simply as 'Nothing comes into being out of nothing', Lucretius in introducing it adds the highly significant word *divinitus*,[12] followed by a justification for its addition (1 149–58):

> principium cuius hinc nobis exordia sumet,
> nullam rem e nilo gigni *divinitus* umquam.   150
> quippe ita formido mortalis continet omnis,
> quod multa in terris fieri caeloque tuentur
> quorum operum causas nulla ratione videre
> possunt, ac fieri divino numine rentur.
> quas ob res ubi viderimus nil posse creari   155 [156]
> de nilo, tum quod sequimur iam rectius inde   [157]
> perspiciemus, et unde queat res quaeque creari   [158]
> et quo quaeque modo fiant opera sine divom.   [155]

> The starting-point [of the study of nature] will take its cue from this: that nothing ever comes to be out of nothing, *through divine causes*. For the reason why all mortals are so gripped by fear is because they witness many things happening on earth and in the heaven whose causes they are quite unable to see, and suppose that they are the work of divine power. That is why, when we see that nothing can be created out of nothing, we will then as a result have a more accurate view of our goal – both what it is that each thing can be created from, and how each thing comes about without the work of the gods.

He then proceeds immediately to his first proof of the thesis. His addition has sometimes been criticised as a mistake. For example, Hans Gottschalk writes:[13]

In this form, his premiss loses its universality and can no longer be inferred from the inductive evidence he adduces; for God is not 'nothing', and the fact that particular things are always seen to come from other particular things, does not prove that there is not a deity (instead of another particular thing) at the beginning of the chain. Moreover, since his avowed purpose is to disprove divine creation (1.159), the presence of this word in his premiss makes the argument

---

[12] The significance of this addition is well brought out by Asmis (1983), p. 57, and Gale (forthcoming). [13] Gottschalk (1996), p. 234.

circular. Lucretius' eagerness to give his demonstration an extra anti-religious twist has betrayed him into formulating his initial postulate in a way that renders it invalid.

I think this criticism is answerable. The word *divinitus* is actually being added to the conclusion of an argument, not to its premise. Lucretius' point is that if things came into being out of nothing – meaning from no material origin whatsoever, not from no cause – there would be no physical stuff to point to as controlling how, when and where they came to be, and the only explanation left to postulate for these regularities would be god: they would come into being *divinitus*. Hence to argue that things do not come to be out of nothing is indeed to forestall one argument for the existence of a controlling god or gods. As he says in the lines just quoted, it is people's inability to find a physical explanation that leads them to reach for a divine one instead. By proceeding to show that generation invariably depends on the right material conditions, Lucretius precludes the need for a further, divine cause.

Again, however, we can see the sense of urgency which governs Lucretius' procedure and differentiates him from Epicurus. In introducing his very first argument, he has to alert us to the long-term outcome to which it is leading us – the exclusion of divine agency. That exclusion will depend, for its eventual success, on many further arguments, right through to the demystification of cosmic phenomena in book VI. But in pointing out that he is already with his first argument removing one prop from the theological edifice, Lucretius is both quite correct, and quite independent of Epicurus' own cautiously progressive methodology. Epicurus, we may now recall, reached his own conclusions on religious belief in book XIII of *On nature*, his final expository book on his physical system (see item (xxxiv) in Chart 1, p. 133, and Chart 2, p. 136), and in Chapter 4 we found no evidence of any theological passage in the opening books.

5. OTHER CHANGES

In view of what we have seen, we should from now on be on the lookout for further methodological departures by Lucretius from his Epicurean original, and especially for transpositions of arguments. One very clear such case (although too fine a detail to have shown up among the arrowed transpositions in Chart 2, p. 136 above) is the final three arguments for the atomicity of the fundamental particles (1 599–634 = arguments 9–11 in Chart 5, pp. 188–9 above). These all appeal in some way to the impossibility of dismantling an atom into its own primary or 'minimal' parts. Now Epicurus' demonstration of the existence of these minimal parts (epitomised at *Ep. Hdt.* 55–9), which closes with the same point about their inseparability, came a good deal later in his exposition than the proofs of atomicity. Lucretius, not very surprisingly, chose to omit so theoretically demanding a part of Epicurean physics from his own exposition in book II; but it seems clear that in doing so he rescued from it these specific points which could be cited in support of atomism in book I, and inserted them there.

Other such transpositions are bound to exist, even if any attempt to identify them can be no more than speculative. For example, if I am even half right about Epicurus' methodology, it would be quite surprising to find him placing the arguments of stages (L1) and (L2) (those for, respectively, microscopic body and hidden vacuum, both of them omitted in his epitome) as early as Lucretius does.[14] For as presented by Lucretius these go beyond the self-evident existence of ordinary phenomenal body and space to argue that minute portions of body (265–328) and hidden stretches of empty space (329–417) are to be found even below the threshold of vision. This sounds like the first stage of refining familiar body and space into the atomic particles and pure vacuum which ultimately underlie them at the lowest level of analysis. Given what we have already seen of Lucretius' willingness to sacrifice methodological orderliness for rhetorical impact, the suspicion must be entertained that he is himself responsible for moving stages (L1) and (L2) to their present early position, Epicurus having himself, I suggest, probably placed them after stage (viii). For Lucretius to make this further move to hasten his readers' descent into the microscopic world illuminated by Epicurus would be entirely of a piece with the strategy we have already witnessed.

In the present state of our evidence this cannot be demonstrated, but it would be unwise to ignore the possibility. Is there perhaps even a telltale sign of the transposition in the text? At 418 Lucretius terminates stages (L1) and (L2), the arguments for microscopic body and hidden vacuum, and effects his transition to the step which I am suggesting would in his Epicurean source have preceded it, namely that the 'all' consists of (ordinary phenomenal) bodies and space. The words marking the transition are *sed nunc ut repetam coeptum pertexere dictis* . . . — 'But now, to return to weaving in words the task on which I embarked . . .' In the context such talk of a 'return' to the main task is hardly anomalous,

---

[14] What follows is an expansion of an idea I have already put forward in Sedley (1996), p. 315.

given that the preceding lines (398–417), in which Lucretius has been urging that if the foregoing arguments for vacuum are insufficient he has plenty more with which to overwhelm Memmius, might appear an incipient digression which he now wishes to halt. Even so, it remains a tempting speculation – and no more than a speculation – that these words may also be his acknowledgement of a return to the order of topics as he found them in his Epicurean original.[15]

6. BACK TO EMPEDOCLES

Whether or not this last guess is correct, a general pattern has nevertheless emerged. Lucretius' strategy of persuasion does not permit the slow and painstaking process established by Epicurus, whereby the atomicity of matter would emerge only after progressive refinement of the world's familiar contents. To generate the excitement of discovery Lucretius needs right from the outset to plunge his readers into a microscopic world few of them can have dreamt of. Both the sequence and the style of his opening arguments are designed to maximise this impact.

The strategy is, if anything, overdetermined. If I am right, Lucretius' procedure is self-explanatory and justified by the immediate task in hand. Yet it also reflects the power exerted on him by his principal literary model, Empedocles. To appreciate this, we may return to the lines of his proem where Lucretius launches his primary elements as protagonists in a natural cycle (54–8):

> nam tibi de summa caeli ratione deumque
> disserere incipiam, et rerum primordia pandam,   55
> unde omnis natura creet res auctet alatque
> quove eadem rursum natura perempta resolvat,
> quae nos . . .

> For I shall embark on explaining to you about the fundamental rationale of the heaven and the gods, and I shall expound the primary particles of things, from which nature creates, develops and nourishes all things, and into which nature destroys and dissolves those same things once more, which it is our practice . . .

And he continues with the list of names for these primary particles which we have already encountered (58–61). He is mimicking the opening book of Empedocles' *On nature*, which at what we now know to be lines 233ff. (see p. 28 above) catalogued his four elements plus the two motive forces

---

[15] See Asmis (1983), p. 61, for much the same suggestion about this line's meaning.

Love and Strife as divinities engaged in a never-ending cycle of birth and death. Even Lucretius' surprising reference to the gods (54) emphasises the link. So does his development of a set of biological metaphors for 'atoms', which has played such an important role in this chapter: was it not Empedocles who set the pattern, by calling his own four elements 'roots' (ῥιζώματα)?

Reflection on this Empedoclean model may help confirm the story I have already told. For Empedocles certainly did not work towards his four elements and two motive forces by argument. He unveiled them at the outset, as divine players in the cosmic drama which he then proceeded to unfold. When Lucretius, departing from Epicurus' methodology, places his own primary elements on centre stage from the start, and when in his very first set of arguments he exploits to the full the imagery which represents them as live procreative powers, it is the Empedoclean model that we should see as holding sway.

Epilogue

The quotation from Cicero with which I began Chapter I remains as acute an evaluation of Lucretius as any. His is indeed a poem which displays many flashes of genius but also much craftsmanship. If I have had more to say about the craftsmanship, my excuse is that genius is best left to speak for itself.

Lucretius' artistry was expended upon the creation of a most remarkable poem. Its main filling is fifteen books' worth of technical physics from Epicurus' *On nature*, painstakingly assembled and systematically reshaped into a poetic masterpiece. The upshot was a dazzlingly delivered message of salvation designed to whet the intellectual appetites of a Roman audience, and to satisfy their emotional needs, without once asking them to compromise their own Romanness.

This filling is sandwiched between two antithetical yet curiously complementary descriptive passages. One is an Empedoclean hymn to birth and life, which, while laying Lucretius' chosen theme of nature before us in all its glory, also locates the poem by reference to fixed co-ordinates on the map of Graeco-Roman poetry. The other is the Thucydidean tableau of pestilence and death, which establishes a further set of co-ordinates, this time chronological: it shows why even in Athens, the cradle of civilisation, it was only the advent of Epicurus' philosophy that could successfully fortify the human spirit against everything that fortune might cast its way.

This complex whole is no less magnificent for the fact, which we have seen amply confirmed, that Lucretius did not live to take his vision through to its final fulfilment. Disappointment at an uncompleted quest would be entirely the wrong way for us to react. Only by seeing what the quest was, and how Lucretius was working towards it, *can* we properly understand and value the poem's second half, and especially its ending. What I hope to have brought into clearer focus is the grand conception by which Lucretius, while remaining loyal to his revered Greek masters (and I mean Empedocles no less than Epicurus), was able to transform their benefactions into something truly new. The fact that he has not erased all traces of earlier strata in the poem's history – from the doxographical imprint of Theophrastus on Epicurus, all the way down to his own abandoned first proem to book IV – enables us the better to appreciate the extraordinary craftsmanship by which he has worked that transformation.

Bibliography

Adams, J., Mayer, R. (1998), eds., *Aspects of the Language of Latin Poetry* (London)

Alberti, A. (1994), ed., *Realtà e ragione* (Florence)

Algra, K. A., van der Horst, P. W., Runia, D. T. (1996), eds., *Polyhistor: Studies in the History and Historiography of Ancient Philosophy* (Leiden)

Allen, R. E., Furley, D. J. (1975), eds., *Studies in Presocratic Philosophy*, II. *The Eleatics and Pluralists* (London)

André, J. M. (1967), *Les Noms d'oiseaux en latin* (Paris)

Angeli, A. (1988), *Filodemo, Agli amici di scuola* (Naples)

Arnim, H. von (1893), 'Der angebliche Streit des Zenon und Theophrastos', *Neue Jahrbücher für Philologie und Paedagogik* 147: 449–67

   (1903–5), *Stoicorum Veterum Fragmenta*, 3 vols., with indexes in vol. IV (1924) by M. Adler (Leipzig)

Arrighetti, G. (1973), *Epicuro, opere*, ed. 2 (Turin)

   (1979), 'Un passo dell'opera "Sulla natura" di Epicuro, Democrito, e Colote', *Cronache Ercolanesi* 9: 5–10

Asmis, E. (1982), 'Lucretius' Venus and Stoic Zeus', *Hermes* 110: 459–70

   (1983), 'Rhetoric and reason in Lucretius', *American Journal of Philology* 104: 36–66

   (1990), 'Philodemus' Epicureanism', in Haase/Temporini (1990) 2369–406

   (1996), 'Epicurean semiotics', in Manetti (1996) 155–85

Atherton, C. (forthcoming), ed., *Form and Content in Didactic Poetry*, Proceedings of the 5th Nottingham Classical Literature Symposium (Nottingham/Bari)

Auvray-Assayas, C. (1992), 'Le livre I du *De natura deorum* et le traité *De signis* de Philodème: problèmes de théologie et de logique', *Revue des Etudes Latines* 69: 51–62

Avotins, I. (1980), 'Alexander of Aphrodisias on vision in the atomists', *Classical Quarterly* NS 30: 429–54

Bailey, C. (1922), *Lucreti De Rerum Natura Libri Sex*, ed. 2 (ed. 1, 1900), Oxford Classical Texts (Oxford)

   (1947), *Titi Lucreti Cari De Rerum Natura Libri Sex*, 3 vols. (Oxford)

Baltes, M. (1976), *Die Weltentstehung des Platonischen Timaios nach den antiken Interpreten* (Leiden)

Barigazzi, A. (1950), 'La μονή della terra nei frammenti ercolanesi', *Studi Italiani di Filologia Classica* 24: 3–19

(1958), 'Cinetica degli εἴδωλα nel περὶ φύσεως di Epicuro', *La Parola del Passato* 13: 249–76

Barnes, J. (1979), *The Presocratic Philosophers* (London)

    (1988), 'Epicurean signs', *Oxford Studies in Ancient Philosophy* suppl. vol.: 91–134

    (1989a), 'Antiochus of Ascalon', in Griffin/Barnes (1989) 51–96

    (1989b), 'The size of the sun in antiquity', *Acta Classica Univ. Scient. Debrecen* 25: 29–41

    (1997), 'Roman Aristotle', in Barnes/Griffin (1997) 1–69

Barnes, J., Brunschwig, J., Burnyeat, M., Schofield, M. (1982), eds., *Science and Speculation: Studies in Hellenistic Theory and Practice* (Cambridge)

Barnes, J., Griffin, M. (1997), eds., *Philosophia Togata II: Plato and Aristotle at Rome* (Oxford)

Barnes, J., Mignucci, M. (1988), eds., *Matter and Metaphysics* (Naples)

Ben, N. van der (1975), *The Proem of Empedocles'* Περὶ φύσεως (Amsterdam)

Bergsträsser, G. (1918), *Neue meteorologische Fragmente des Theophrast arabisch und deutsch* (Heidelberg)

Bignone, E. (1936), *L'Aristotele perduto e la formazione filosofica di Epicuro* (Florence)

    (1945), *Storia della Letteratura Latina* II (Florence)

Bloch, H. (1940), 'L. Calpurnius Piso Caesoninus in Samothrace and Herculaneum', *American Journal of Philology* 44: 485–93

Bollack, J. (1959), 'Lukrez und Empedokles', *Die neue Rundschau* 70: 656–86

    (1965–9), *Empédocle*, 4 vols. (Paris)

Bollack, J., Laks, A. (1976), eds., *Etudes sur l'épicurisme antique* (Cahiers de Philologie 1; Lille)

    (1978), *Epicure à Pythoclès* (Cahiers de Philologie 3; Lille)

Bonitz, H. (1870), *Index Aristotelicus* (Berlin)

Boyancé, P. (1963), *Lucrèce et l'Epicurisme* (Paris)

Brieger, A. (1882), *Epikurs Brief an Herodot 68–83* (= Jahresbericht des Stadtgymnasiums zu Halle 14)

Bright, D. F. (1971), 'The plague and the structure of the *De rerum natura*', *Latomus* 30: 607–32

Brunschwig, J. (1977), 'L'argument d'Epicure sur l'immutabilité du tout', in *Permanence de la philosophie* (Mélanges Joseph Moreau; Neuchâtel) 127–50; repr. in Brunschwig (1995) 15–42, and republished as 'Epicurus' argument on the immutability of the all' in Brunschwig (1994) 1–20

    (1994), *Papers in Hellenistic Philosophy* (Cambridge)

    (1995), *Etudes sur les philosophes hellénistiques* (Paris)

    (1996), 'Le fragment DK 70 B 1 de Métrodore de Chio', in Algra/Horst/Runia (1996) 21–38

Buffière, F. (1956), *Les Mythes d'Homère et la pensée grecque* (Paris)

Burkert, W. (1972), *Lore and Science in Ancient Pythagoreanism* (Cambridge, Mass.)

Burnyeat, M. F. (1976), 'Protagoras and self-refutation in later Greek philosophy', *Philosophical Review* 85: 44–69

    (1978), 'The upside-down back-to-front sceptic of Lucretius IV 472', *Philologus* 122: 197–206

(1997), 'Antipater and self-refutation: elusive arguments in Cicero's *Academica*', in Inwood/Mansfeld (1997) 277–310

Caizzi, F. Decleva (1992), 'Aenesidemus and the Academy', *Classical Quarterly* NS 42: 176–89

Capasso, M. (1981), "I *Problemi di filologia filosofica* di Mario Untersteiner', *Elenchos* 2: 375–404

    (1989), 'Primo supplemento al *Catalogo dei papiri ercolanesi*', *Cronache Ercolanesi* 19: 193–264

Casson, L. (1974), *Travel in the Ancient World* (Baltimore)

Castner, C. J. (1987), '*De rerum natura* 5.101–103: Lucretius' application of Empedoclean language to Epicurean doctrine', *Phoenix* 41: 40–9

    (1988), *A Prosopography of Roman Epicureans* (Frankfurt am Main)

Cavallo, G. (1983), *Libri scritture scribi a Ercolano* (*Cronache Ercolanesi* suppl. 1, Naples)

Cavini, W., Donnini Macciò, M. C., Funghi, M. S., Manetti, D. (1985), *Studi su papiri greci di logica e medicina* (Accademia Toscana di Scienze e Lettere 'La Colombaria', *Studi* 74) (Florence)

Classen, C. J. (1986), ed., *Probleme der Lukrezforschung* (Hildesheim)

Clay, D. (1983), *Lucretius and Epicurus* (Ithaca)

Commager, H. S., Jr (1957), 'Lucretius' interpretation of the plague', *Harvard Studies in Classical Philology* 62: 105–21

Comparetti, D., De Petra, G. (1883), *La villa ercolanese dei Pisoni. I suoi monumenti e la sua biblioteca* (Turin; repr. Naples 1972)

Courtney, E. (1987), 'Quotation, interpolation and transposition', *Hermathena* 143: 7–18

Grönert, W. (1975), *Studi ercolanesi* (Naples)

Daiber, H. (1992), 'The *Meteorology* of Theophrastus in Syriac and Arabic translation', in Fortenbaugh/Gutas (1992) 166–293

De Lacy, P. (1948), 'Lucretius and the history of Epicureanism', *Transactions of the American Philological Association* 79: 12–35

    (1993), review of M. Capasso, *Manuale di papirologia ercolanese*, in *American Journal of Philology* 114: 178–80

De Lacy, P. and E. (1978), *Philodemus, On Methods of Inference*, ed. 2 (Naples)

Delattre, D. (1996), 'Les mentions de titres d'œuvres dans les livres de Philodème', *Cronache Ercolanesi* 26: 143–68

Diano, C. (1946), *Epicuri ethica* (Florence)

Diels, H. (1879), *Doxographi Graeci* (Berlin)

    (1901), *Poetarum Philosophorum Fragmenta* (Berlin)

    (1903), *Die Fragmente der Vorsokratiker* (Berlin)

Diels, H., Kranz, W. (1951–2), *Die Fragmente der Vorsokratiker*, ed. 6 (Berlin)

Dillon, J. M. (1977), *The Middle Platonists* (London)

Dorandi, T. (1982), 'Filodemo, Gli Stoici (PHerc. 155 e 339)', *Cronache Ercolanesi* 12: 91–133

    (1990), 'Gli arconti nei papiri ercolanesi', *Zeitschrift für Papyrologie und Epigraphik* 84: 121–38

(1991), *Ricerche sulla cronologia dei filosofi ellenistici* (Stuttgart)

(1997), 'Lucrèce et les Epicuriens de Campanie', in Schrijvers/Koenen/ Algra (1997) 35–48

Drexler, F. (1935), 'Aporien im Prooemium IV des Lukrez', *Athenaeum* 13: 73–100

Düring, I. (1957), *Aristotle in the Ancient Biographical Tradition* (Göteborg)

Edelstein, L. (1940), 'Primum Graius homo (Lucretius 1.66)', *Transactions of the American Philological Association* 71: 78–90

Edelstein, L., Kidd, I. G. (1989), *Posidonius*, vol. 1: *The Fragments*, ed. 2 (ed. 1 1972) (Cambridge)

Edwards, M. J. (1989), 'Lucretius, Empedocles and Epicurean polemic', *Antike und Abendland* 35: 104–15

Erler, M. (1994), 'Erstes Kapitel: Epikur', 'Zweites Kapitel: Die Schule Epikurs', 'Drittes Kapitel: Lukrez', in Flashar (1994) 29–490

Ernout, A., Robin, L. (1962), *Lucrèce, De rerum natura, commentaire exégétique et critique*, ed. 2 (Paris)

Farrell, J. (1991), *Virgil's 'Georgics' and the Traditions of Ancient Epic* (New York/Oxford)

Ferrari, W. (1937), ' La doppia redazione del proemio IV di Lucrezio', *Atene e Roma* 39: 188–200

Ferrary, J.-L. (1988), *Philhellénisme et impérialisme* (Rome)

Flashar, H. (1994), ed., *Die Philosophie der Antike 4: Die hellenistische Philosophie* (Basel)

Fortenbaugh, W., Gutas, D. (1992), eds., *Theophrastus: His Psychological, Doxographical and Scientific Writings* (Rutgers University Studies in Classical Humanities 5; New Brunswick)

Fortenbaugh, W. W., Huby, P. M., Sharples, R. W., Gutas, D. (1992), *Theophrastus of Eresus: Sources for his Life, Writings, Thought and Influence*: cited as 'FHS&G' (Leiden/New York/Cologne)

Fortenbaugh, W., Steinmetz, P. (1989), eds., *Cicero's Knowledge of the Peripatos* (Rutgers University Studies in Classical Humanities, 4; New Brunswick)

Fowler, P. G. and D. P. (1996), 'Lucretius', in *Oxford Classical Dictionary*, ed. 3 (Oxford) 888–90

Furley, D. J. (1966), 'Lucretius and the Stoics', *BICS* 13: 13–33; repr. in Classen (1986) 75–95, and in Furley (1989a) 183–205

　　(1967), *Two Studies in the Greek Atomists* (Princeton)

　　(1970), 'Variations on themes from Empedocles in Lucretius' proem', *BICS* 17: 55–64; repr. in Furley (1989a) 172–82

　　(1978), 'Lucretius the Epicurean: on the history of man', *Entretiens Hardt* 24: 1–37; repr. in Furley (1989a) 206–22

　　(1989a), *Cosmic Problems* (Cambridge)

　　(1989b), 'The dynamics of the earth: Anaximander, Plato, and the centrifocal theory', in Furley (1989a) 14–26

Gale, M. (1994a), *Myth and Poetry in Lucretius* (Cambridge)

　　(1994b), 'Lucretius 4.1–25 and the proems of the *De rerum natura*', *Proceedings of the Cambridge Philological Society* 40: 1–17

(forthcoming), comments on Sedley (forthcoming), in Atherton (forthcoming)
Gallo, I. (1980), *Frammenti biografici da papiri. Volume secondo, La biografia dei filosofi* (Rome)
Giancotti, F. (1959), *Il preludio di Lucrezio* (Messina)
Giannantoni, G., Gigante, M. (1996), eds., *Epicureismo greco e romano*, 3 vols. (Naples)
Gigante, M. (1976), 'Polemonis Academici Fragmenta', *Rendic. Archeol. / Lettere e Belle Arti Nap.* 51: 91–144
(1979), ed., *Catalogo dei papiri ercolanesi* (Naples)
(1981), *Scetticismo e epicureismo* (Naples)
(1995), *Philodemus in Italy: the Books from Herculaneum*, tr. D. Obbink (Ann Arbor)
Gigante, M., Capasso, M. (1989), 'Il ritorno di Virgilio a Ercolano', *Studi Italiani di Filologia Classica* NS 7: 3–6
Gilbert, W. (1600), *De Magnete* (London)
Giussani, C. (1896–8), *T. Lucreti Cari De rerum natura libri sex. Revisione del testo, commentario e studi*, 4 vols. (Turin)
Glucker, J. (1978), *Antiochus and the Late Academy* (Göttingen)
Godwin, J. (1986), *Lucretius: 'De Rerum Natura' IV* (Warminster)
(1991), *Lucretius: 'De Rerum Natura' VI* (Warminster)
Görler, W. (1994), 'Fünftes Kapitel: Älterer Pyrrhonismus. Jüngere Akademie. Antiochus aus Askalon', in Flashar (1994) 717–989
Gottschalk, H. (1996), 'Philosophical innovation in Lucretius', in Algra/Horst/Runia (1996) 231–40
Goulet, R. (1980), *Cléomède, théorie élémentaire* (Paris)
(1989–), ed., *Dictionnaire des philosophes antiques* (Paris)
Graeser, A. (1975), *Zenon von Kition: Positionen und Probleme* (Berlin)
Graham, D. W. (1988), 'Symmetry in the Empedoclean cycle', *Classical Quarterly* NS 38: 297–312
Griffin, M. (1989), 'Philosophy, politics and politicians at Rome', in Griffin/Barnes (1989) 1–37
(1995), 'Philosophical badinage in Cicero's letters to his friends', in Powell (1995b) 325–46
Griffin, M., Barnes, J. (1989), eds., *Philosophia Togata* (Oxford)
Grilli, A. (1963), 'διαστροφή', *Acme* 16: 87–101
Guthrie, W. K. C. (1969), *A History of Greek Philosophy*, vol. II (Cambridge)
Haase, W., Temporini, H. (1990), *Aufstieg und Niedergang der römischen Welt*, II 36.4 (Berlin/New York)
Habicht, C. (1995), *Athen. Die Geschichte der Stadt in hellenisticher Zeit* (Munich)
Hadot, P. (1987), 'Théologie, exégèse, révélation, écriture, dans la philosophie grecque', in M. Tardieu (ed.), *Les Règles de l'interprétation* (Paris 1987) 13–34
Hardie, P. (1986), *Virgil's Aeneid. Cosmos and Imperium* (Oxford)
(1995), 'The speech of Pythagoras in Ovid *Metamorphoses* 15: Empedoclean *epos*', *Classical Quarterly* NS 45: 204–14
Hartung, H. J. (1970), *Ciceros Methode bei der Übersetzung griechischer philosophischer Termini* (diss., Hamburg)

Henrichs, A. (1974), 'Die Kritik der stoischen Theologie im PHerc. 1428', *Cronache Ercolanesi* 4: 5–32

Hinds, S. E. (1987), 'Language at breaking point: Lucretius 1.452', *Classical Quarterly* NS 37: 450–3

Hölscher, U. (1965), 'Weltzeiten und Lebenszyklus', *Hermes* 93: 7–33

House, D. K. (1980), 'The life of Sextus Empiricus', *Classical Quarterly* NS 30: 227–38

Inwood, B. (1981), 'The origin of Epicurus' concept of void', *CP* 76: 273–85
(1992), *The Poem of Empedocles* (Toronto)

Inwood, B., Mansfeld, J. (1997), eds., *Assent and Argument: Studies in Cicero's Academic Books* (Leiden)

Jobst, F. (1907), *Über das Verhältnis zwischen Lukretius und Empedokles* (diss., Munich)

Jocelyn, H. D. (1977), 'The ruling class of the Roman republic and Greek philosophers', *Bulletin of the John Rylands University Library of Manchester* 59: 323–66

Kahn, C. H. (1960), 'Religion and natural philosophy in Empedocles' doctrine of the soul', *Archiv für Geschichte der Philosophie* 42: 3–35

Kenney, E. J. (1970), 'Doctus Lucretius', *Mnemosyne* 4.23: 366–92
(1971), *Lucretius: De rerum natura Book III* (Cambridge)
(1977), *Lucretius* (= *Greece and Rome* New Surveys in the Classics 11; Oxford)

Kerschensteiner, J. (1955), 'Der Bericht des Theophrast über Heraklit', *Hermes* 83: 385–411

Kidd, I. G. (1996), 'Theophrastus fr. 184 FHS&G: some thoughts on his arguments', in Algra/Horst/Runia (1996) 135–44

Kingsley, P. (1995), *Ancient Philosophy, Mystery, and Magic: Empedocles and Pythagorean Tradition* (Oxford)
(1996), 'Empedocles' two poems', *Hermes* 124: 108–11

Kirk, G. S. (1954), *Heraclitus, the Cosmic Fragments* (Cambridge)

Kleve, K. (1966), 'Lukrez und Venus (*De rerum natura* I, 1–49)', *Symbolae Osloenses* 41: 86–94
(1978), 'The philosophical polemics in Lucretius', *Entretiens Hardt* 24: 39–71
(1989), 'Lucretius in Herculaneum', *Cronache Ercolanesi* 19: 5–27

Kollman, E. D. (1971), 'Lucretius' criticism of the early Greek philosophers', *Studii Clasice* 13: 79–93

Kranz, W. (1944), 'Lukrez und Empedokles', *Philologus* 96: 68–107

Kuhrt, A. (1987), 'Berossus' *Babyloniaka* and the Seleucid rule in Babylonia', in A. Kuhrt, S. Sherwin-White (eds.), *Hellenism in the East. The Interaction of Greek and Non-Greek Civilizations from Syria to Central Asia after Alexander* (London) 32–56

Lackenbacher, H. (1910), 'Zur Disposition und Quellenfrage von Lukrez IV 1–521', *Wiener Studien* 32: 213–38

Langslow, D. (1998), 'The language of poetry and the language of science: the Latin poets and "medical Latin"', in Adams/Mayer (1998)

Lapidge, M. (1978), 'Stoic cosmology', in Rist (1978) 161–86

Laursen, S. (1987), 'Epicurus, *On nature* book XXV', *Cronache Ercolanesi* 17: 77–8

(1988), 'Epicurus, *On nature* xxv (Long–Sedley 20B, c, and j)', *Cronache Ercolanesi* 18: 7–18

(1992), 'The summary of Epicurus, *On nature* book 25', *Papyrologica Lupiensia* 1: 143–54

(1995), 'The early parts of Epicurus, *On nature*, 25th book', *Cronache Ercolanesi* 25: 5–109

Leone, G. (1984), 'Epicuro, *Della natura*, libro xiv', *Cronache Ercolanesi* 14: 17–107

Lévêque, P. (1959), *Aurea Catena Homeri* (Paris)

Lévy, C. (1992), 'Cicéron créateur du vocabulaire latin de la connaissance: essai de synthèse', in *La Langue latine, langue de la philosophie* (Ecole française de Rome) 91–106

(1997), 'Lucrèce avait-il lu Enésidème?', in Schrijvers/Koenen/Algra (1997) 115–24

Lewis, N. (1959), *Samothrace, the Ancient Literary Sources* (London)

Lloyd, G. E. R. (1966), *Polarity and Analogy* (Cambridge)

(1987), *The Revolutions of Wisdom* (Berkeley/Los Angeles)

Long, A. A. (1966), 'Thinking and sense-perception in Empedocles: mysticism or materialism?', *Classical Quarterly* ns 16: 256–76

(1974), 'Empedocles' cosmic cycle in the 'sixties', in Mourelatos (1974) 397–425

(1975–6), 'Heraclitus and Stoicism', Φιλοσοφία 5–6: 133–53; repr. in Long (1996a) 35–57

(1988a), 'Reply to Jonathan Barnes, "Epicurean signs"', *Oxford Studies in Ancient Philosophy* suppl. vol.: 135–44

(1988b), 'Socrates in Hellenistic philosophy', *Classical Quarterly* ns 38: 150–71; repr. in Long (1996a) 1–34

(1992a), review of Segal (1990), *Ancient Philosophy* 12: 493–9

(1992b), 'Stoic readings of Homer', in R. Lamberton, J. J. Keaney (eds.), *Homer's Ancient Readers* (Princeton 1992) 41–66; repr. in Long (1996a) 58–84

(1996a), *Stoic Studies* (Cambridge)

(1996b), 'Theophrastus' *De sensibus* on Plato', in Algra/Horst/Runia (1996) 345–62

(1997), 'Lucretius on nature and the Epicurean self', in Schrijvers/Koenen/Algra (1997) 125–39

Long, A. A., Sedley, D. N. (1987), *The Hellenistic Philosophers*, 2 vols. (Cambridge)

Longo Auricchio, F. (1978), 'La scuola di Epicuro', *Cronache Ercolanesi* 8: 21–37

(1988), *Ermarco, frammenti* (Naples)

Lück, W. (1932), *Die Quellenfrage im 5. und 6. Buch des Lukrez* (diss., Breslau)

McDiarmid, J. B. (1940), 'Theophrastus on the eternity of the world', *Transactions of the American Philological Association* 71: 239–47

MacKay, L. (1955), '*De rerum natura* 1.717 sqq.', *Latinitas* 3: 210

Manetti, G. (1996), ed., *Knowledge through Signs: Ancient Semiotic Theories and Practices* (Brussels)

Mansfeld, J. (1989), 'Gibt es Spuren von Theophrasts *Phys. op.* bei Cicero?', in Fortenbaugh/Steinmetz (1989) 133–58

(1990), 'Doxography and dialectic. The *Sitz im Leben* of the "Placita"', in Haase/Temporini (1990) 3056–229

(1992a), 'A Theophrastean excursus on god and nature and its aftermath in Hellenistic thought', *Phronesis* 37: 314–35

(1992b), '*Physikai doxai* and *Problemata physika* from Aristotle to Aëtius (and beyond)', in Fortenbaugh/Gutas (1992) 63–111

(1994a), 'Epicurus Peripateticus', in Alberti (1994) 28–47

(1994b), 'A lost manuscript of Empedocles' *Katharmoi*', *Mnemosyne* 47: 79–82

(1995), 'Aenesidemus and the Academics', in L. Ayres (ed.), *The Passionate Intellect* (New Brunswick/London) 235–48

Martin, A., Primavesi, O. (1998), *L'Empédocle de Strasbourg (P. Strasb. gr. Inv. 1665–1666). Introduction, édition et commentaire* (Strasbourg/Berlin)

Mewaldt, J. (1908), 'Eine Dublette in Buch IV des Lucrez', *Hermes* 43: 286–95; repr. in Classen (1986) 31–40

Milanese, G. (1989), *Lucida carmina. Comunicazione e scrittura da Epicuro a Lucrezio* (Milan)

Millot, C. (1977), 'Epicure, De la nature, livre xv', *Cronache Ercolanesi* 7: 9–39

Moraux, P. (1951), *Les Listes anciennes des ouvrages d'Aristote* (Louvain)

Mourelatos, A. P. D. (1974), ed., *The Presocratics* (New York)

Muehll, P. von der (1922), *Epicurus, Epistulae Tres et Ratae Sententiae* (Teubner text; Stuttgart)

Munro, H. A. J. (1886), *T. Lucreti Cari De Rerum Natura Libri Sex*, ed. 4 (London)

Norden, E. (1893), 'Über den Streit des Theophrast und Zeno περὶ ἀφθαρσίας κόσμου', *Jahrbücher für Classische Philologie*, suppl. 19: 440–52

Obbink, D. (1995), ed., *Philodemus and Poetry: Poetic Theory and Practice in Lucretius, Philodemus, and Horace* (Oxford)

(1996), *Philodemus On Piety, Part I* (Oxford)

O'Brien, D. (1969), *Empedocles' Cosmic Cycle* (Cambridge)

(1981), *Pour interpréter Empédocle* (Paris/Leiden)

(1995), 'Empedocles revisited', *Ancient Philosophy* 15: 403–70

Ophuijsen, J. M. van, Raalte, M. van (1998), *Theophrastus: Reappraising the Sources* (Rutgers University Studies in Classical Humanities 8; New Brunswick)

Osborne, C. (1987), 'Empedocles recycled', *Classical Quarterly* NS 37: 24–50

Owen, G. E. L. (1973), 'Plato on the undepictable', in E. N. Lee et al. (eds.), *Exegesis and Argument* (Assen 1973) 349–61; repr. in G. E. L. Owen, *Logic, Science and Dialectic* (London 1986) 138–47

Panchenko, D. (1994), 'ΟΜΟΙΟΣ and ΟΜΟΙΟΤΗΣ in Thales and Anaximander', *Hyperboreus* 1: 28–55

Parker, R. (1983), *Miasma* (Oxford)

Pearson, A. C. (1891), *The Fragments of Zeno and Cleanthes* (London)

Pease, A. S. (1955–8), *M. Tulli Ciceronis De natura deorum libri III*, 2 vols. (Cambridge, Mass.)

Pigeaud, J.-M. (1981), 'La physiologie de Lucrèce', *Revue des Etudes Latines* 58: 176–200

Pizzani, U. (1959), *Il problema del testo e della composizione del De rerum natura di Lucrezio* (Rome)

Powell, J. G. F. (1995a), 'Cicero's translations from Greek', in Powell (1995b) 273–300

    (1995b), ed., *Cicero the Philosopher* (Oxford)

Price, D. de Solla (1975), *Gears from the Greeks* (New York)

Primavesi, O. (forthcoming), *Kosmos und Dämon bei Empedokles. Der Papyrus P. Strasb. gr. Inv. 1665–1666 und die indirekte Überlieferung* (Hypomnemata 116; Göttingen)

Puglia, E. (1987), 'PHerc. 1420/1056: un volume dell'opera "Della natura" di Epicuro', *Cronache Ercolanesi* 17: 81–3

    (1988), *Demetrio Lacone: Aporie testuali ed esegetiche in Epicuro* (Naples)

Radl, A. (1988), *Der Magnetismus in der Antike. Quellen und Zusammenhänge* (Stuttgart)

Rawson, E. (1982), 'The life and death of Asclepiades of Bithynia', *Classical Quarterly* NS 32: 358–70

    (1985), *Intellectual Life in the Late Roman Republic* (London)

Reiley, K. C. (1909), *Studies in the Philosophical Terminology of Lucretius and Cicero* (New York)

Reitzenstein, E. (1924), *Theophrast bei Epikur und Lukrez* (Heidelberg)

Rist, J. M. (1978), ed., *The Stoics* (Berkeley/Los Angeles)

Romeo, C. (1979), 'Demetrio Lacone sulla grandezza del sole (PHerc. 1012)', *Cronache Ercolanesi* 9: 11–35

Rösler, W. (1973), 'Lukrez und die Vorsokratiker: doxographische Probleme im 1. Buch von "De rerum natura"', *Hermes* 101: 48–64; repr. in Classen (1986) 57–73

Runia, D. T. (1986), *Philo of Alexandria and the Timaeus of Plato* (Leiden)

    (1989), 'Plato, *Timaeus* 30 B 6–C 1', *Elenchos* 10: 435–43

    (1997), 'Lucretius and doxography', in Schrijvers/Koenen/Algra (1997) 93–103

Sambursky, S. (1959), *Physics of the Stoics* (London)

Sandbach, F. H. (1985), *Aristotle and the Stoics* (Cambridge Philological Society, suppl. vol. 11, Cambridge)

Schmalzriedt, E. (1970), *Peri Physeos: zur Frühgeschichte der Buchtitel* (Munich)

Schmid, W. (1936), *Epikurs Kritik der platonischen Elementenlehre* (Leipzig)

Schmidt, J. (1990), *Lukrez, der Kepos und die Stoiker* (Frankfurt am Main)

Schofield, M. (1975), 'Doxographica Anaxagorea', *Hermes* 103: 1–24

Schrijvers, P. H. (1976), 'La pensée d'Epicure et de Lucrèce sur le sommeil (*DRN*, IV, 907–961, Scolie *ad* Epicure *Ep. ad Her.* 66). Un chapitre des *Parva naturalia* Epicuriens', in Bollack/Laks (1976): 231–59

    (1983), 'Sur quelques aspects de la critique des mythes chez Lucrèce', in ΣΥΖΗΤΗΣΙΣ: *studi sull'epicureismo greco e latino offerti a Marcello Gigante* (Naples) 353–71

    (1992), 'Philosophie et paraphrase: Lucrèce et les sceptiques', in *La Langue latine, langue de la philosophie* (Ecole française de Rome) 125–40

    (1994), 'Intertextualité et polémique dans le *De rerum natura* (V 925–1010): Lucrèce vs. Dicéarque de Messène', *Philologus* 138: 288–304

    (1996), 'Lucretius on the origin and development of political life (*De rerum natura* 5.1105–1160)', in Algra/Horst/Runia (1996) 220–30

(1997), 'L'homme et l'animal dans le *DRN*', in Schrijvers/Koenen/Algra (1997) 151–61

Schrijvers, P. H., Koenen, M. H., Algra, K. A. (1997), eds., *Lucretius and his Intellectual Background* (Amsterdam)

Sedley, D. (1973), 'Epicurus, *On Nature*, Book XXVIII', *Cronache Ercolanesi* 3: 5–83

(1974), 'The structure of Epicurus, *On nature*', *Cronache Ercolanesi* 4: 89–92

(1976a), 'Epicurus and his professional rivals', in Bollack/Laks (1976) 119–59

(1976b), 'Epicurus and the mathematicians of Cyzicus', *Cronache Ercolanesi* 6: 23–54

(1981), 'The end of the Academy', *Phronesis* 26: 67–75

(1982), 'On signs', in Barnes et al. (1982) 239–72

(1983), 'Epicurus' refutation of determinism', in ΣΥΖΗΤΗΣΙΣ: *studi sull'epicureismo greco e romano offerti a Marcello Gigante* (Naples) 11–51

(1984), 'The character of Epicurus' *On Nature*', in *Atti del XVII congresso internazionale di papirologia* (Naples) 381–7

(1988), 'Epicurean anti-reductionism', in Barnes/Mignucci (1988) 295–327

(1989a), 'The proems of Empedocles and Lucretius', *GRBS* 30: 269–96

(1989b), 'Philosophical allegiance in the Greco-Roman world', in Griffin/Barnes (1989) 97–119

(1992a), 'Sextus Empiricus and the atomist criteria of truth', *Elenchos* 13: 21–56

(1992b), 'Empedocles' theory of vision in Theophrastus, *De sensibus*', in Fortenbaugh/Gutas (1992) 20–31

(1996), 'The inferential foundations of Epicurean ethics', in Giannantoni/Gigante (1996) 313–39; repr. in S. Everson (ed.), *Ethics* (Cambridge 1998)

(1997a), 'The ethics of Brutus and Cassius', *Journal of Roman Studies* 87: 41–53

(1997b), 'How Lucretius composed the *De rerum natura*', in Schrijvers/Koenen/Algra (1997) 1–19

(1998a), 'Theophrastus and Epicurean physics', in Ophuijsen/Raalte (1998) 333–56

(1998b), 'Lucretius' use and avoidance of Greek', in Adams/Mayer (1998) 227–46

(forthcoming), 'The sequence of argument in Lucretius 1', in Atherton (forthcoming)

Seele, A. (1995), *Römische Übersetzer, Nöte, Freiheiten, Absichten: Verfahren des literarischen Übersetzens in der griechisch-römischen Antike* (Darmstadt)

Segal, C. (1990), *Lucretius on Death and Anxiety* (Princeton)

Sharples, R. W. (1992), *Alexander of Aphrodisias, Quaestiones 1.1–2.15* (London)

Skutsch, O. (1985), *The Annals of Quintus Ennius* (Oxford)

Smith, M. F. (1966), 'Some Lucretian thought processes', *Hermathena* 102: 73–83

(1975), *Lucretius, 'De Rerum Natura'*, with an English translation by W. H. D. Rouse, revised with new text, introduction, notes and index (Loeb Classical Library; London / Cambridge, Mass.)

(1993), *Diogenes of Oinoanda, The Epicurean Inscription* (Naples)

(1996), 'An Epicurean priest from Apamea in Syria', *Zeitschrift für Papyrologie und Epigraphik* 112: 120–30

Snyder, J. M. (1972), 'Lucretius' Empedoclean Sicily', *Classical World* 65: 217–18

Solmsen, F. (1951), 'Epicurus and cosmological heresies', *American Journal of Philology* 72: 1–23; repr. in Solmsen (1968) 461–83

(1953), 'Epicurus on the growth and decline of the cosmos', *American Journal of Philology* 74: 34–51; repr. in Solmsen (1968) 484–501

(1961a), 'αἴσθησις in Aristotelian and Epicurean thought', *Mededelingen der Koninklijke Nederlandse Akademie van Wetenschappen, Afd. Letterkunde* 24 no. 8: 241–62; repr. in Solmsen (1968) 612–33, and in Classen (1986) 151–72

(1961b), 'Greek philosophy and the discovery of the nerves', *Museum Helveticum* 18: 150–97; repr. in Solmsen (1968) 536–82

(1965), 'Love and strife in Empedocles' cosmology', *Phronesis* 10: 109–48; repr. in Solmsen (1968) 274–313, and in Allen/Furley (1975) 221–64

(1968), *Kleine Schriften* vol. 1 (Hildesheim)

Staden, H. von (1989), *Herophilus* (Cambridge)

Steckel, H. (1968), 'Epikuros', *RE* suppl. XI: 579–652

Tatum, W. J. (1984), 'The Presocratics in book one of Lucretius' *De rerum natura*', *Transactions of the American Philological Association* 114: 177–89

Tepedino Guerra, A. (1991), *Polieno, frammenti* (Naples)

Townend, G. B. (1979), 'The original plan of Lucretius' *De rerum natura*', *Classical Quarterly* NS 29: 101–11

Tyrrell, R. Y. (1885–1901), *The Correspondence of M. Tullius Cicero*, 7 vols. (Dublin)

Usener, H. (1887), *Epicurea* (Leipzig)

(1977), *Glossarium Epicureum*, ed. M. Gigante, W. Schmid (Rome)

Vallance, J. T. (1990), *The Lost Theory of Asclepiades of Bithynia* (Oxford)

Vander Waerdt, P. A. (1985), 'Peripatetic soul-division, Posidonius, and Middle Platonic moral psychology', *Greek, Roman and Byzantine Studies* 26: 373–94

(1988), 'Hermarchus and the Epicurean genealogy of morals', *Transactions of the American Philological Association* 118: 87–106

(1989), 'Colotes and the Epicurean refutation of scepticism', *Greek, Roman and Byzantine Studies* 30: 225–67

Vlastos, G. (1950), 'The physical theory of Anaxagoras', *Philosophical Review* 59: 31–57; repr. in Allen/Furley (1975) 323–53, and in Vlastos (1993) 303–27

(1993), *Studies in Greek Philosophy*, vol. 1: *The Presocratics* (Princeton)

Vogliano, A. (1928), *Epicuri et Epicureorum Scripta in Herculanensibus Papyris Servata* (Berlin)

(1940), *I resti dell' XI libro del Περὶ φύσεως di Epicuro* (Cairo)

(1953), 'I resti del IIᵒ libro del Περὶ φύσεως di Epicuro', *Prolegomena* 2: 59–98

Wallace, R. (1996), '"Amaze your friends!" Lucretius on magnets', *Greece & Rome* 43: 178–87

Wardy, R. (1988), 'Lucretius on what atoms are not', *Classical Philology* 83: 112–28

Waszink, J. H. (1950), 'The proem of the *Annales* of Ennius', *Mnemosyne* 4.4: 215–40

Weise, F. O. (1882), *Die griechischen Wörter im Latein* (Leipzig)

West, D. (1970), 'Virgilian multiple-correspondence similes and their antecedents', *Philologus* 114: 262–75

    (1975), 'Lucretius' methods of argument (3. 417–614)', *Classical Quarterly* NS 25: 94–116

Wiersma, W. (1940), 'Der angebliche Streit des Zenon und Theophrast, *Mnemosyne* 3.8: 235–43

Woltjer, J. (1877), *Lucreti Philosophia cum Fontibus Comparata* (Groningen)

Woolf, G. (1994), 'Becoming Roman, staying Greek: culture, identity and the civilizing process in the Roman east', *Proceedings of the Cambridge Philological Society* 40: 116–43

Wright, M. R. (1981), *Empedocles: the Extant Remains* (New Haven)

Young, D. (1971), *Theognis* (Leipzig)

Zeller, E. (1876), 'Der Streit Theophrasts gegen Zeno über die Ewigkeit der Welt', *Hermes* 11: 422–9

Index locorum

General index

Academics, 62–3, 67, 74n, 76–8, 79–82, 84n, 85n, 90n, 153
Aenesidemus, 72n, 86n, 89–90, 92
aether, 2n, 8, 15
Aetius, 157–9
allegory, 74–5
Amafinius, 38
analogy
  argument by 11, 67, 83–4, 107
  alphabetic, 39, 48n, 190–1, 195
Anaxagoras, 48, 73–4, 124–6, 145–6, 183, 191
Anaximander, 19, 80n, 82n, 178
Anaximenes, 74
Andronicus, 63
Antikythera mechanism, 83
Antiochus, 62–4, 77–8, 85n, 87n, 89n
Antipater, 87n
Apollonius of Rhodes, 9
Aratus, 1, 50n
Arcesilaus, 85–6, 87n
Archimedes, 83, 91
Aristarchus, 91
Aristion, Epicurean tyrant, 62
Aristotle, 79, 86, 178–9
  re-emergence at Rome, 63–4
  on teleology, 19
  influence on doxography, 20, 124–5, 183, 151n
  school treatises little known in Hellenistic period, 63, 91–2, 183–4
  Physics 104, 186
  on location of mind, 68
  De philosophia, 168n
Asclepiades, 69n, 72n
Athenodorus, 63–4
Athens
  Lucretius on, 57, 160–1, 203
  as philosophical centre, 62–4, 67, 129–30
atoms, Latin vocabulary for, 28, 38–9, 193–8, 202

Atticus, friend of Cicero, 64
Atticus, Platonist philosopher, 179
Aurispa, G., had copy of Empedocles' *Katharmoi*, 3
authority, philosophical, 18, 21, 67–8, 68–9

Berosus, 90–1
Boethus, 75
Bolos, 90n
Brutus, 63

Caesar, Julius, 62n, 64–5
Calcidius, 93n
Calliope, 22, 24
Carneades, 74n, 87n
Cassius, 39, 64
Catius, 39, 42, 140
Cato the Younger, 63
Chrysippus, 68–9, 167
Cicero, xvii, 66n, 86, 89
  letter about Lucretius, 1–2, 22, 203
  philosophical works, 36–7, 43–4, 67, 77–8, 81, 82
  and translation of Greek philosophical terms, 36–9, 42, 43–4, 49
  philosophical position and contacts, 63–5
Cleanthes, 73n
Cleomedes, 84, 93n
Colotes, 18n, 86n, 89n
compound adjectives, 24–5, 51, 54n, 59
Crantor, 76n, 78n
Crassus, 64
Cratippus, 64
creation, 75–8, 80–1, 82–3, 153
Critias, 121
Cyzicus, mathematical school of, 83

Demetrius of Laconia, 70, 84n
Democritus, 178
  as forerunner of scepticism, 86–7

228

Index of modern scholars

Printed in the United States
20494LVS00006B/259-273